Sleeping Bear

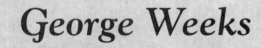

George Weeks

Preface by James Ridenour,
Director, National Park Service, 1989–93

Sleeping Bear

YESTERDAY and TODAY

*Including Ghost Towns, Lighthouses, and
Shipwrecks of Sleeping Bear Dunes
National Lakeshore*

The University of Michigan Press
and
Petoskey Publishing Company

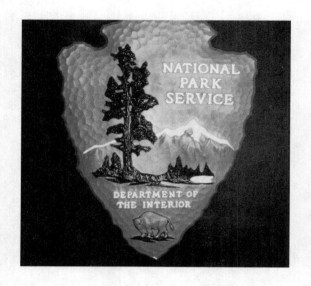

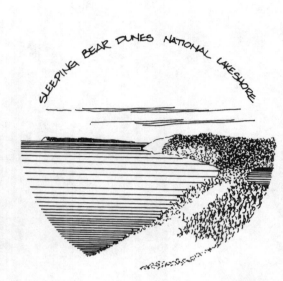

(National Park Service)

ISBN 0-472-03031-0
Don Weeks, Contributing Author, Chapters 8 and 11

Designed by Don Ross and William Kalvin
Cover photograph by Ken Scott
Typeset by Delmas Typesetting, Ann Arbor, MI

CONTENTS

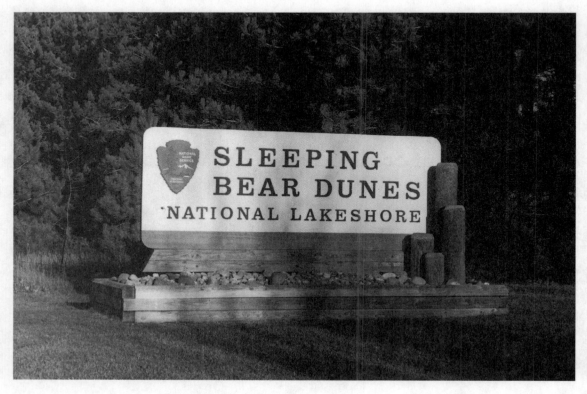

(George Weeks)

ACKNOWLEDGMENTS

Large portions of this book are not the words of the author. They are the words of the prehistoric first people of Sleeping Bear, passed on through legends and oral tradition; of explorers and settlers; of the keepers of lighthouses and life-saving stations; of the pioneer families of Sleeping Bear whose recollections are preserved in the excellent libraries and museums of Leelanau and Benzie counties; of authors who chronicled segments of Sleeping Bear's yesterdays; of today's residents of the area; of the National Park Service and its many studies and publications of the Sleeping Bear Dunes National Lakeshore.

The staffs of Lakeshore Superintendents Richard Peterson (1980–90), Ivan Miller (1990–2001) and Dusty Shultz (2001–) provided research, graphic and other help. Special thanks to the Lakeshore's Bill Herd, keeper/ interpreter of much of the Lakeshore's heritage.

Many of the recollections and pictures came from descendents of the pioneer families, including Marion Warnes, daughter of Glen Haven's "King David"—D. H. Day; D. H. Day, III, a grandson; Robert Travis; another grandson of Day; and Jack Barratt, great grandson of Carson Burfiend, the first settler of Port Oneida.

The Michigan Travel Bureau was a valuable source of pictures, as were Grace and Fred Dickinson, George Shilling, Gary Jones, Rich Brauer, and Chris Byron and Tom Wilson of Vintage Views. Jed Jaworski made major contributions to one of the objectives of this book—presenting new discoveries of old shipwrecks. Thanks also to Scott Peters of the Michigan Historical Museum.

Special thanks to contributing author Don Weeks; Julie Weeks for review and editing; and Mollie Weeks, founder and former owner of the Cottage Book Shop of Glen Arbor for research material, pictures and encouragement.

The author appreciates the early support of A&M Publishing, and, for this updated edition, Anne and Brian Lewis of Petoskey Publishing Co., and Mary Erwin of the University of Michigan Press.

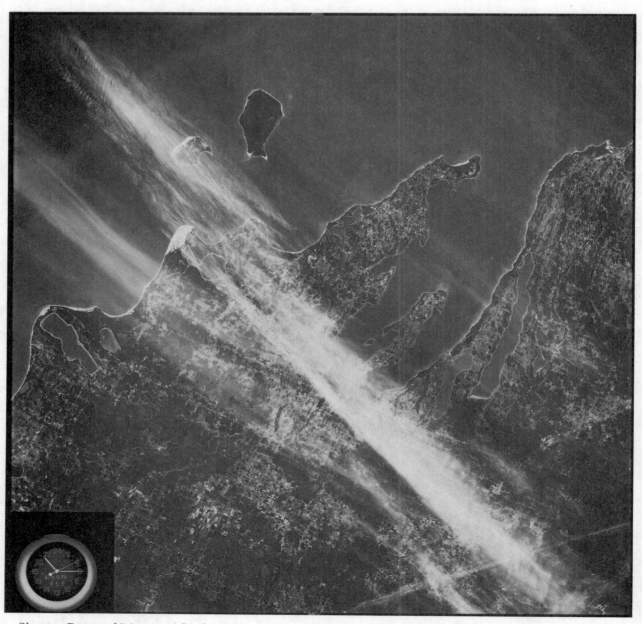

Sleeping Bear and Manitou Islands, as viewed from 234 miles by Skylab 3 in 1973.

(Environmental Research Institute of Michigan)

PREFACE

Since the authorizing legislation for Sleeping Bear Dunes National Lakeshore passed the Congress in 1970, the National Park Service has been charged with the responsibility for protecting the resources there and providing access for travelers. Today, visitors find meadows, forests, dunes, islands, beaches, lakes and streams as they travel throughout the park. There is a hint of man's presence in the farms, orchards, lighthouses, summer homes and logging trails that are part of the park landscape. The legend of Sleeping Bear speaks of an earlier time when native people traveled through the region on foraging trips.

Under the administration of the National Park Service, modern intrusions into the natural scene are being removed and Nature is encouraged to reclaim her realm. Historic resources are being preserved so that future generations may understand their story. As areas surrounding the park are developed to meet man's current needs, we can see that our children and their children will be able to enjoy the Sleeping Bear Dunes much the same as today's visitors.

Reading about national parks is a popular pasttime for many visitors and greatly increases appreciation for park resources. Set in the heart of the Great Lakes, Sleeping Bear Dunes is truly one of the jewels of the National Park System, worthy of a visit or study in any season.

The National Park Service is pleased to acknowledge the publication of this book in recognition of the twentieth anniversary of the creation of the Sleeping Bear Dunes National Lakeshore by Congressional Act on October 21, 1970.

James Ridenour
Director (1989–93)
National Park Service
United States Department of the Interior

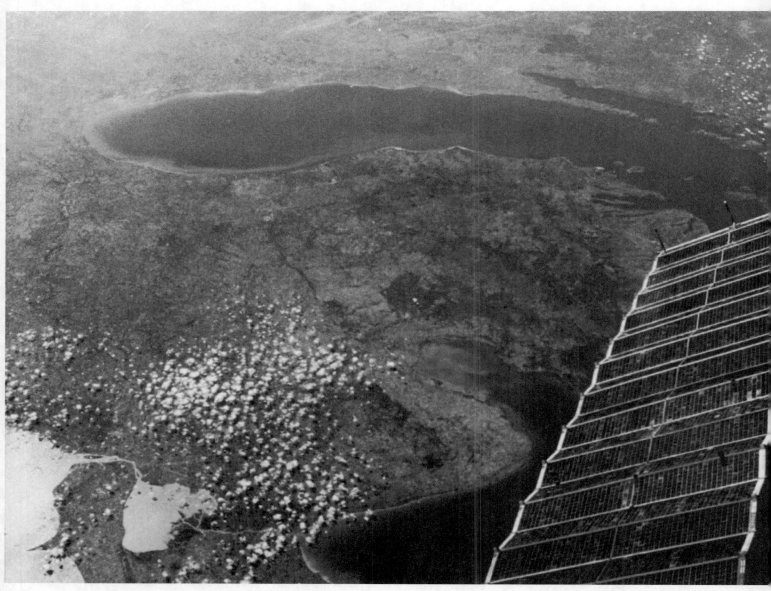

In this highly unique picture of Michigan taken by astronaut Jerry Linenger in 1997 aboard the Russian Space Station Mir, the Sleeping Bear Dunes is a white speck along Lake Michigan at the base of the Leelanau Peninsula. Mir's solar panel juts across the northern Lower Peninsula. Linenger found the dunes "just spectacular—a beautiful white relief, very visible to the naked eye." Linenger, who retired to Leelanau County, had a rare eye on the dunes, from outer space and up and close personal—from 2,000 Earth orbits during five months aboard a Russian space station, and from climbing the dunes before and after his flight. (Jerry Linenger/NASA)

INTRODUCTION

From Ice Age to Space Age

The natural splendor of Sleeping Bear can be readily seen. It has been sculptured by glaciers, honed by wind and water, and preserved and presented as a jewel of the national parks. Less evident, but no less splendid, is its human heritage.

William Penn Mott, Jr., the 1985–1989 director of the National Park Service, called the Sleeping Bear Dunes National Lakeshore "truly one of America's treasures. . . . The landscape reveals intriguing stories of geology, ecology and human history. From the earliest Native Americans to modern vacationers, people came here because of the unique relationship of land and water. Sailors, loggers, and farmers all had close ties with nature. The story of the people has become part of the story of the land."[1]

This book tells the story of the people and the land, the human history, and the natural history. It includes the story of the first people of Sleeping Bear as presented in my 1988 book, *Sleeping Bear: Its Lore, Legends and First People*. This book then picks up where that book left off and continues the human story through the first settlers to today. It also presents the natural history of Sleeping Bear, and the attractions and activities of today's Lakeshore.

Sleeping Bear's first human inhabitants were migrating American Indians whose lives and leg ends embellish its heritage and mystique. Today's hikers can retrace paths of the first inhabitants, visit the Manitou islands where early writers said Indians were afraid to dwell but where archaeologists have discovered they did dwell; and picnic on a Benzie County river bank that was used by Indians for seasonal activities for at least 1,000 years starting within a few centuries after the birth of Christ.

The 1826 completion of the Erie Canal, linking middle America with Atlantic seaboard states, brought rapid development and rapid growth of commercial shipping on the Great Lakes. It was this highway of water, not land trails, that led to settlement of Sleeping Bear country. Docks were built along the Lakeshore to serve as cord wooding stations for the steamers, and then to serve homestead-seeking immigrants, the lumber industry and vacationers.

Now the docks have disappeared, as have most of the towns from which the docks extended. Today's Lakeshore visitors can see some of the lighthouse and life-saving facilities that served early sailors. They also can see the Glen Haven Historic Village, the turn-of-the-century company lumbering town that may well be the Great Lakes' best-preserved example of a frontier wooding station and steamboat stop. Among the buildings are the Sleeping Bear Inn, erected in

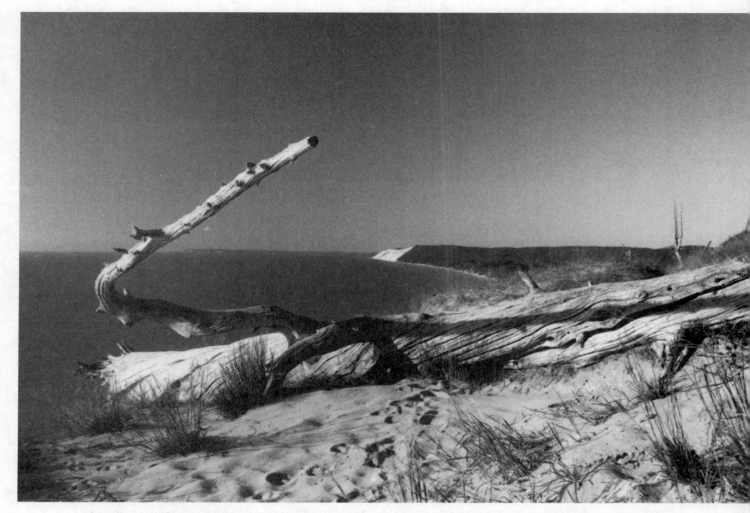

Ghost Trees of Sleeping Bear lean from the Empire Bluffs north toward South Bar Lake and the dunes. (Michigan Travel Bureau)

1857, and the D. H. Day Store, the "castle" of King David of the North.

Sleeping Bear's narrow and dangerous Manitou Passage, between the islands and a long and weaving shoreline, was both the early shipwreck triangle of Lake Michigan, and magnet for first settlements of Leelanau and Benzie counties. French naturalist Francis Count de Castlenau, who traveled the Manitou Passage in 1838, wrote of Lake Michigan: I have seen the storms of the Channel, those of the Ocean, the squalls off the banks of Newfoundland, those on the coasts of America, and the hurricanes of the Gulf of Mex- ico. Nowhere have I witnessed the fury of the elements comparable to that found on this fresh water sea."[2]

The remains of many a ship are in the Manitou Passage and along the shore, sometimes exposed on beaches by shifting shorelines; often visible to offshore snorkelers and boaters; and available to divers at various points within one of Michigan's most popular bottomland preserves, where in the late 1980s there were new discoveries of old wrecks. Artifacts from shipwrecks are on display at the Sleeping Bear Point Coast Guard Station Maritime Museum.

The museum is a centerpiece of the Sleeping Bear Dunes National Lakeshore created in 1970 to preserve one of the natural wonders of America's heartland. Specifically, Congress voted to preserve "outstanding natural features, including forests, beaches, dune formations and ancient glacial phenomena . . . for the benefit, inspiration, education, recreation, and enjoyment of the public."[3]

At the time, considerable opposition to this legislation arose from local units of government that were to lose portions of their tax base, and from those forced to sell their property to the federal government. Many pieces of private property exist within the park's authorized boundary, and the National Park Service urges visitors to respect all property owners' rights.

The Lakeshore's headquarters and Visitor Center in Empire is named after the legislator primarily responsible for creation of the Lakeshore, Senator Philip A. Hart. Prominent area citizens are honored by designation of the D.H. Day Campground and the Pierce Stocking Scenic Drive. The drive includes a view from atop the dunes that in 1990 was selected Michigan's "Best Scenic View" by *Michigan Living*, the official publication of the Automobile Club of Michigan.

The shimmering whiteness of the Sleeping Bear Dunes was a landmark and beacon to Lake Michigan's first travelers, and, centuries later, an earthmark to space travelers.

"Sleeping Bear really stands out from space," noted U. S. astronaut Jack Lousma, who climbed the dunes as a boy growing up in Michigan and viewed them from 200 and 275 miles away as pilot of the *Skylab 3* mission in 1973 and commander of the third orbital flight of the space shuttle *Columbia* in 1982. "There is a sharp contrast between the white of the dunes, and the vast aqua blue of Lake Michigan, the deep blue of Glen Lake and the green of the forests. "[4]

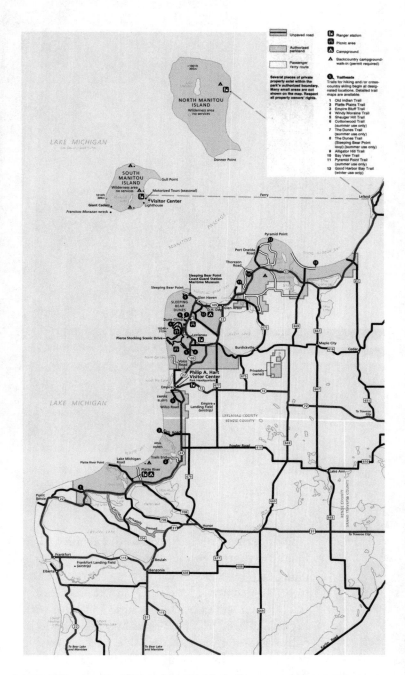

Map of Sleeping Bear Dunes National Lakeshore (National Park Service)

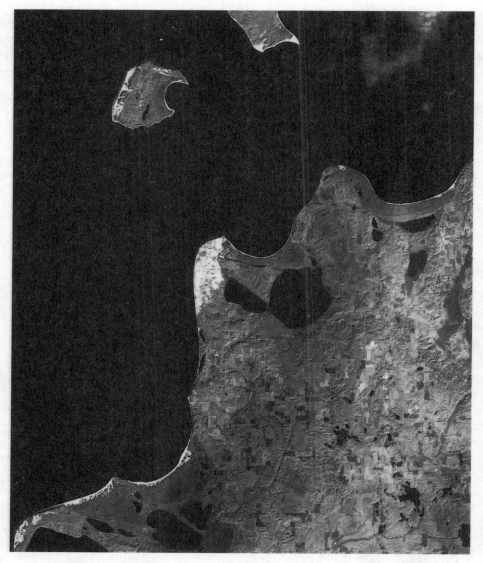

Sleeping Bear from space (Environmental Research Institute of Michigan)

A most unique perspective of Sleeping Bear Dunes is that of retired Leelanau County astronaut Jerry Linenger—up close and personal, and from outer space. He relishes "strong memories" of climbing the dunes as a youth and later with his son; viewed and photographed them periodically on more than 2,000 Earth orbits during five perilous months aboard the Russian Space Station *Mir* in 1997; and then, as part of his rehabilitation from loss of bone density caused by weightlessness of space, had a regimen of climb-

ing Sleeping Bear's steepest slope—sometimes as many as six times a day.

Reflecting on his unique perch traveling more than 50 million miles in space, Linenger said: "Nothing on the globe was more recognizable than the Great Lakes, particularly northwestern Michigan with its deep, aqua-colored lakes and bays contrasted by the green of its woods. The dunes were just spectacular—a beautiful white relief, very visible to the naked eye."[5]

Many a Michigan governor has climbed the

dunes. Among them was Governor Jennifer Granholm, who, on a 2003 Leelanau County visit during her first year in office, called Sleeping Bear "one of the most unusual areas of Michigan." She noted that on most Michigan beaches, "the sand is narrow, yet all of a sudden rising from the earth are these fabulous dunes, which makes it, I want to say anachronistic. It's not out of time; it's out of place. I think that's really part of the magic of the dunes—that they are *so* unusual. So the notion that over time the wind has blown these shafts into our land, and when you combine them with the Indian legends about the dunes, there is a magnetic appeal."[6]

William G. Milliken, Michigan's longest-serving governor (1969–1982), grew up in nearby Traverse City and, as have generations of area students, used to come to the dunes on class outings. His successor, Governor James J. Blanchard (1983-1990), climbed the dunes as a boy, and later brought his family back to climb them again. Said Blanchard: "I love the Sleeping Bear Dunes and Glen Lake—to stand up there and look at them . . . It's like being governor of Paradise."[7]

Paradise. An American treasure. A jewel of the National Park Service. Scenic splendor:

Sleeping Bear Dunes National Lakeshore is all of this, as the following words and pictures will reflect.

George Weeks
Glen Arbor, MI
2004

Endnotes—Introduction

1. William Penn Mott, Jr., *Sleeping Bear: Its Lore, Legends and First People*, (Glen Arbor, MI: The Cottage Book Shop, 1988), v.
2. Myron H. Vent, *South Manitou Island: From Pioneer Community to National Park*, (Nassau, Del.: Manitou Publications, 1973), 16.
3. Public Law 91–479 (84 Stat. 1075), approved 21 October 1970.
4. Jack Lousma, interview with the author, 1 February 1988. (Grand Rapids-born Lousma was raised in Ann Arbor and worked there at the Environmental Research Institute of Michigan after retiring from the space agency and making an unsuccessful bid for the U.S. Senate.)
5. Jerry Linenger, interview with the author, 2003.
6. Governor Jennifer Granholm, interview with the author, 2003.
7. Governor James J. Blanchard, interview with the author, 1989.

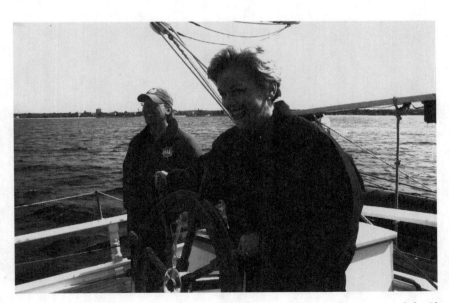

Gov. Jennifer Granholm, while sailing off the Leelanau Peninsula on a 2003 tour that promoted the Sleeping Bear Dunes and other tourist attractions, at the helm of the Malabar, *replica of the tall ships that plied Lake Michigan.*

(John Russell)

CHAPTER I

The Folklore of Sleeping Bear

Long ago, a mother bear and her two cubs fled a Wisconsin forest fire by swimming across Lake Michigan. The mother reached shore and climbed to the top of a bluff to watch and wait. But the exhausted cubs drowned. When the mourning mother died, the Great Spirit Manitou marked her resting place with a solitary forested dune called Sleeping Bear. Her cubs are the Manitou Islands.
—Chippewa legend

Sleeping Bear Country is steeped in the legends of American Indians, whose tales of mighty Mishe-Mokwa*, the Great Bear, embellish folklore of the Great Lakes. When the first white explorers plied Lake Michigan (then called Lake of the Illinois), they found that the dunes forming the lake's most striking scenic landscape had already been named in Chippewa folklore.

*This is the spelling used by Henry Wadsworth Longfellow in Song of Hiawatha. Gitchi Mukwa is the proper term, according to Basil Johnson's Lexicon of the Ojibway Language.

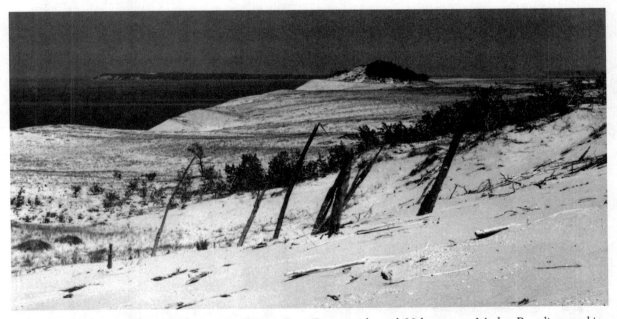

FOLKLORE VIGIL: *High atop shimmering Sleeping Bear Dunes in the mid-20th century, Mother Bear lies watching over South Manitou Island, one of her two cubs in the Chippewa Legend of Sleeping Bear.* (Fred Dickinson)

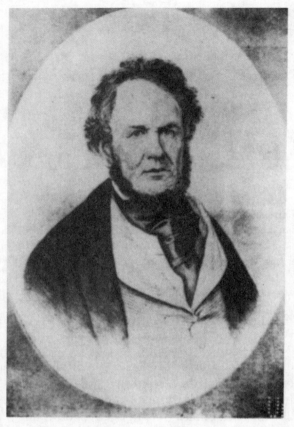

Henry Rowe Schoolcraft, Michigan's Superintendent of Indian Affairs, chronicled the lore and legends of Sleeping Bear and provided inspiration for Henry Wadsworth Longfellow's Song of Hiawatha.
(Historical Society of Michigan)

North and South Manitou Islands, to the mainland Indians who gazed out upon them, were embodiments of the dominating Great Spirit, as was Sleeping Bear Point. In Algonquin, the linguistic family of the Chippewa and Ottawa along Michigan's western shore, manitou* is a term for spirit, a supernatural being or deity that controls Nature. Antoine de la Mothe Cadillac, who lived among the Ottawa from 1694 to 1698 and in 1701 founded Fort Pontchartrain at the present site of Detroit, said of the Indian view of manitou

*Spelled a variety of ways since the sixteenth century, including: manito, manido, maneto, moneto, manitoo, manitu, menitto, and mantoac

This spirit, in which he trusts, is sometimes a raven, an eagle, an otter, a bear, a fox, or other animal; but each holds his own in esteem, and it is always the one which has appeared to him in his dreams and visions; so that, if during their sleep; they have visions of their enemies, at certain times and places, and if finally their vision is favorable, they take it as a good omen and conclude that they *will* succeed in their attack on their enemies.[1]

The Indian became aware of a personal manitou during the initial fast at the age of puberty. The process was described by ethnologist Henry Rowe Schoolcraft. Schoolcraft, the first American to provide a written record of having seen the Sleeping Bear region, wrote extensively on the history and conditions of Indian tribes. He was federal Indian agent at Sault Ste. Marie and for thirty years lived and studied among the Ojibways (Chippewas). In 1823, he married Jane Johnston, whose mother was the daughter of Chippewa Chief Wabojeeg. In 1828 he was co-founder of the Historical Society of Michigan with Territorial Governor Lewis Cass, an architect of U.S. Indian policy who negotiated twenty-two treaties during 1814–1831. One of Schoolcraft's sources on Northwest Michigan was Ishqua-gonabi, chief of the Chippewas on Grand Traverse Bay. Schoolcraft's monumental mid-nineteenth century 4,955-page report on the history and conditions of American Indians was an important inspirational source of legends for Henry Wadsworth Longfellow's lyric epic, *The Song of Hiawatha*. Schoolcraft wrote of the Indian's manitou: "When revealed in dreams . . . he adopts that revelation, which is generally some bird or animal, as his personal or guardian Manito. He trusts it in war and peace; and there is no exigency in life, in or from which he believes it cannot help or extricate him."

Unfortunately, Schoolcraft noted, "the Indian is never sure that his neighbor is not under the guardianship of a Manito stronger than his own . . . thus the Indian, who believes in a passive Great Spirit, or Gezha Manito, with no other attributes but goodness and ubiquity, is left in a perpetual and horrible state of fear."[2]

Some of the interpretations by Schoolcraft and earlier European writers about the spiritual connotations of Michigan's indigenous peoples are disputed by modern-day ethnologists, as well as by American Indian leaders who say the writings reflect a cultural bias, and in some cases, were used to build the nineteenth century case for re-locating Indians from northwest Michigan to western lands. Manito is not voodoo. Long before discovery of atoms and molecules, Native Americans had their own beliefs about the nature of biological phenomena and other forms of life.

The Algonquins, according to Schoolcraft, "believe a soul alike pervades all animate creation, the brute as well as the human ... Every animal is supposed to be endowed with a reasoning faculty ... according to their theory, a bear reasons as well as a man."[3]

This is beautifully illustrated in *The Song of Hiawatha*, where, in "The Four Winds," a warrior says:

> Hark you, Bear! you are a coward
> And no Brave, as you pretended;
> Else you would not cry and whimper
> Like a miserable woman! Bear! You
> know our tribes are hostile Long
> have been at war together; Now you
> find that we are strongest, You go
> sneaking into the forest . . . [4]

The Algonquin tribes believed that the world was created by a Supreme Spirit, called, according to Schoolcraft, "Monedo, and Ozheaud, the Maker, and who is specifically addressed under the prefix of Gezha, the Benevolent or Merciful, and Gitchi, the Great."[5] There is neither a good nor bad meaning to manitou, unless used with a prefix or qualifying expression. Jesuit missionary Claude Allouez, who came to Michigan in 1665, said the Ottawa, while worshiping and venerating manitous, recognized no sovereign master of heaven and earth.' But Grand Traverse Indian historian A.J. Blackbird, son of an Ottawa chief, wrote in 1887:

Ottawa and Chippewa Indians were not what we would call entirely infidels and idolaters; for they believed that there is a Supreme Ruler of the Universe, the Creator of all things, the Great Spirit, to which they offer worship and sacrifices in a certain form.[7]

It was customary every spring for them to gather all cast off garments that had been worn during the winter "and rear them up on a long pole while they were having festivals and jubilees to the Great Spirit."

Blackbird said their individual deities, or manitous, were "supreme only to the extent that they had power over the land where they presided. These deities were supposed to be governed by the Great Spirit above." The manitou often appeared as an animal, but also in higher phenomena of the atmosphere. Beneficent manitous

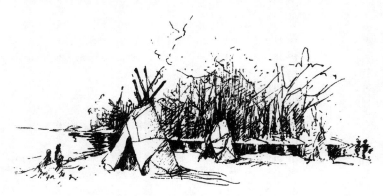

(Glen Arbor artist Suzanne Wilson)

were the sun, moon, takes, rivers and woods. Malevolent ones were the adder, dragon) cold, and storms.[8]

In The Indians of the Western Great Lakes, W. Vernon Kinietz noted that "an Ottawa wishing to acquire a manito usually took the first animal that appeared to him during sleep. Afterward, he killed an animal of this kind, put its skin or its feathers in the most conspicuous part of his cabin and made a feast in its honor, during which he addressed it in most respectful terms. From that time on it was recognized as his manito, and he carried its skin to war, to the hunt, and on journeys, believing that it would preserve him from every danger and cause all his undertakings to succeed."[9]

Legends

Schoolcraft called Indian legends the "scattered bones of aboriginal lore"—bones fortunately preserved in large measure by Schoolcraft's own writings. The legend of naming of Sleeping Bear Dunes is well known by area residents and is quickly learned by visitors. In fact, Indian folklore with its rich historical heritage contributes to understanding this area.

Those who today view the awe-inspiring magnificence of what Nature sculptured along the shores and inland vistas of Sleeping Bear, and those who have seen a sunset behind the Manitou Islands or the eerie northern lights over Lake Michigan, can appreciate why Indians not only viewed the natural phenomena with awe, but endowed them with the supernatural and paid homage to them in ceremonies. "Almost everything, animate or inanimate, that seemed unusual was believed manido," Gertrude Prokosch Kurath wrote in *Michigan Indian Festivals*. "Certain lakes, hills, and points such as Sleeping Bear Point were manido."[10]

Sand and great bodies of water have special places in Indian folklore. One legend—which can be imagined as a Sleeping Bear variation of Adam and Eve—cited by Kurath, says that in the very beginning, "Indians discovered themselves standing on the shore of a great water. They were standing in the sand and the sand covered their feet and came up to their ankles. They finally worked themselves loose and walked around. That's where their mind started. These people were fullgrown; there were no children. They began to move around and walk around the shore. " It goes on to describe how voices came to them instructing how to hunt, and how to start a fire.[11]

The Gift of Corn

Sleeping Bear figures among the many stories about how Indians got the gift of corn, or mon-daw-min.* One such story comes from the Ottawa who roamed the area:

Sleeping Bear Point used to be a stopping place for traveling Indians. One time an Indian was going by there. As night was falling, he made preparations to camp.

Then he heard a call for help. It sounded like a woman. After listening for the direction of the voice, he climbed a hill. He got into the woods. Then he saw a very beautiful maiden. She was slender. She had long, yellow hair, like ribbons. He thought she was lost. He looked about and saw no signs of people. He asked: "What are you doing in this wild country?"

She said: "I live here. I am not lost. My name is Mindamin, Corn." He said: "I will take you home." As he took her by the arm, instead of a maiden, he held a stalk of corn. He took an ear of corn home. He had never seen anything like the corn.

When he arrived home, he showed it around. After a while an old man said, "Taira! This is corn. A long time ago I heard my ancestors, far away, tell about this. It comes from apungishmok, out west. We've heard, if you will plant this, more will come out. When it matures, then it is supposed to be eaten."

—Fred Ettawageshik 1947[12]

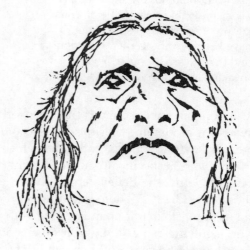

(Michigan Bureau of History)

---

*Compound from mondo, spirit; min, a grain or berry; and iaw, the verb substantive. Also spelled mindamin.

Much of the lore of Sleeping Bear has been preserved through generations of the Ettawageshik family of Harbor Springs, descendants of eighteenth and nineteenth century Ottawa who traveled the northeastern shores of Lake Michigan. They recall, for example, hearing their elders tell of how young Indian men would come to Sleeping Bear to climb the dunes from the shore at their highest point.

"It was not a rite of manhood, but it was something the young men would do," said Frank Ettawageshik, whose forebears spent summers at Harbor Springs and winters near Big Rapids. "If you could make the climb, you would have a long life." He heard the story from his great grandfather, Louis Chingwa ("Louie the Bear"), who made the climb and lived to the age of eighty-nine.[13]

Ettawageshik also said the Sleeping Bear legend about the mother bear and her two cubs who became the Manitou Islands "is not a tourist promotion thing. It is a favorite story of generations of my people."

The Beautiful Maiden of Sleeping Bear

Contributing to the mystique of Sleeping Bear Country is the Algonquin tale of Petta Kway, or The Tempest, as recounted by Schoolcraft. Here is an abbreviated version:

> There once lived a woman called Monedo Kway on the sand mountains called Sleeping Bear of Lake Michigan, who had a beautiful daughter. She was so handsome that her mother feared she would be carried off. To prevent it, the mother put her in a box on the lake, which was tied by a long string to a stake on the shore. Every morning the mother pulled the box ashore, and combed her daughter's long, shining hair, gave her food, and then put her out again on the lake.
>
> A handsome young man came by one day while the mother was tending to the maiden. He wanted to marry the daughter but was rebuffed by the mother. The pride and haughtiness of the mother was talked of by the spirits living on that part of the lake. They met

together and determined to exert their power in humbling her. For this purpose they resolved to raise a great storm on the lake. The water began to toss and roar, and the tempest became so severe, that the string broke, and the box floated off through the straits down Lake Huron, and struck against the sandy shore at its outlet.

The place where it struck was near the lodge of a superannuated old spirit called Ishkwon Daimeka, or the keeper of the gate of the lakes. He opened the box and let out the beautiful daughter, took her into his lodge, and married her.

After long cries of lament by the mother, the spirits took pity, and raised another storm to bring her back. It was a greater one than the first. The daughter leaped into the box, and the waves carried her back to Sleeping Bear. The mother was startled to learn the beauty of the daughter had almost all departed. She then sent a message, offering the hand of her daughter to the man who earlier wanted to marry her. The man haughtily rebuffed the offer.

The storm that brought the daughter back was so strong and powerful it tore away a large

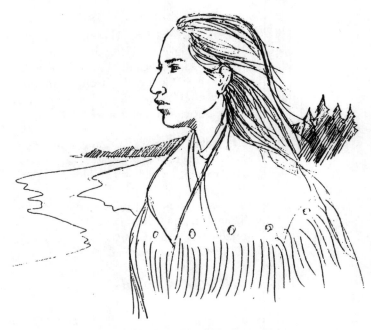

Leelinau—The Lost Daughter (Laura Schultz)

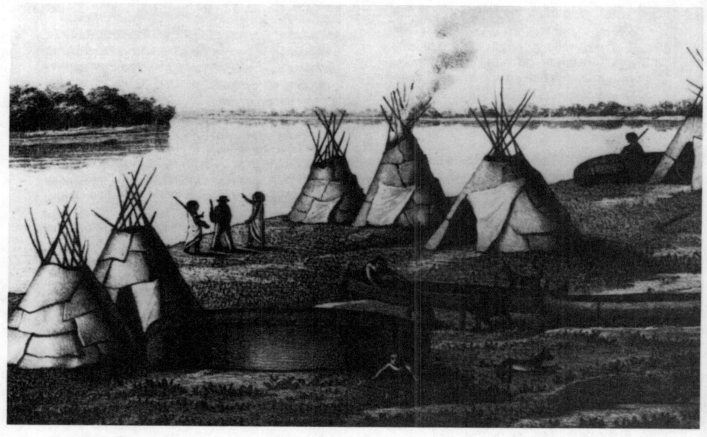

Typical early Ottawa temporary summer village in Northern Michigan (State Archives of Michigan)

part of the shore of Lake Huron, and swept off Ishkwon Daimeka's lodge, the fragments of which formed the beautiful islands now scattered in the St. Clair and Detroit rivers. Buried under the islands are the bones of the old man, who can be heard to lament:

> The waves, the waves, the angry waves,
> Have borne my bless'd away,
> And cast me forthall reft and lone,
> With wrecks of wood and clay …
> Yet shall I triumph; for the storm
> That sounds my funeral knell,
> Shall lands, and coasts, and islands form
> Where joy and peace shall dwell.[14]

Leelinau—The Lost Daughter

Leelanau was one of 21 unorganized counties in Michigan given names by Schoolcraft in 1840

when he was U.S. Indian Commissioner. He said the translation of Leelinau (the i was later changed to a) was "delight of life." He earlier had compiled a collection of legends that included "Leelinau, or the Lost Daughter, an Odjibwa Tale."[15] It tells of a pensive maiden, living on the shores of Lake Superior, who worries her family by continually leaving home to spend time among the pines of a sylvan haunt called Manitowak, or the Sacred Grove. On one such visit she was heard to plea:

> Spirit of the dancing leaves
> Hear a throbbing heart that grieves,
> Not for joys this world can give,
> But for the life that spirits live …
> Spirits hither quick repair,
> Hear a maiden's evening prayer.

Her prayer was answered. Showing "buoyant

6

delight," she disappeared from home and went to live in her enchanted "fairy haunted grove."*

Fables of Fancy: The Legends Vary

The Ottawa and Chippewa Indians of the Grand Traverse region, according to Schoolcraft, lacked knowledge of a recorded history. He wrote:

> They often cover the deficiency with a legend, or an allegory. These tales and allegories do not, generally, agree, but differ widely in their details, which arises from the narrator having no sure standard, and attempting to supply from fancy, what he, perhaps, cannot extract from memory. [16]

There are considerable variations in popularized versions of The Legend of Sleeping Bear. Some Ottawa story-tellers say the bears fled a famine, not a fire. Another version says the Great Spirit Manitou raised the two drowned cubs above the water as islands and named them North and South Manitou after himself.

According to an Indian legend described by Leelanau author Edmund M. Littell, both islands were inhabited by evil spirits. He wrote in 1965:

> Originally, says the legend, there were two powerful tribes, one in the Upper Peninsula and one on the lower, who were at war. The northern band attacked the southern band, and under the impression that they had killed them all, returned to the camp on the island. They left behind, however, seven survivors of the southern tribe, who under the cover of darkness came to the island and practically wiped out the northerners, retiring without being seen. The northerners who survived consequently blamed the loss of the others on evil spirits, with the result that no Indians lived on the islands afterward. [17]

As told by Schoolcraft, and re-told and reshaped by Longfellow, and lesser lights through the ages, the oral literature of American Indians underwent considerable poetic license. There were revisions to suit popular tastes, as well as the authors' own literary tastes.

Schoolcraft himself made modifications during the three decades from when he first began publishing tales in 1826 in manuscript magazines circulated among his friends, to the time in 1856 when he published *The Myth of Hiawatha* as a popularized and enlarged version of his 1839 *Algic Researches*.

Longfellow said he drew "from the various and valuable writings of Mr. Schoolcraft, to whom the literary world is greatly indebted for his indefatigable zeal in rescuing from oblivion so much of the legendary lore of the Indians."[18] Schoolcraft himself said that the Indian legends awaited the "arranger" who could touch them "with the spear of truth and cause the skeleton of their ancient society to arise and live."[19]

While Schoolcraft presumably was referring to a literary arranger, it is the archaeologist who has brought spears of evidence to historical consideration of the prehistoric society of Sleeping Bear Country.

Endnotes—Lore

1. W. Vernon Kinietz, *The Indians of the Western Great Lakes* 1615–1760 (Ann Arbor: The University of Michigan Press, 1965), 251.
2. Henry Rowe Schoolcraft, *Historical Reports*, Vol. I, 34–35.
3. Schoolcraft, 658.
4. Henry Wadsworth Longfellow, *The Song of Hiawatha*, (New York: Bounty Books, 1982), 15. (facsimile reprint of 1890 edition).
5. Schoolcraft, Vol. V, 402.
6. Kinietz, 285.
7. Andrew J. Blackbird, *History of the Ottawa and Chippewa Indians of Michigan* (1887), (Petoskey: Little Traverse Regional Historical Society, 1977), (Reprint of 1887 edition), 14. (When D.C. Leach of Traverse City was Indian Agent, Blackbird served as U.S. Interpreter, and later became postmaster of Little Traverse, now Harbor Springs. His father was Chief Macka-de-pe-nessy of L'Arbre Croche [The Crooked Tree], now Good Hart).
8. Kinietz, 285.
9. Kinietz, 288.
10. Gertrude Prokosch Kurath, *Michigan Indian Festivals*, (Ann Arbor: Ann Arbor Publishers, 1966), 7. The University of Michigan, A Sesquicentennial Publication.

*See Appendix for full text of legend of "Leelinau."

11. Kurath, 2 (attributed to Anthony Chingman).

12. Kurath, 10. (Fred Ettawageshik and his wife Jane, collaborated with Gertrude Kurath on the book).

13. Frank Ettawageshik, interview in Karlin, MI, with the author, 1987. (Frank Ettawageshik, son of Fred and Jane, is an artist, known especially for traditional Woodland Indian pottery.)

14. Henry Rowe Schoolcraft, *Algic Researches*, (New York: Harper & Brothers, 1839), I, 129–133 (includes the full text of the legend, and all eight verses of Ishkwon Daimeka's Lament). A selection of this and other legends from Algic Researches, as well as other Schoolcraft writings, can be found in a more contemporary work, *Schoolcraft's Indian Legends*, edited by Mentor L. Williams, (Westport, Conn.: Greenwood Press, 1974), originally published in 1956 by Michigan State University Press, East Lansing).

15. Schoolcraft, II, 77–84.

16. Schoolcraft, V, 192.

17. Edmund M. Littell, *100 Years in Leelanau*, (Leland, MI: The Print Shop, 1965), 2.

18. Longfellow, 230.

19. Mentor L. Williams, *Indian Legends* (Westport, Conn.: Greenwood Press, 1974), xxi.

CHAPTER 2

Prehistoric Times— The First Visitors and Dwellers

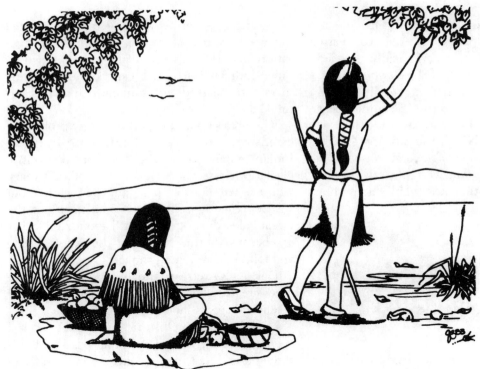

*O Great Spirit
Whose voice I hear in the winds,
And whose breath gives life to
   all the world . . .
Let me learn the lessons
You have hidden in every leaf and rock.*

—Indian prayer,
Immaculate Conception Church,
Peshawbestown

(Drawing by Jolene Barber, courtesy of Native American Arts & Crafts Council)

Hidden under the leaves and rocks of Sleeping Bear Country is evidence that its first human inhabitants used it much as it is used today—for seasonal activity. There is considerable evidence of periodic use of the area by prehistoric Indians about 3,000 years ago, and some evidence that it began even earlier. Archaeological discoveries in the 1970s and 1980s pushed back in time the periods in which prehistoric Indians were thought to have used the region.

After retreat of the glaciers, the area became available for human occupation about 11,300 to

11, 000 years ago—or approximately 9, 000 B.C. But it was an inhospitable heap of rubble, and it took some time before the area produced the plants and animals that lured humans.

Although evidence about the time and circumstance of the first use is scant, accelerated archaeological research prompted by establishment of the Sleeping Bear Dunes National Lakeshore provided new information about the area's cultural past. As with any archaeological record, the glimpses are only occasional and extremely limited, but even the most meager prehistoric artifacts offer important clues about the area's first visitors and dwellers.

In Michigan, as elsewhere in North America, there is archaeological evidence of human life before the end of the ice age. The first human populations migrated to North America nearly 40,000 years ago across a periodically exposed land bridge in the vicinity of the Bering Straits. According to Dr. William A. Lovis in a 1984 archaeological report on the Sleeping Bear Dunes National Lakeshore prepared for the National Park Service (NPS), the crossing 40,000 years ago "was only one of several episodes of migration of people from Siberia into the Western hemisphere, and that it is highly likely that

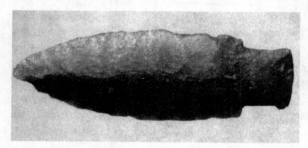

This late Paleo-Indian projectile point, dated about 6, 000 B.C., was among 1987 discoveries that changed the picture archaeologists have drawn of prehistoric Michigan.
(Northern Michigan University)

there was a major influx of people about 14,000 years ago. Due to the longevity of glacial and postglacial activity across the Great Lakes in general and Michigan in particular, however, human occupation of the state initiates about 13,000 years ago or 11,000 B.C."[1] The Lovis

report tabulates the evolution of human occupation of the Lakeshore as follows:

Paleo Indian	11,000+ B.C	to	8,000 B.C.
Early Archaic	8,000 B.C.	to	6,000 B.C.
Middle Archaic	6,000 B.C.	to	3,000 B.C.
Late Archaic	3,000 B.C.	to	600 B.C.
& Early Woodland	600 B.C.	to	300 B.C.
Middle Woodland	300 B.C.	to	500/600 A.D.
Late Woodland	500/600 A.D.	to	1620 A.D.
Historic Contact	1620 A.D.	to	1830 A.D.

Paleo-Indian Period (11,000 + B.C. to 8,000 B.C.)

During this era, a warming trend prompted northward retreat of the ice, restoration of vegetation and the migration of groups known as Paleo-Indians into Michigan to hunt grazing mammoth, mastodon, bison, caribou and white-tailed deer.

The area's complex glacial history prohibited extensive use of Sleeping Bear Country by Paleo-Indian populations. The last, or Wisconsin, glaciation lasted about 10,000 to 50,000 years, with the ice disappearing from the region about 11,000 years ago. The final adjustment of the Great Lakes did not occur until about 2,000 years ago because of fluctuations of the waters during and following retreat of the ice.

During its retreat, the great Wisconsin ice sheet created the Manitou Islands as well as the Fox and Beaver island chains.

Most sites of prehistoric occupation of the area are currently submerged under Lake Michigan, and much of the evidence of any preglacial life on land was ground out by the enormous sheets of ice. But, scant as it is, Lovis notes some evidence of Paleo-Indians in the region. He said "most of this evidence is confined to scattered surface finds of distinctive spear points on the moraines."

These include both the very typical 'fluted' points as well as unfluted but beautifully flaked late Paleo-Indian spearpoints typical of northern Wisconsin and other northern areas.

"The great mobility of these hunters is

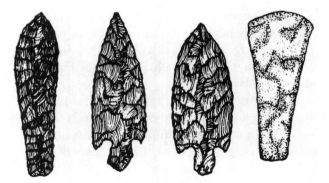

Late Archaic blades and knives. (Michigan Bureau of History)

attested to by the use of both local flint, as well as flint from as far away as Bay Port, Michigan, on Saginaw Bay. Their camps were temporary, and appear to have been used primarily for the butchering and skinning of game animals, since large leaf-shaped chipped stone knives, and hide-scraping implements dominate the tool kits of these people."[2]

What may be the oldest known event in Michigan history took place during the Paleo-Indian period. James E. Fitting relates this story:

Beneath the sparse spruce cover, a silent man watched the clearing on either side of the small cold stream that flowed into the shallow lake to his east. The time was fall, and the first snowflakes were in the air. Suddenly he saw them: a herd of thousands of deer, the great barren ground caribou. Quickly he ran back to camp and gathered his fellow hunters, a small group of six men all related by blood or marriage. He had hunted with them before, Sometimes with luck and sometimes without, and he knew that he could trust them to do their share.

The men returned to the bank and slew the caribou with spears as they came out of the water. The air was now full of the sounds of animals and men as stone tipped lances pierced the hides of the fat fall animals returning from the summer meadows of the north to the winter forest cover of the south.

The men were a hard lot, descendants of the big game hunters that had crossed to this new land out of Asia only a few generations before. They had chosen to live in the new lands recently opened by the retreating glacial ice. They followed the animals and learned their

ways. Their reward was survival; failure meant death. This kill was good, and the meat of the caribou was roasted and eaten in camp that night.[3]

This conjectured tale is based on discovery north of Detroit of the earliest known Michigan habitation site for Paleo-Indian hunters identi-

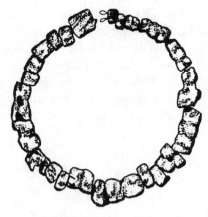

Late Archaic copper beads. (Michigan Bureau of History)

fied by their lanceolate projectile points. Shifting the sands of an old beach ridge, archaeologists found the broken tools, caribou bone, and fire inhabitants of North America and roamed Michigan as the Wisconsin ice sheet retreated northward.

While no such extensive find had been discovered by then in Sleeping Bear Country, a 1987 discovery in the Upper Peninsula further defines the time of northern Michigan human habitation and provides an important piece in

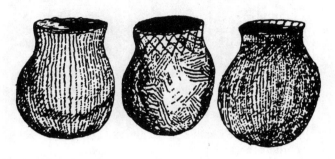

Late Woodland pottery vessels. (Michigan Bureau of History)

11

the Michigan archaeological puzzle of which Sleeping Bear is an intriguing part.

Northern Michigan University anthropologist Marla M. Buckmaster reported finding more than 80 Paleo-Indian points and fragments at a site on a drained lake bed in northern Marquette County. She dated them at about 6,000 B.C., and said "this pushes the time of first human habitation of the Upper Peninsula back some 4,000 years. . . . Knowing that the Paleo-Indians inhabited the Lake Superior country changes the whole picture archaeologists have drawn of prehistoric Indian settlement Patterns."[4]

Among the artifacts unearthed was a six-inch-long point of quartz-like Hixton silicified sandstone which came from southwestern Wisconsin.

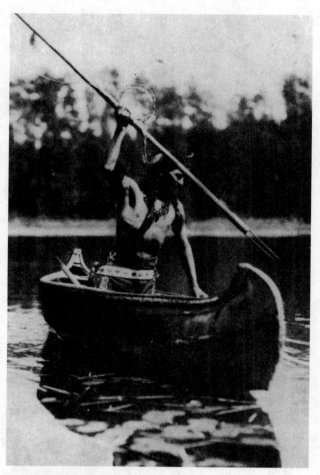

Chippewa and Ottawa shared several hunting and fishing territories including the Sleeping Bear area.

(State Archives of Michigan)

This site apparently was used for cremation burials in which many of the artifacts were buried with the body. There is evidence that the Indians probably migrated to Michigan from as far west as present-day Wyoming.

Thus, from fragmentary discoveries in the immediate area, and more extensive finds to the north and south of Sleeping Bear Country, a hazy picture emerges of first human use of the Lakeshore.

Most experts agree that people were passing through Sleeping Bear in Paleo-Indian times, and hunting close to the edge of retreating glaciers near the Grand Traverse region.[5]

The Archaic Period (8,000 B.C. to 600 B.C.)

Because of periodic raising and lowering of water levels, little is known of the archaeology of the Lakeshore during the Early (8,000 B.C. to 6,000 B.C.) and Middle (6,000 B.C. to 3,000 B.C.) Archaic periods. Between 8,000 B.C. and 7,000 B.C., retreat of the ice allowed the lakes to drain eastward rather than to the south down the Mississippi as they had in Paleo-Indian times. By 7,000 B.C., the Michigan basin takes were nearly 400 feet lower than they are today.[6]

While most evidence of prehistoric Lakeshore inhabitants is submerged, the National Park Service survey by Lovis said:

> We know from other parts of Michigan and the Midwest . . . that these people were probably adapting to changes in vegetation during post-glacial times. In the Lakeshsore area, these changes would have included a shift toward more mixed conifer and broadleaf forests typical of a transition between northern and southern biotic communities. We know from southeastern Michigan and the Saginaw Valley that Michigan's prehistoric populations were related at least in terms of their artifact styles to southern traditions from as far away as the Carolinas.[7]

By 2,000 B.C., the lakes were high again, the rivers filled with fish, and the forests were becoming more like they are today. As Fitting observed:

> Men moved back into the state from the south, bringing with them a rich ceremonial life centered around a burial cult. Between 2,000 B.C. and 500 B.C. they had not yet learned the art of pottery making, hunted deer in the fall and winter and hunted small animals and fished in the summer.[8]

From about 4,700 years ago, at the beginning of the Late Archaic Period (3,000 B.C. to 500 B.C.), there is direct evidence of occupation in the Lakeshore. Lake elevations were again high, and beachlines from this period still exist across the Lakeshore. According to Lovis:

> During this period, known as the Nipissing stage, Platte Lake, Glen Lake, Crystal Lake and other smaller lakes were actually connected with Lake Michigan as shallow bays, creating protected and favorable lakeshore environments. In addition, there is good evidence from North and South Manitou Islands revealing that these areas were also favored by Late Archaic peoples.
>
> The Late Archaic period across the Eastern United States is characterized by a complex series of transformations in technology, social organization, and economics. Human groups began to schedule their use of a wide range of animal and plant foods on a seasonal basis, and in this (Lakeshore) region move between these different resources from season to season.[9]

Trade, or exchange, of locally rare high status items such as flint from Indiana, copper from Lake Superior, and conch shells from the Gulf Coast of Florida reflects wide-ranging social contacts. At a discovered burial site known as the Dunn Farm Site on the eastern shore of Big Glen Lake, artifacts made from exotic materials from across the Midwest and Great Lakes were found amidst cremated human bone.

At a site on North Manitou Island, one of the Lakeshore's richest sources of archaeological discovery, a large copper awl was found. Significant Late Archaic artifacts were also found at a site

now covered by a beech and maple forest along bluffs on the north end of the island.

Lovis said "it is clear that these are local people. They are using local flint from the vicinity of Norwood, Michigan, and their styles of artifacts are local as well. They provide us with our first archaeological glimpse of a local, indigenous, occupation of the Sleeping Bear Dunes National Lakeshore."[10]

The Woodland Period (600 B.C. to A.D. 1620)

The last prehistoric period before European contact is called the Woodland, a time when archaeologists define cultural boundaries in terms of types of pottery, which people started making at the time. There are two other ceramic traditions in the Great Lakes region (the Upper Mississippian and the Mississippian), but Woodland is by far the dominant one.

As described by Helen Hornbeck Tanner's *Atlas of Great Lakes Indian History*, Woodland pottery is most often tempered with coarse grit and the surface has a cord-roughened finish produced by malleting the pot with a cordwrapped paddle. The upper portions of the globular vessels often have pronounced shoulders and collars. Decoration is done with repeated application of twisted cords, punctates, or incised lines placed in geometric patterns on the upper rim and lips.[11]

The earliest of the Woodland occupations in Sleeping Bear Country is represented at a Fisher Lake site east of Glen Arbor, which had pottery dating between A.D. 200 and A.D. 600—the late Middle Woodland Period-and has been interpreted as a short-term fishing station.[12]

Lovis, noting that it is most likely that the site represents a northern pottery tradition, concluded:

> It is clear that during the Middle Woodland that the Sleeping Bear Dunes area is being occupied by populations from further north in the Michigan basin.
>
> Subsequent Late Woodland occupation of the Lakeshore is present at about a dozen

known sites that variously date between A.D. 600 and A.D. 1620. These occur on the mainland shore, on interior lakes and streams, and on both North and South Manitou Islands. A wide range of habitats are being exploited during this period. Distinctive Late Woodland pottery, thin, crumbly containers tempered with finely crushed granite and decorated with different kinds of cord, twine, and fabric impressions, have been found at least three sites in the Lakeshore.[13]

At the Fisher Lake and South and North Manitou Island sites, the decorations reveal origins from the Straits of Mackinac, Wisconsin's Door Peninsula and Michigan's Mason and Oceana counties. The arrow points are from Norwood flint found in the Charlevoix vicinity. Much of the chippage from stone tool manufacture is from the Saginaw Bay area. "Apparently there is continued exchange, and perhaps intermarriage and other contact, during this period," Lovis said in his 1984 survey for the National Park Service.[14]

Further indication of the links between Sleeping Bear Indians and the Mackinac area comes from one of the most important Woodland archaeological sites in the Lakeshore-the campground on the Platte River near the M-22 bridge. Artifacts indicate the riverbank was used by Woodland Indians for at least 1,000 years, starting about A.D. 500.

As Lakeshore Superintendent Richard R. Peterson reported to the Sleeping Bear Dunes National Lakeshore Advisory Commission in 1987: "What this site depicts is not a village but rather relatively small social units, probably a few related families, utilizing this area on a seasonal basis actually very much like what campers are doing today in this area."[15]

These activities were indicated by pottery, stone tools and large quantities of waste flakes which are the by-product of manufacture of stone tools. Of particular importance was discovery of Hopewell pottery, reflecting the Indian culture which emerged about 500 B.C. in the lower Midwest.

During the Late Woodland (A.D. 500–600 to 1620) period, summer agricultural activities flourished to the south of Sleeping Bear and an autumn fishery to the north.

In the Lakeshore, the last prehistoric centuries apparently were characterized by short-term sites used primarily for seasonal hunting, with some fishing and gathering of wild rice and berries.

While Lovis concluded that "it is unlikely that major settlements exist in the Lakeshore," clearly the Late Woodland period was the most pronounced period of occupation and activity in Sleeping Bear Country's prehistoric period, with most of the area's known archaeological sites being associated with that time.[16]

"Let me learn the lessons You have hidden in every leaf and rock," says the prayer of today's Native Americans in Leelanau. Through the language of archaeology, their ancestors speak from the soil, providing lessons about the region's past, however fragmentary and uncertain, that have been hidden for centuries.

There is the lesson of the Manitou Islands. While embodiments of the Great Spirit, they were not off bounds for occupation. As noted in the previous chapter, some nineteenth and twentieth century writers say they were. Archaeology and ethnological research tell us otherwise.

Charles E. Cleland, curator of Anthropology at the Michigan State University Museum, in a 1967 report on an archaeological survey of North Manitou Island indicated that it

> was far from being the foreboding spirit-haunted burial place of modern Indian folklore. Indeed, this island was the home of many Indian peoples.
> . . . (it) was probably inhabited by primitive peoples by at least 1, 000 B.C. and was certainly occupied again sometime between A.D. 1,000 and the coming of the Europeans to the Lake Michigan basin.[17]

Executive Director William Church of the Michigan Indian Affairs Commission said archaeological discoveries of prehistoric activity in the Sleeping Bear area helped provide "a hazy view into the distant past." He said the statement by Lovis about people passing through Sleeping

Bear in Paleo-Indian times "makes a whole lot of sense."[18]

Endnotes—Prehistoric Times

1. William A. Lovis, *Sleeping Bear Dunes National Lakeshore: Archaeological Survey,* (Denver, Colo.: National Park Service, 1984), 2–3.

2. Lovis, 4.

3. Fitting, James E., "Archaeology in Michigan," Great Lakes Informant, Michigan History Division, Lansing, September 1984, p. 1.

4. Buckmaster, Marla M., "Valuable Artifacts Found," press release from Northern Michigan University, Marquette, Dec. 10, 1987.

5. Lovis, in a Jan. 7, 1988, comment to the author. (See also William A. Lovis, Robert Mainfort and Vergil E. Nobel, "An Archaeological Inventory and Evaluation of the Sleeping Bear Dunes National Lakeshore, Leelanau and Benzie Counties, Michigan," the National Park Service, June 30, 1976.) Buckmaster, comment to the author Jan. 6, 1988. Jeff Richner, comment to the author, Midwest Archaeological Center, National Park Service, Lincoln, Nebraska, Jan. 7, 1988.

6. Fitting, 2.

7. Lovis, 5.

8. Fitting, 2.

9. Lovis, 6.

10. Lovis, 7.

11. Helen Hornbeck Tanner, *Atlas of Great Lakes Indian History,* (Norman, Oklahoma: University of Oklahoma Press, 1987) 25.

12. Lovis, 8.

13. Lovis, 8–9.

14. Lovis, 9.

15. Richard R. Peterson, Lakeshore superintendent, statement at July 31, 1987 meeting of the Sleeping Bear Dunes National Lakeshore Advisory Council attended by author.

16. Lovis, 9. James Muhn, *Historic Resource Study, Sleeping Bear Dunes National Lakeshore,* (Denver, Colo.: National Park Service, Branch of Historical Preservation, 1979), 5.

17. Charles E. Cleland, "A Preliminary Report on the Prehistoric Resources of North Manitou Island submitted to William R. Angel Foundation, Detroit, 1967, 1, 11.

18. William Church, Executive Director of the Michigan Indian Affairs Commission, statement to the author, May 5, 1988.

CHAPTER 3

"Michigamies"—The Historic Period Begins

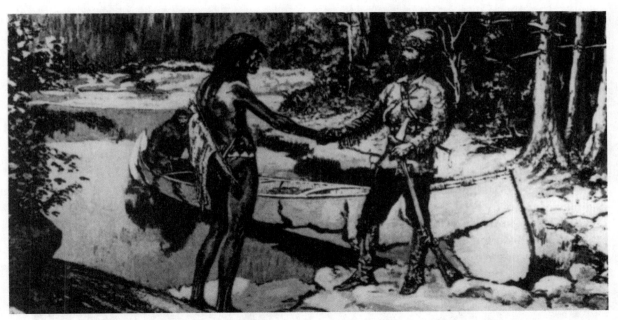

Arrival of trappers and other white men brought change to Indian life in Michigan. (State Archives of Michigan)

There is a mountain there which the savages call the sleeping bear, because it is shaped like one. They say that after the flood the canoe which saved their fathers ran aground there and stopped.
—*Antoine Denis Raudot, describing Lake Michigan in his 1710* Memoir
Concerning the Different Indian Nations North America.[1]

There does not appear to be a marked break between the prehistoric inhabitants of Sleeping Bear Country and the Indians living there when the first French discovers arrived. But Indian life changed markedly with arrival of the white men and start of "historic times"—so called because writers like Raudot began recording it. For one thing, the new arrivals gave a European slant to the history of Native Americans as missionaries tried to convert them, and white Americans later tried to re-locate them.

In truth, the "savages" gave white men' much of value that was produced long before European arrival. As Michigan historian George N. Fuller observed in the early twentieth century:

> Maize or Indian corn was perhaps the most valuable of all agricultural products which the Indians passed on to the white people. . . . White men learned by imitating the Indian how to live off the products of the wilderness, and how to penetrate most easily the wilderness barriers. The birchbark canoe of the Indian has been called the most perfect vehicle of its kind. Without this canoe and with Indians to paddle it and carry it around the portages, the French would not have discovered the Great Lakes so early as they did.[2]

The footpaths of Native Americans blazed the trails for fur traders, settlers and the road-builders whose ribbons of concrete and asphalt now bring modern day visitors to the Lakeshore. The two most important Indian trails in Michigan were the Sauk Trail, which U.S. 12 generally follows between Detroit and Chicago today, and the Saginaw-Mackinac Trail, a branch of which came into the Grand Traverse Region.

As the prehistoric period ended early in the 1600's, tribal warfare inhibited Indian occupancy of the Lower Peninsula. During much of the 17th

century, the powerful Five Nations Iroquois from upstate New York dispatched war parties to gain control of Michigan's fur trade, forcing the Potawatomi, Sauk and Foxes to flee westward. The Iroquois aggression virtually depopulated the peninsula, making it a "no man's land" between themselves and tribes occupying the Upper Peninsula and Wisconsin.[3]

The Ottawa and Chippewa—First Families of Sleeping Bear

The Chippewa spread across the Upper Peninsula and around Lake Superior, while the Ottawa occupied shores of Lake Huron. During the mid-

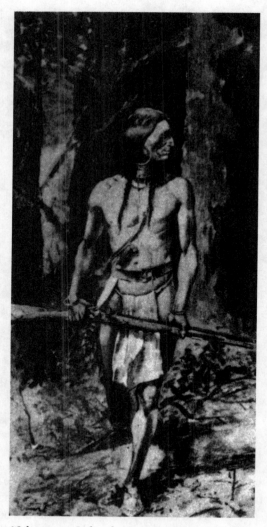

An 18th century Indian hunter. (State Archives of Michigan)

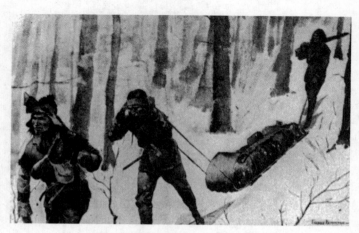

Tobaggans and snowshoes helped winter travel.
(State Archives of Michigan)

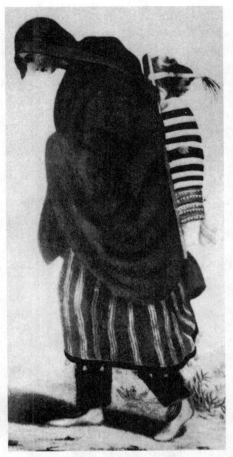

A deerskin strap over a Chippewa mother's head enabled her to carry a child in a cradle board made with moss and rabbit fur. (State Archives of Michigan)

fields. After considering several other sites, including the Grand Traverse area, in 1742 they selected L'Arbre Croche, so named after a crooked pine tree, north of what is now Petoskey.[5]

The original L'Arbre Croche is now Good Hart. The term later covered the entire coastal region from Little Traverse Bay to Cross Village, and the Ottawas named a second village New L'Arbre Croche at what is now Harbor Springs.

The founding of L'Arbre Croche was an important factor in Sleeping Bear history because it led to shift of the center of Ottawa populati on from eastern to western Michigan.

The Michigamies

"Michigamies" is a term the French applied to several tribes and bands of Indians of the Algonquin lineage who clustered around the borders of Lake Michigan. As Schoolcraft observed in the 1850's, "The lake itself takes its name from them, being a compound of two words which signify great and lake."[6]

At Schoolcraft's writing, some of the Algonquins had already disappeared, including the Muskoda. In this account, Schoolcraft refers to their defeat and the alternating Ottawa and Chippewa occupations on Lake Michigan's eastern shore:

> Ishqua-gonabi, chief of the Chippewas on Grand Traverse Bay, and a man knowing traditions, denotes the war against Muskoda men or dwellers on Little Prairie or Plains, to have been carried on by the Chippewas and Ottawas, and in this manner he accounts for the fact that villages of Chippewas and Ottawas alternate at this day on the eastern shores of Lake Michigan. Ossigunac, an Ottawa chief of note of Penetauguishine, says that the Ottawas went at first to live among the men called the Potawatomies, about the southern shores or head of Lake Michigan; but the latter used bad medicine, and when complained of for their necromancy, they told the Ottawas they might go back towards the north if they did not like them.[7]

seventeenth century, Ottawas migrated westward across the peninsula, farming, fishing and hunting principally for deer, bear and beaver. In what are now Benzie and Leelanau counties, much of agriculture focused on corn and wild rice, and there were camps for gathering of maple sugar. Apart from seasonal migrations, Indians moved their settlements occasionally, out of fear of hostile tribes or because of unproductiveness of unfertilized soil, and did not hunt the same region each year. For example, the Glen Lake area was visited once every three years.[4]

While Sleeping Bear Country was a favorite seasonal hunting ground, it was not among the places considered when the Ottawa at Mackinac contemplated moving elsewhere for more fertile

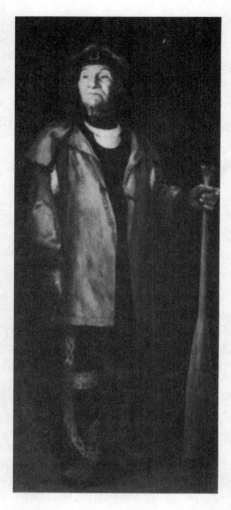

Shop-Ne-Gon, a Chippewa born near Saginaw, became a favored trapper and guide when 19th century lumbering brought an influx of whites into northern Michigan.
(Detroit Institute of Arts)

"The Battle for The Bear"

A vivid, but unverified, account of a fierce two-day 1803 Indian battle at Sleeping Bear was provided by Flavius Josephus Littlejohn, a nineteenth century circuit-riding judge, president pro-tem of the state Senate and an unsuccessful candidate for governor. Based on accounts provided by what he called "Michigan scouts," Littlejohn described how the Ottawa fought off an invasion by the Sauk and Fox tribes of Wisconsin and the Chippewas of the Upper Peninsula. Thousands of spent arrows were said to have been left scattered on the ground, in trees and along shores of Lake Michigan and Glen Lake, then known as Bear Lake. Archaeologists to date have found no physical evidence of such an epic

battle, and it appears to have escaped mention of contemporary writers or the acceptance of subsequent Michigan historians.

While noting the lack of verification, twentieth century Glen Arbor writer Rob Rader said, "many details are accurate, particularly descriptions of the geographical locations of his stories."[8]

The Three Brothers

The Potawatomi, Ottawa and Chippewa were called the "three brothers" of the Algonquin family, and were loosely organized in the Three Fires Confederacy. As the Potawatomi migrated south, the Chippewa and Ottawa, in general, co-

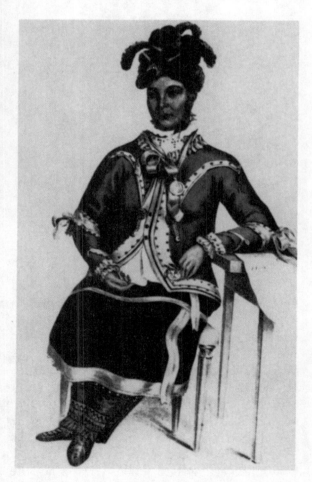

Tshusick, a Chippewa woman from Michigan, wore fancy clothing with traditional moccasins and leggings on an 1826 visit to Washington. (State Archvies of Michigan)

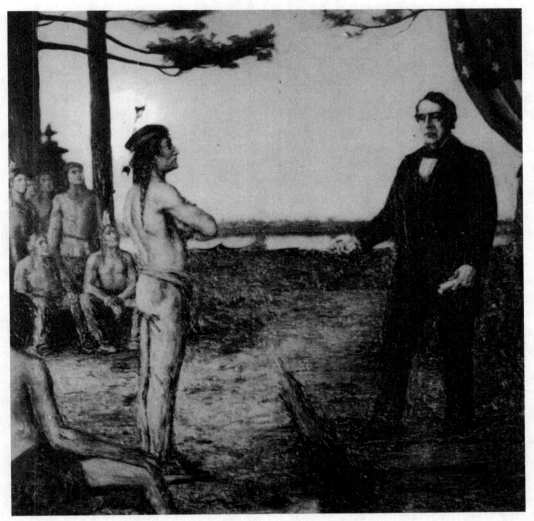

Territorial Governor Lewis Cass negotiates with Chippewa Chief Kishkaukou before making the 1819 Treaty of Saginaw that gained about six million acres of northeastern land for Michigan. (State Archives of Michigan)

mingled peacefully in northern Michigan. They shared several hunting and fishing territories, including the Sleeping Bear area. Chippewa is an English corruption of Ojibwa, a word variously referring to 1) the practice of recording information by drawing glyphs and signs on birch bark, and 2) the puckered seam characteristic of moccasins. Also, in some usage, called Ojibway, Odjibwa, Outchibous, Otchipwe.

Ottawas were also called Outaouacs, Ottowas, Odawas, Utawawas, and Otawawas. Modern day Northwestern Michigan Ottawa appear to favor the pronunciation O-dah-wah. Kinietz said application of the term is as diverse as its spelling, including designation of Ottawa as a band "who have come from the nation of the raised hair." It is also said that French traders knew the Ottawa as people who had gone "Outaways," according to Ethel Rowan Fasquelle in *When Michigan Was Young.*

Potawatomies was described by Schoolcraft as meaning "makers of fire—a symbolic phrase, by which is meant they who assume separate sovereignty by building a council-fire for themselves. "

One notable exception to friendly relations—the stabbing of a young Chippewa by a young Ottawa in a dispute over some fishing nets in the Straits of Mackinac—is said to have resulted in transfer of Sleeping Bear Country from Ottawas to Chippewas.

Indian writer Andrew Blackbird said, "The Chippewas proposed war to settle the question of murder, while the Ottawas proposed compromise and restitution for the murder. Finally the Ottawas succeeded in settling the difficulty by ceding part of their country to the Chippewa nation, which is now known and distinguished as the Grand Traverse Region."

He said this involved "A strip of land which I believe to have extended from a point near Sleeping Bear, down to the eastern shore of the Grand Traverse Bay, some 30 or 40 miles wide, thence between two parallel lines running southeasterly until they strike the head waters of Muskegon River, which empties into Lake Michigan not very far below Grand Haven."[9]

Although there was considerable migration in and out of the area, Sleeping Bear was off the main path of travel by early Great Lakes Indians. From the Mackinac Straits, the main route south was along the north shore of Lake Michigan to Green Bay, and then down the Fox-Wisconsin waterway to the Mississippi River. An alternate southern route from Mackinac was along the west shore of Lake Michigan to Chicago.[10]

While Indian villages were the recognized home bases for their inhabitants, the villages, unlike white settlements, were seldom fully occupied during the entire year.[11]

Schoolcraft expressed this view on the migrations:

> An Indian considers 100 miles but a short distance, and 1,000 miles as not a long one to march, when the purpose he has in view is to glut his vengeance, or gratify himself. He is not a man who pines for the enjoyments of home, there is not much to attach him to it; to camp in the woods is his delight, and the wilderness is, comparatively, his dwelling. Time passes lightly with him, its pace never wearies him; and anything that cheats him of the very idea of its passage is pleasant. To journey . . . for the trifling present of a gun, a blanket, or a kettle, a pound of powder, a gorget, or a flag, was, in point of enterprise, considered as nothing for an Indian chief. To him, to whom time is nothing, and

wandering pleasure, the toil is ten times overpaid by the reward.[12]

Schoolcraft was an important, yet controversial, figure in the history of Sleeping Bear Country. He chronicled its lore and legends (see Chapter One), and was the first American to make a shoreline survey of Sleeping Bear and to provide a written record of having seen it (see Chapter Four). As Michigan's Superintendent of Indian Affairs, he helped prepare the way for the 1836 Treaty of Washington, under which the Chippewa and Ottawa ceded to the United States the northwestern lower peninsula, including Sleeping Bear Country, and the eastern half of the Upper Peninsula.

The treaty removed an obstacle to Michigan's 1837 admission to statehood, and, as revised by the Senate, provided for re-location of Indians to western lands.

But there were dissenting views in the nineteenth century about the treaty, as there are debates today about the interpretations of Michigan's prehistoric civilizations.

Of the treaty, Andrew Blackbird wrote in 1887:

> . . . my people—the Ottawas and Chippewas—were unwilling parties, but they were compelled to sign blindly and ignorant of the true spirit of the treaty and the true import of some of its conditions. They thought when signing the treaty that they were securing reservations of lands in themselves and their children in the future; but before six months had elapsed from the time of signing this treaty, or soon after it had been put in pamphlet form so that all persons could read it and know its terms, they were told by their white neighbors that their reservations of land would expire in five years, instead of being perpetual, as they believed."[13]

The Ottawa were particularly effective in organizing public support for opposition to being moved from a woodland environment to the prairies of Kansas. Their success meant a continuing presence in northwest Michigan, and prompted James M. McClurken of the Michigan State University Museum to comment:

> The successful struggle of the Ottawa to remain in their homeland, by adapting to the expanding American economy and political system often on their own culturally defined terms, demonstrated that the Ottawa were the antithesis of the poor, downtrodden, and defeated Indians so frequently described in historical literature.[14]

This controversy about indigenous prehistory is pointedly addressed by the Grand Rapids Inter-Tribal Council's Michigan Indian Press in its authorized history, *People of The Three Fires: The Ottawa, Potawatomi and Ojibway of Michigan:*

> . . . native peoples do not always subscribe to academic interpretations of their respective histories and beliefs. For centuries, scholars have been attempting to theoretically explain the origins of American Indians. In contrast, it should be remembered that native peoples have formalized traditions that describe their existence in diverse regions. American Indians explain their life and past as an act of creation rather than as a stage in evolutionary theory. All peoples have an undeniable right to spiritual interpretation of life and purpose. These beliefs are the very core of Native American societies and must be considered as viable alternatives to continuously changing "scientific" explanations.[15]

In noting that the historic dates assigned to Native American civilizations are constantly being revised, the book observed that "American Indian influence on the North American continent is now thought to have been more pervasive and much older than previously believed."

This is the case in Sleeping Bear Country.

Endnotes—The Historic Period Begins

1. W. Vernon Kinietz, *The Indians of the Western Great Lakes, 1615–1760*, (Ann Arbor: University of Michigan Press, 1965), 380.
2. George N. Fuller, *Michigan, A Centennial History of the State and Its People*, (Chicago: The Lewis Publishing Co., 1939), I, 6.
3. Muhn, 6.
4. Kinietz, 236–37.
5. Kinietz, 230.
6. Schoolcraft, V, 191.
7. Schoolcraft, I, 308.
8. Rader, Rob, The Small-Towner Magazine, Glen Arbor, (August 1985), 56–59, based on F. J. Littlejohn's *Legends of Michigan and the Old North West*, (Allegan, Mi.: Northwestern Bible and Publishing Co., 1875).
9. Andrew Blackbird, 97.
10. Tanner, 7.
11. Tanner, 7.
12. Schoolcraft, VI, 208.
13. Blackbird, 97.
14. James M. McClurken, "Ottawa Adaptive Strategies to Indian Removal," *The Michigan Historical Review*, (Spring 1986), 55.
15. James A. Clifton; George L. Cornell; and James M. McClurken, *People of The Three Fires: The Ottawa, Potawatomi and Ojibway of Michigan*, (Grand Rapids: Grand Rapids Inter-Tribal Council), v.

CHAPTER 4

Days of Discovery—
European Explorers and
American Expeditions

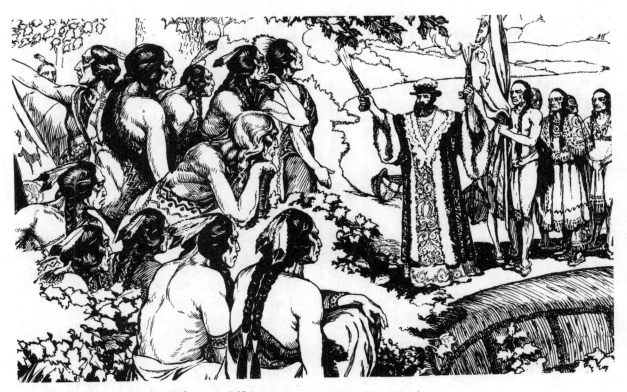

Jean Nicolet discovered Lake Michigan in 1634. (Mackinac Island Park Commission)

Seas of Sweet Water
—Jesuit description of the unchartered Great Lakes

Sleeping Bear Country was late to he discovered, and was only vaguely known, during initial exploration of the Great Lakes.

The first people of the Sleeping Bear, those present before European exploration and later American settlement, drastically impacted those who came second. The first white men known to have visited the Sleeping Bear area were the French, who came to the Great Lakes via the St. Lawrence River in the seventeenth century as fur traders, missionaries and Orient-seeking explorers. While searching for a route to Asia from Quebec, Jean Nicolet discovered Lake Michigan in 1634, some 12 years after French explorers had discovered Lake Superior. He wore a mandarin's robes embroidered with poppies and birds of paradise when he went ashore at Green Bay, thinking the "Seas of Sweet Water" had led him to the Orient.

The first white man known to have visited Michigan's Lower Peninsula was trapper-explorer Adrien Jolliet, who came to the peninsula's eastern shores in 1669. Fur trappers may have preceded them, but it was in 1675 that the first non-Indians were recorded to have seen the Sleeping Bear area. They were Pierre Porteret and Jacques Largilier, attendants of Father Jacques Marquette, the famous French Jesuit missionary who established missions in 1668 at Sault Ste. Marie (oldest permanently occupied settlement in Michigan) and St. Ignace in 1671, and was co-discoverer of the Mississippi in 1673 on a trip that began the recorded history of Chicago.

Porteret and Largilier had accompanied Marquette on his last canoe voyage (1674–1675) from St. Ignace, hub of French activities in the western Great Lakes, to start a mission among Illinois Indians. They went south by the customary route along the western shore on the Wisconsin side of Lake Michigan, but made the northward return trip along the lake's eastern shore after Marquette became mortally ill and wanted to take advantage of northwardly currents to return to St. Ignace before he died. The route was relatively unknown to the French because seventeenth century intertribal warfare, as well as Iroquois animosity toward the French, made much of Michigan's Lower Peninsula inhospitable.

According to Father Claude Dablon, superior of the Jesuits in Canada, it was the first trip along Lake Michigan's eastern shore for Marquette, who was "so feeble and exhausted that he was unable to assist or even to move himself, and had to be handled and carried about like a child."[1.] His companions continued northward after Marquette, at age thirty-eight, died May 18, 1675, ashore near the mouth of a river south of the Dunes. just how far south has been a matter of dispute. For decades, the most widely-accepted version is that Marquette died at the present site of Ludington along the river now called the Pere Marquette. Subsequently, support was gained for the contention that he died at the mouth of the Betsie River at what is now Frankfort, just south of the Lakeshore. The strongest arguments for the Frankfort site are outlined by Catherine L. Stebbins in the September 1965 issue of *Michigan History* magazine. The state of Michigan gave Frankfort a marker appearing to support its claim. (see Chapter Five).

LOUIS JOLLIET

On his 1673 trip, Marquette was accompanied by fur trader Louis Jolliet, younger brother of Adrien Jolliet and a skilled navigator and mapmaker. In Jolliet's 1673 map of eastern North America, Michigan looked more like a stubby finger than a mitten. The Leelanau Peninsula was not discernible. The map included five unnamed islands in the northern part of *Lac des Illinois ou Michigami,* as Lake Michigan was then called. There is dispute whether the Manitous were among the five. (South Manitou Island authority Myron H. Vent said French missionaries "were certainly aware" of the Manitous at the time, and they were shown on the map. NPS researcher James Muhn, in a 1978 historical survey of the area, said the southern most of the islands "probably are one of the Fox Islands," and the map "shows that Jolliet knew little about the true geographical character of Lake Michigan's east shore.")

LA SALLE AND TONTY

Among the famous explorers of the Great Lakes was Robert Cavelier de La Salle, who in

1682 claimed the whole Louisiana Territory for King Louis XIV. La Salle was a protege of Louis de Buade, Comte de Frontenac, a longterm seventeenth century governor of New France, which then included Michigan.

It was La Salle who built the first sailing vessel to ply the upper Great Lakes, naming it the *Griffin* after the fabled winged beasts that appeared in Fronenac's coat-of-arms. La Salle's superintendent for 1679 construction of the *Griffin* was Henry de Tonty, an Italian-born French soldier who became La Salle's most trusted aide and an explorer credited with helping map Sleeping Bear country.

Late in 1679, while LaSalle led a group of men down Lake Michigan's western shore to establish a settlement in the Illinois country, Tonty led twenty men by canoe down the lake's eastern shore. At one point, according to Tonty's memoir on the trip, "the violence of the waves was such that our canoe was upset. We were, however, saved, but everything that was in the canoe was lost, and for want of provisions we lived for three days on acorns." On another Lake Michigan trip, Tonty's men had to "grub up wild onions from frozen ground to save themselves from starving."[3]

It is probable that Tonty was the source of information for Lake Michigan's eastern shoreline for French cartographer jean Baptiste Louis Franquelin's Great Map of 1688, which was reproduced for King Louis XIV and contains history's first geographical record of the Sleeping Bear Dunes area.[4] It specifically records "L'ours qui dort"—the Sleeping Bear—and shows what likely were the Manitou islands.

ST. COSME

In 1698, Canadian missionary Jean Francois Buisson de St. Cosme accompanied Tonty on a trip from Mackinac to the lower Mississippi, using Lake Michigan's western shore—which was referred to as the northern route because it involved crossing the lake at its northern end. Late seventeenth century conditions in Michigan along the lake's eastern shore were reflected

in a report that St. Cosme sent to his bishop in Quebec:

> We should have gone by the south side, which is much finer than the north, but as it is the route usually followed by the Iroquois, who, not long before, had made an attack on the soldiers and savages proceeding to the country of the Miamis, this compelled us to take the north side, which is not as agreeable nor so well stocked with game, though it is easier, I believe, in the autumn because one is sheltered from the northwest winds.[5]

St. Cosme's report also had this account of the perils of traveling the length of Lake Michigan by canoe:

> One must be very careful along the lakes, and especially Lake Michigan, whose shores are very low, to take to the land as soon as possible when the waves rise on the take, for the rollers become high in so short a time that one runs the risk of breaking his canoe and of losing all it contains.[6]

CHARLEVOIX—
"The Bear Lying Down"

A 1721 description of Sleeping Bear was recorded by Jesuit historian-explorer Pierre Francois Xavier Charlevoix on his extraordinary eighteenth century canoe trip through the interior of America. Commissioned by King Louis XV to report on the French colonies, Charlevoix spent almost three years journeying up the St. Lawrence and through the Great Lakes to the south end of Lake Michigan at Fort St. Joseph, down the Mississippi to the Gulf of Mexico.[7]

Charlevoix, after whom the city and county are named, saw on a large dune along Lake Michigan's eastern shore a "kind of bush" shaped like a reclining animal. His journal said "The French call it L'ours qui dort (the sleeping bear) and the Savages the Bear Lying Down."[8]

SCHOOLCRAFT AND DOUGLASS

Henry Rowe Schoolcraft was the first American to make a topographical and geological shoreline survey of Sleeping Bear and to then publish a written account of it.

Geologist Schoolcraft, whose writings and role in Michigan history are described in Chapter One, accompanied Territorial Governor Lewis Cass in 1820 on his epic expedition of more than 4,200 miles by canoe from Detroit via Lakes Huron and Superior to explore the Old Northwest and to seek the source of the Mississippi River. When they got to Chicago (then a village described by Schoolcraft as having "ten or twelve dwelling houses, with an aggregate population, of probably, sixty souls"[9]) on the return trip, Cass returned to Detroit by horseback. Schoolcraft continued by canoe northward up the eastern shore of Lake Michigan to complete its topographical and geological survey.

Schoolcraft's party left Chicago 31 August and on 6 September, after covering forty-five miles on a rainy day, stopped to camp at Point Betsie. Describing the encampment, and the next day's journey past Sleeping Bear, Schoolcraft wrote (His punctuation and spelling are retained):

> There is a great uniformity in the appearance of the coast, which is characterized by sand banks, and pines. In some instances, a stratum of loam, is seen beneath the sand, and the beech and maple are occasionally intermixed with the predominating pines of the forest; but our impressions in passing along the coast, are only those produced by barren scenery or uncultivated woods.

> "No hamlet smoking through the mists of dawn,
> No garden blushing with its fostering dew,
> No herds wild browsing on the daisied lawn—
> No busy village charms the admiring view."

> CVII. Day. (September 7)—The weather still remained cloudy. We embarked at early daylight. In going thirteen miles, we passed a small stream called Plat [Platte] river; and nine miles beyond reached a noted point, on the east shore of the lake, called the Sleeping Bear. The shore of the lake here, consists of a bank of sand, probably two hundred feet high, and extending eight or nine miles, without any vegetation,

except a small hillock, about the centre, which is covered with pines and poplars, and has served to give name to the place, from a rude resemblance it has, when viewed at a distance, to a couchant bear. There are two islands off this part of the coast, in plain view from the shore, which are called the Sleeping Bear [Manitou] islands.

> Fifteen miles beyond the Sleeping Bear, we passed Carp river, a small stream; and a like distance beyond it, encamped at the southern cape of Grande Traverse Bay, which is the most considerable indentation in the eastern shore of Lake Michigan, being nine miles wide, and about twenty or twenty-five miles in length, narrowing toward its head, where it receives the Ottoway [Boardman] river . . . [10]

Another prominent member of the Cass expedition, and the party that surveyed the Lake Michigan shoreline, was topographer David Bates Douglass, a West Point professor and Army civil engineer who made voluminous notes and sketches during the expedition. His journal and an account of the preparations and aftermath of the expedition were published in 1969 by Northern Michigan University Press in *American Voyageur: The Journal of David Bates Douglass*.[11]

In his entry for 6 September Douglass said that before overnighting at Point Betsie, the party "passed some Indian graves a few miles before camping over which a flag was flying—apparently British." The next entry:

> September 7—Thermometer 67x at sunrise, 76x at 2 P.M. Clear. Wind, south fresh, south east light, and at evening west with appearance of rain. Water of the lake 68x. Heard pigeons on the shore of Grand Traverse Bay. Collected some small shells—observed the water to fall along shore at dusk 4 to 5 inches and rise again in the course of the night. Fifty canoes of Indians said to have been lost long since in passing from the main to Great Manitou Island—none escaped. They have a superstitious fear of that island ever since. Camped on the shore of Grand Traverse Bay—having made nearly 60 miles progress this day. . . . [12]

Douglass' map shows "Great Manitou" to have been North Manitou, and the 7 September campsite to have been at the northern tip of the Leelanau peninsula. Accounts of loss of large numbers of Indian canoes and superstitions about the Manitou Islands circulated among early white travelers through Sleeping Bear Country.

Throughout the days of discovery, there were varying accounts about the lives of the first people of Sleeping Bear. Little was preserved of earlier human history of Sleeping Bear. The first people left no written records. Their ancestors did pass along folklore, which varied greatly in the telling—and retelling through the ages.

A clearer picture of the area emerges from the days of settlement, but even in historical accounts of the period, as in modern journalism, there are variations in the telling.

Endnotes—Days of Discovery

1. Louise Phelps Kellogg, editor, *Early Narratives of the Northwest: 1634–1699*, (New York: Charles Scribner's Sons, 1917), 272.
2. Kellogg, 288.
3. Francis Parkman, *La Salle and the Discovery of the Great West*, (Boston: Little, Brown & Co., 1907), 174.
4. Muhn, Chapter II, 3.
5. Kellogg, 343.
6. Kellogg, 346.
7. Milo M. Quaife, *Lake Michigan*, (New York: The Bobbs-Merrill Co., 1944), 285.
8. Muhn, 8. (Cites J. B. Plym, editor, "Fort St. Joseph Historical Leaflet," No. 1, Niles, MI, May 1942).
9. Henry Rowe Schoolcraft, *Narrative Journals of Travels Through the Northwestern Regions of the United States Extending from Detroit Through the Great Chain of American Lakes to the Sources of the Mississippi River in the Year 1820*, (Albany, NY: E. & E. Hosford, 1821). Reprint, edited by Mentor L. Williams, Michigan State College Press, 1953, 250.
10. Schoolcraft, 401.
11. Excerpts from Douglass' journal were scanned by Governor James J. Blanchard during a 3,288-mile Great Lakes shoreline tour in 1989. On occasion, he referred in speeches in shoreline communities to Lewis Cass' expedition as chronicled by Douglass. Cass took about four months for his expedition. The Blanchard odyssey—made by plane, helicopter and power boat, and including speeches in 39 cities—covered portions of six days. Blanchard visited Frankfort and Leland, and flew over the Sleeping Bear Dunes that he used to climb as a youth.

    In a 1989 interview with the author, Blanchard spoke of returning as an adult to take his son Jay on a dunes hike "throughout the 'Sharaha'—It was really a hot day, too—all the way to Lake Michigan." He said: "I always liked Sleeping Bear Sand Dunes and the Leelanau peninsula. . . . I love Sleeping Bear and Glen Lake—to stand up there and look at them." Recounting his visits to shoreline communities, he said "It's just like being governor of Paradise."
12. David Bates Douglass, *American Voyageur: The Journal of David Bates Douglass*, (Marquette, MI: Northern Michigan University), 110.

PART II *Days of Settlement and Today's Lakeshore*

CHAPTER 5

Benzie and Leelanau: The Counties of Sleeping Bear Country

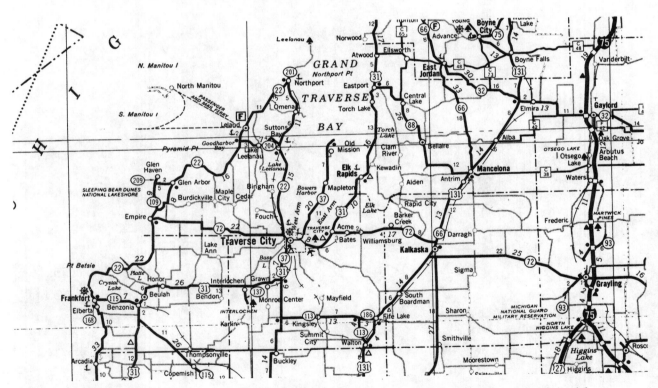

COASTAL COUNTIES: *The prominence of Benzie and Leelanau counties on the Lake Michigan shoreline of the Grand Traverse region is shown here on the Sesquicentennial map of Michigan in 1987—the 150th anniversary of the state's admittance to the union. Although statehood came in 1837, Leelanau was not organized as a county until 1863, and Benzie in 1869.* (Michigan Department of Transportation)

Even before a modern bond was forged when portions of Benzie and Leelanau counties were incorporated into the Sleeping Bear Dunes National Lakeshore, these neighbors had a long kinship. (The authorized size of the Lakeshore is about 72,000 acres, including about 3,600 that as of 1990 were in private or other than federal ownership. Leelanau County contains 56,621 acres of the Lakeshore, including about 20,000 on the Manitou islands. The 15,307 authorized acres in Benzie County include 1,128 that may not be acquired because they were for a disputed scenic corridor. The 72,000 acres include nearly 12,000 acres of surface water within the boundary that extends a quarter mile out from the Lake Michigan shore.)

The two counties share a heritage of shores that attracted their first visitors and first settlers.

Shipping spurred settlement of both. Some of their communities were named after, and settled as a result of, early schooners that came to their shores.

Centuries before county lines were drawn, the first people of Sleeping Bear ranged between prehistoric sites in Benzie and Leelanau counties. Both counties were included in the recognized territory of the Ottawa and Chippewa Indian tribes. Early Indians established trails up and

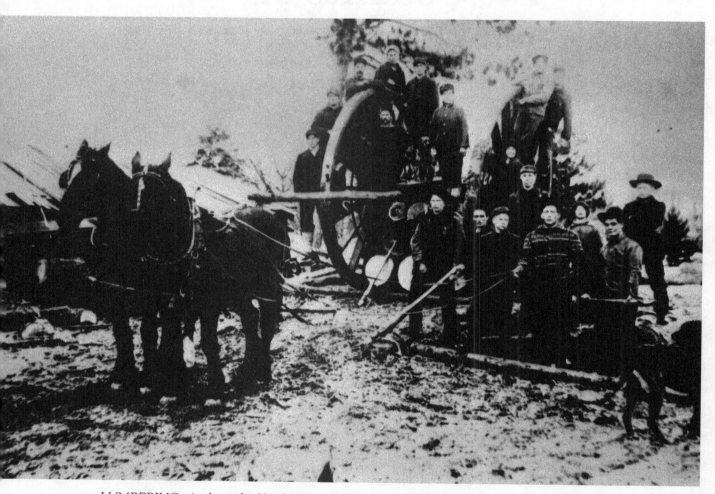

LUMBERING: *At the peak of lumbering, Benzie County had mill operations in a dozen communities. The Big Wheels, invented by Cyrus Overpack of Mainstee, were among Michigan innovations of the 1870s that increased logging production. They provided an alternative to sleds, allowing transportation to continue out of the forests during snowless seasons. Logs were chained beneath the axle.*

Here is a 1908 crew with Big Wheels at Edgewater by the northern corner of Big Platte Lake. The Edgewater Sawmill, which registered its marks at the Benzie County Courthouse in 1893, continued operation until it burned about 1910. The community around the mill slowly dissolved, thus leaving yet another northern ghost town.

(National Park Service)

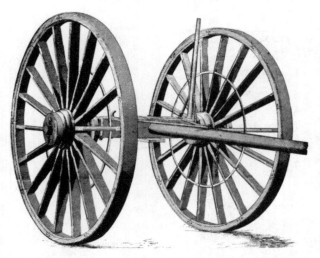

Big Wheels at the Michigan Historical Museum in Lansing. (Michigan Historical Museum)

down the Lake Michigan coastline, and to and from the shore where they made camps and fished. Some of the roads that today link the two counties follow these trails, including the Benzonia Trail that links Leelanau's Empire Township and Benzie's Platte Township.

The Platte River area was the site of a nineteenth century Indian settlement in present day Benzie County. In Leelanau, there were settlements at Leland, Northport, Cat Head Bay, Omena and Peshawbestown. There were encampments in the Sleeping Bear area.

Some early white settlers lived one time or another on both sides of what is now the Benzie-Leelanau border. Development of both rippled inland from Lake Michigan, and was fostered during the 1860s after passage of the Homestead Act of 1862. This act enabled a person to receive 160 acres of government land for a small fee by residing on the land for five years. Lumbering and commercial fishing operations spanned the two counties. Primarily because of the lumbering boom, the two counties had a combined total of more than 40 communities with post offices. Many became ghost towns. By 1990, there were only fifteen post offices in the two counties.

Benzie and Leelanau periodically were within one county. At the time Michigan attained statehood in 1837, they both were in Michilimackinac County, which had Mackinaw City as

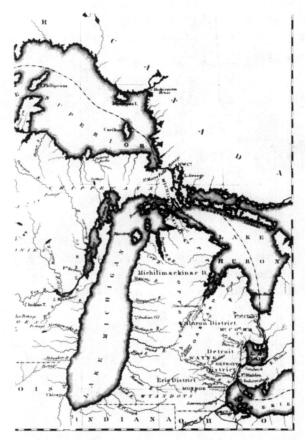

Benzie and Leelanau did not exist as counties in Michigan's territorial days. As shown on this map from the collection at the University of Michigan's Hatcher Library, Sleeping Bear was part of the Michilimackinac District. (Historical Society of Michigan)

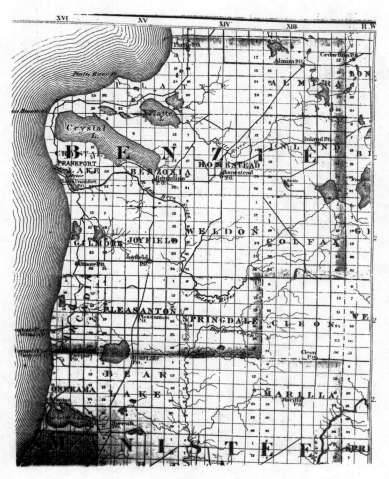

19th CENTURY BENZIE: *Most of the postal towns (designated by P.O.) on this 1873 Atlas of Michigan by H. F. Walling no longer exist. In the late 19th century, there were 15 post offices in Benzie County. There are six today. Platte, which is within what is now the Sleeping Bear Dunes National Lakeshore, was a stop on the stage coach between Frankfort and Leelanau County's Glen Arbor. What shows as Platte Township at the upper left of this map is now a center of hiking, cross-country skiing, canoeing and other Lakeshore activities. What was called South Frankfort in 1873 is now Elberta. Beulah was not on the 1873 map but today is the county seat and a bustling shopping center.* (Cottage Book Shop of Glen Arbor)

its county seat and originally included three-quarters of Michigan's Lower Peninsula. In 1853, Benzie and Leelanau counties were attached to the township of Leelanau within Grand Traverse County.

It is not the intention here to offer a comprehensive history of each county, but to note their common heritage and provide a brief overview of each. The overview emphasizes those communities in the most immediate area of the Sleeping Dunes National Lakeshore.

BENZIE COUNTY

Benzie was established as a county in 1869, with ten organized townships (now twelve). Frankfort, Benzonia, and Homestead all sought

to be the county seat. As a result of a series of elections and court rulings, the county seat at various times was in five different communities before the permanent site of Beulah was chosen in 1916.

Although Michigan's smallest county with 316.2 square miles, Benzie's population surpasses a dozen of the state's eighty-two other counties. The year-round population is about 12,000, a figure multiplied in the summer. Benzie is one of the most popular spots on Michigan's "Golf Coast," with Frankfort's Crystal Downs being rated in 1989 by *Golf Digest* magazine as Michigan's number one course. The Crystal Mountain Resort Golf Course in 1984 was rated by *Travel Weekly* magazine as one of the world's best resort courses. The 1,000-acre resort near Thompsonville also has twenty-two downhill ski runs and thirty kilometers of cross-country ski trails.

Benzie has more than 17,000 acres of lakes and streams, and 25 miles of Lake Michigan shoreline. Crystal Lake, eight miles long and three wide, is the largest of Benzie's fifty-four inland lakes. The Platte River, one of the first Michigan streams planted with Coho salmon, provides what the Michigan United Conservation Clubs described as "some of the midwest's greatest fishing." More than 100,000 Coho salmon return each fall to the river and Platte Bay for spawning, producing "some of the world's most fabulous fishing."[1]

The most widely accepted explanation of the county name is that Benzie is a derivative of the French name first applied by explorers to *La Riviere de Bec Scies*, the River of the Sawbill Ducks, or mergansers—now the Betsie River. The name was first applied to the river, changed to Betsey, and finally Benzie. Contemporary French accounts said the Indian name of the river, Uns-zig-o-ze-bee, had the same meaning.

The First Settlements

Benzie's development began in the 1850s. The first settler, believed to be Joseph Oliver, a hunter and trapper from Pennsylvania, built a log cabin at the mouth of the Betsie River. Several accounts place him there in 1850. Another said he came with his wife to "Manitou Island" in 1846, to Manistee in 1848 and then to the Betsie in 1851 or 1852.[2] Benzie's first sawmill was built on Lower Herring Lake in the early 1850s by Harrison Averill, who later moved his operations to Frankfort.

A lake storm helped stimulate Benzie's settle-

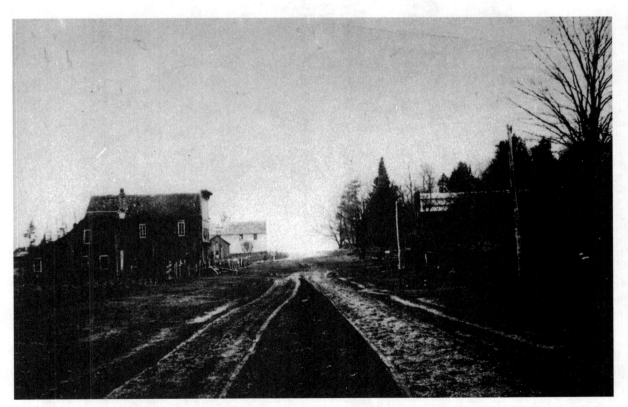

GHOST TOWN: *Looking west at the turn of the century on the main street Of Aral, a lumber town that no longer exists. On the left in the foreground is the Hathaway Store. The large white building was used as a boarding house for the House of David. On the right is the Bancroft Store and home of Bertie Bancroft. Circa 1908–9.*

(National Park Service)

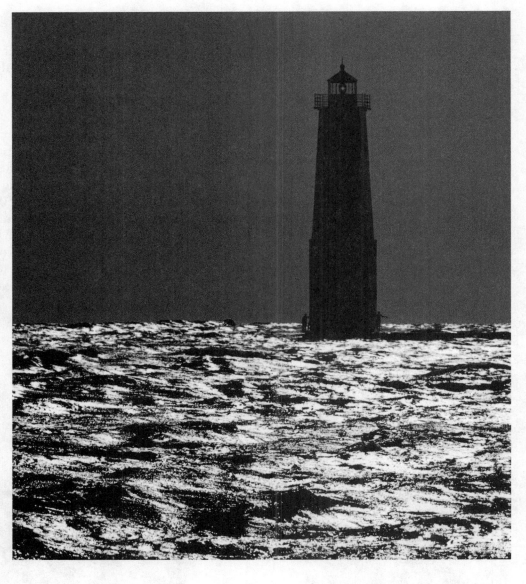

FRANKFORT SENTINEL:
Looming above reflective waters of Lake Michigan in 1978, this light is at the entrance of one of the two harbors that flank the Sleeping Bear Dunes National Lakeshore. Frankfort is south of the park; Leland to its north.
(Michigan Travel Bureau)

ment. In late November 1854, a schooner skippered by a Captain Snow, heading from Buffalo to Chicago to pick up a cargo of corn, was caught off the mouth of the Betsie River "in a terrible gale from the west. It became unmanageable and was being blown toward the shore with imminent danger to passengers, crew and vessel." But the captain found safety in Betsie Lake "to his great delight and gratification and everlasting salvation of passenger, crew and ship."[3]

As Captain Snow spread the word about the harbor, purchases of land were made by investors from Detroit and Chicago.[4] Among the buyers

was the vessel's owner, George W. Tifft of Chicago.

One early settler with Benzie and Leelanau ties was physician Alonzo J. Slyfield. He was a South Manitou Island lighthouse keeper in the 1850s before moving to Frankfort in the 1860s to resume practice, travelling to area villages to treat the ill. The hardships of the day sometimes made this a difficult circuit. Slyfield, during one particularly hard winter in a day of no bridges, " waded the county's Platte River eighteen times, undressing and dressing each time, and continuing his journeys through snow four feet deep."[5]

He later returned to lighthouse keeping, holding the job at Point Betsie for twenty years until the 1880s.

Benzonia-Beulah

In 1858, the Reverend John Bailey arrived on the banks of the Betsie River with a group of Congregational followers from Oberlin College to establish "a temperance, anti-slavery, educational Christian colony" at what is now Benzonia. In 1862, they chartered what became Grand Traverse College and produced teachers for the entire region. It became Benzonia College in 1891. The struggling institution by the turn of the century was converted to a secondary school called Benzonia Academy. One of its students was Benzie County's most celebrated son, historian Bruce Catton, whose father served as the academy's last headmaster before the school and

one of the county's most interesting chapters closed in 1918. Much of the county's past is reflected in displays in the Benzie Area Historical Museum, located in Benzonia's old Congregational Church.

In 1873, there was a poorly-conceived attempt to build a canal to provide a waterway between Crystal Lake and the Betsie River. When water drained into the canal, all that was created was an unnavigable swamp. Although the original idea failed, lowering of the level of Crystal Lake exposed beaches that today make the lake one of Michigan's most popular. The project also drained an area that became the site for the village of Beulah.

Today, the adjoining communities of Beulah and Benzonia southeast of the Lakeshore are centers for shopping and other attractions, including the studio of renowned artist and writer Gwen Frostic.

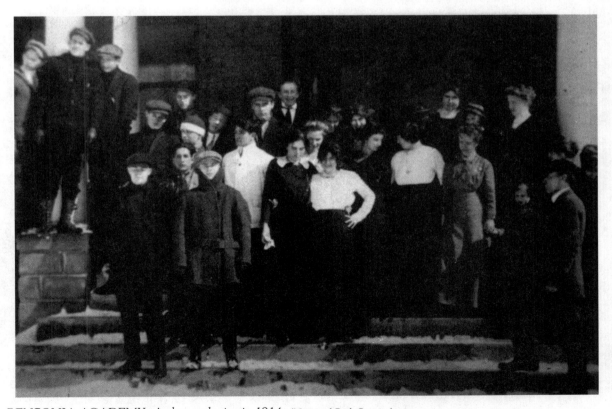

BENZONIA ACADEMY: A class gathering in 1914. (National Park Service)

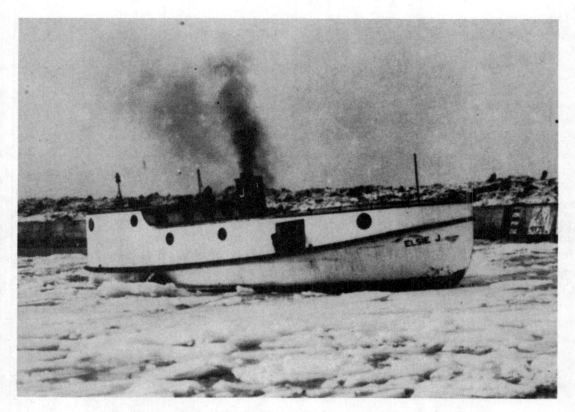

FISHING: *The Olsons were among the prominent commercial fishing families out of Frankfort during the first half of the 20th century. This undated picture from the collection of Ole E. Olson, who took over operation of Ed Olson & Co. from his father, illustrates the all-weather nature of the industry.*

Although few boats were as homely as a Great Lakes gill net fish tug, none was better designed for the work required of it. It had to resist a gale, shed tons of water and protect the crew as it played more than two miles of nets out the rear doors. The enclosed deck not only sheltered the crew, but prevented the tug from being swamped in a storm. Powered net lifters hauled the full nets aboard. (National Park Service)

Frankfort-Elberta

What is now Frankfort got its first major boost toward development when Louis A. Dauby and Alvinzi S. Dow brought crews in 1859 to improve the channel from Betsie Bay (also referred to as Betsie Lake on some contemporary maps to Lake Michigan and build a sawmill and piers for the Frankfort Land Company. Frankfort's first permanent settler, William H. Coggshall, ran a boarding house for Dauby and remained after Dauby left. Coggshall, another of the human links in Benzie-Leelanau history, brought his family to Frankfort from Glen Arbor.

In 1965, Frankfort won a victory in a long controversy when the Michigan Historical Commission presented a marker there indicating that evidence supports the town's claim that it was the death site and first burial place of Father Jacques Marquette, the French missionary-

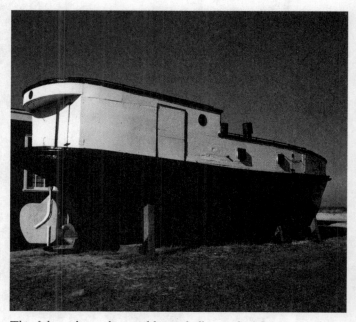

This fish tug has a deep and heavy hull typical of the sea-worthy boats that operated out of Frankfort and Leland. The low center of gravity, along with powerful engines, strong oak timbers and metal plating to help crunch through ice, made these boats functional and amazingly sea-worthy. This tug, the Aloha built in 1937, has been preserved by the National Park Service in a maritime display in Glen Haven. (Cottage Book Shop of Glen Arbor)

explorer (See Chapter Four). Visible today at the Commission's Registered Site Number 269 is a marker with this message:

On May 18, 1675, Father Jacques Marquette, the great Jesuit Missionary and explorer, died and was buried by two French companions somewhere along the Lake Michigan shore of the Lower Peninsula. Marquette had been returning to his mission at St. Ignace which he had left in 1673 to go on an exploring trip to the Mississippi and Illinois country. The exact location of Marquette's death has long been a subject of controversy. Evidence presented in the 1960's indicates that this site, near the natural outlet of the Betsie River, is the Marquette death site and that the Betsie is the Riviere du Pere Marquette of early French accounts and maps. Marquette's bones were reburied at St. Ignace in 1677.

On the south shore of Betsie Bay is Elberta, once known as South Frankfort. It caters to fishermen, and those who come to the Elberta Bluff for hang gliding and watching the sun set on Lake Michigan.

The Elberta-Frankfort area had a long history as a link in the system of the Ann Arbor Railroad between Ohio and Wisconsin. On 24 November 1882 a wooden steamship carrying four train cars

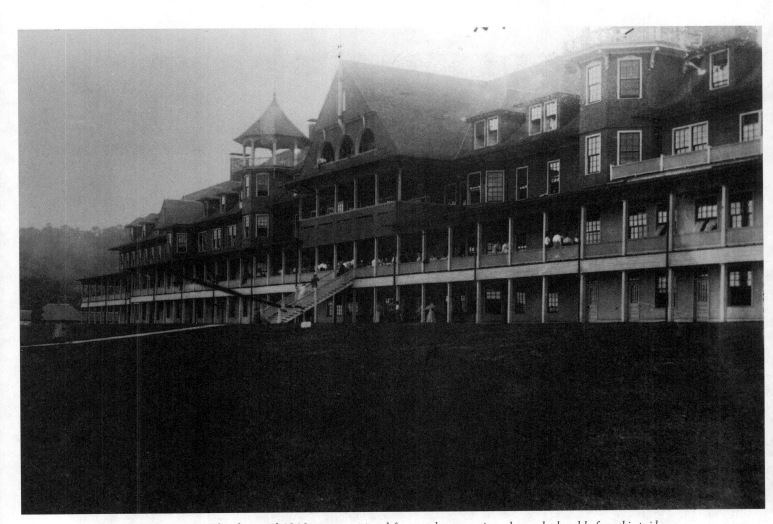

ROYAL FRONTENAC: *This damaged 1910 picture, printed from a glass negative, shows the hotel before this pride of Frankfort burned in 1912.* (National Park Service)

full of coal made an historic voyage from Frankfort harbor to Kewaunee, Wisconsin—the first crossing of a vessel with loaded freight cars across a body of water as wide as Lake Michigan. By 1928, the Ann Arbor Railroad had six vessels making more than 3,000 trips a year to Manitowoc and Kewaunee in Wisconsin, and Menominee and Manistique in Michigan's Upper Peninsula. The *Ann Arbor* carried cars and passengers as well as freight cars, but the national decline in rail service hit the line. The State of Michigan subsidized and operated the ferry service for a period, but phased it out in the 1980s.

Near the site where the Father Marquette maker now stands, the Ann Arbor Railroad in 1901 built the Royal Frontenac, a shoreline hotel that for a decade was the pride of Frankfort and one of the grand hotels of the Midwest. It was destroyed by a mysterious fire in 1912.

Before the decline of commercial fishing in Lake Michigan, Frankfort had one of the most active fishing operations on the eastern shore. Tugs from Frankfort and Leland were a common sight in the Sleeping Bear area, including Sleeping Bear Bay and the Manitou islands, from 1920 to about 1970. Some also came from Charlevoix and Beaver Island, and occasionally from Wisconsin. By 1934, more than 700 gill net tugs fished Lake Michigan. But change in

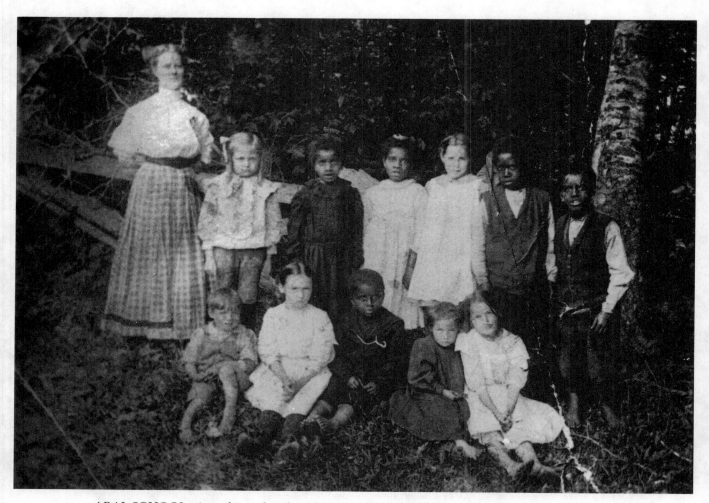

ARAL SCHOOL: *A teacher and students in 1906.* (National Park Service)

fish populations led to sharp curtailment of gill net fishing.

In the 1980s, Frankfort had one of the shoreline's busiest charter fishing operations. About 30 boats operated from there, beginning in May with trout and other shallow water fishing, and concluding in September with large salmon and coho in deeper water.

The Platte River Basin

The Platte River area, which contains some of northwest Michigan's most important archaeological discoveries of prehistoric activity (see Chapter Two), is today one of the major attractions of the Sleeping Bear Dunes National Lakeshore. Visitor activities include camping, hiking, canoeing, tubing, kayaking, swimming,

steelhead fishing in the spring, and salmon fishing in the fall.

By the end of the 1980s, the Lakeshore's Platte River Campground was attracting about 24,000 visitors a year. Known as the Benzie State Park before advent of the Lakeshore, the campground is located on the east bank of the Platte River where M-22 crosses it about one mile inland from Platte Bay on Lake Michigan. Also in the vicinity are a KOA campground and a privately owned canoe livery that provides a leisurely, family-style trip on the lower Platte that ends at Lake Michigan, and a more challenging fast-water trip on the upper Platte.

The mouth of the Platte River, which provides a sweeping view of the Sleeping Bear Dunes to the north, is the center of varied activities, including swimming, fishing, a township

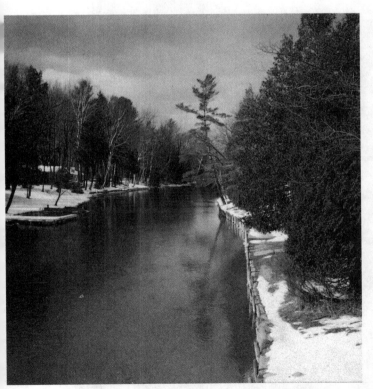

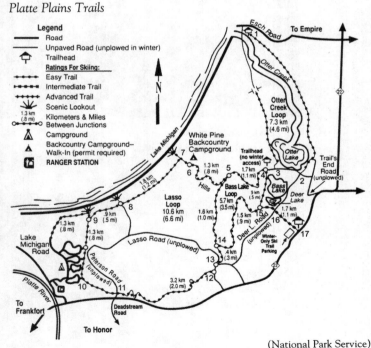

Platte Plains Trails

(National Park Service)

PLATTE RIVER, *above, with campground to the right.*
(Cottage Book Shop of Glen Arbor)

PLATTE RIVER CAMP-GROUND: *This popular site, located where M-22 crosses the river, is used for seasonal activities much as it was by prehistoric Indians. When the National Park Service made an archaeological survey on the land between this sign and the river, it found evidence of use by Indians for at least 1,000 years starting within a few centuries after the birth of Christ.*
(Cottage Book Shop of Glen Arbor)

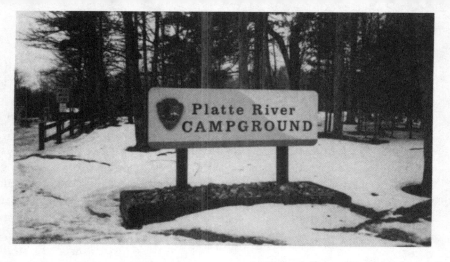

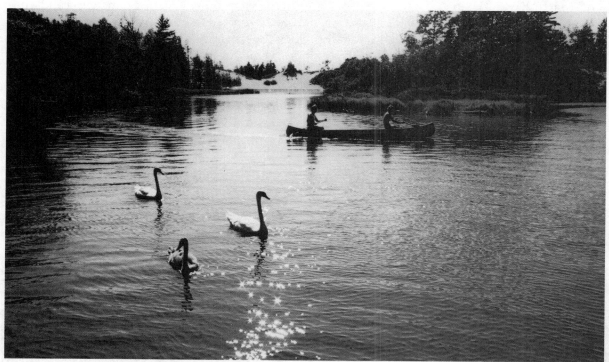

Canoe and swans share the Platte River at sunset.
(Riverside Canoes)

With Lake Michigan and the Sleeping Bear Dunes behind them, vacationers return to their Platte River canoe.
(Riverside Canoes)

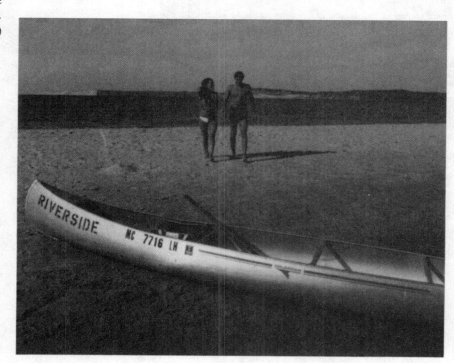

lumber from Platte Lake to a loading dock on Lake Michigan.

Ghost Towns

The Platte area includes remains of the storied ghost town of Aral, a lumbermill town between Empire and Frankfort that had a population of about 200 in the mid-1880s. It was long known as Otter Creek, for the nearby stream. But authorities rejected this name for a post office because there already was a southern Michigan town by that name. For the same reason, postal officials declined to accept naming it after Robert Bancroft, the area's first white settler. In 1883, it was named after the inland Aral Sea located in the Soviet Union.[6]

Adding to the mystique of Aral was one of northwest Michigan's most celebrated nineteenth century murders—in fact, a double murder. In 1889, Charles T. Wright, president of Otter Creek Lumber Company, had a tax dispute with the county. When deputy sheriff Neil Mar-

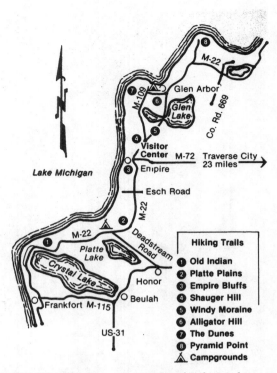

BENZIE TRAILS: *Between M-22 and Lake Michigan in the Platte Plains are two popular hiking and cross country ski trails: Old Indian (1) and Platte Plains (2). In between is the Platte River Campground, which also was the site of Prehistoric seasonal camps.*

(National Park Service)

park and a county-owned boat launch ramp. A fish weir operated by the Michigan Department of Natural Resources halfway between M-22 and the mouth of the river provides control of the number of migrating fish.

Two Lakeshore trails are also popular. The Old Indian Hiking Trail generally follows crests of tree-covered ancient beach dunes considerably inland from today's shoreline. The Platte Plains Trail traverses a former lakebed and includes a section along the bed of an abandoned narrow gauge railroad once used by trains hauling

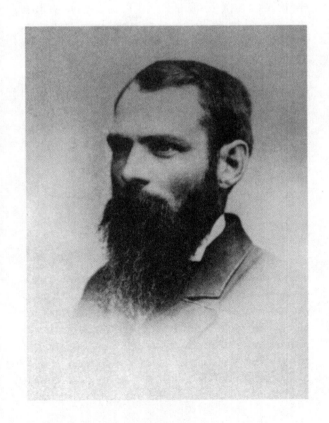

SLAIN: *Shot in the head, Lake Township Treasurer Frank Thurber was one of two men killed in 1869 by a hot-tempered lumberman resisting their attempts to seize his logs in a tax dispute.* (National Park Service)

shall and Dr. Frank Thurber, a physician and Lake Township treasurer, delivered a writ of attachment on the mill's logs, they were shot. Wright fled and hid, but was found, convicted and sent to prison, where he served only twelve years because his sentence was commuted by Governor Hazen S. Pingree.

For several years after the turn of the century, Aral had a brief resurgence when a store and saw mill were operated by members of "King" Ben Purcell's House of David. By about 1940, the last of Aral's original buildings had been leveled.

Edgewater, South of Aral at the northwest corner of Big Platte Lake, is another lumber and postal town that no longer exists. This also was an area Government surveyors in 1839 noted evidence of Indian activity.

Two other early Platte area postal towns were Osborn, which had a school, several stores and service on the Empire & South-Eastern Railroad, and Platte, which had several buildings, a wagon-shop, blacksmith and twice-weekly stage service to Frankfort and Glen Arbor. Like many communities in the region, the towns eventually lost their post offices after Rural Free Delivery, first introduced in 1896, came to northern Michigan. Osborn was then served by Empire, and Platte by Honor.

In 1890, there were fifteen Benzie County communities with post offices. In 1990, there were six. One community that had a nineteenth century post office was the Lake Ann milltown of Success, which did not maintain success or the post office very long.

LEELANAU COUNTY

Established as a county in 1863, Leelanau encompassed three organized townships (now eleven). Originally, Northport was designated the county seat, but no building was built to house the county offices, which were located in rooms over a store. In 1883, Leland was made the county seat.[7]

Although commercial fishing operations that flourished in Leland have sharply declined, its

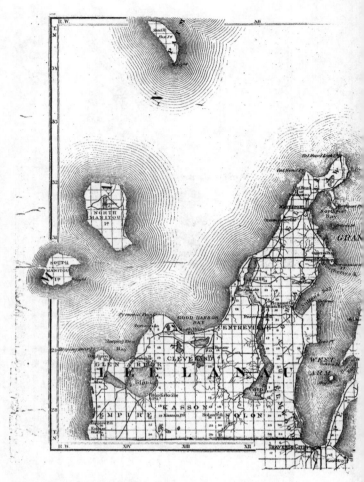

19TH CENTURY LEELANAU: Gone are many of the towns shown on this 1873 Atlas of Michigan. Settlements such as Onomensville, Port Oneida, North Unity and Good Harbor are ghost towns; what was Cat Head Village or Waukazoo to small bands of Indians was in an area that now attracts summer visitors and owners of second homes; the Indian village of Eagletown is now called Peshawbestown and is headquarters of the federally-recognized, six-county tribe of Grand Traverse Band of Chippewa and Ottawa Indians; Burdickville long ago lost its post office and place on the State of Michigan map but regained the map designation in 1983.

(The Cottage Book Shop)

historic "Fishtown" is part of a busy retail and dining center. Leland's harbor is one of the most popular on Lake Michigan, and serves the Manitou Islands.

The 376 square-mile county, because of its peninsula jutting between Grand Traverse Bay to the east and Lake Michigan to the west, is known as the "little finger" in Michigan's geographic mitten. With 98 miles of Great Lakes shoreline, 43 inland lakes, and 58 miles of streams, the county has attractions that greatly expand its year-round population, near 16,000. Its climate is ideal for growing fruit. Leelanau is Michigan's leading producer of cherries, and a major contributor to the state's expanding wine industry.

Leelanau's inland lakes possess a total water surface of 16,532 acres, and include "some of America's most beautiful lakes," according to the Michigan United Conservation Clubs.[8] Eight of the lakes exceed 200 acres, and four exceed 1,000. The largest are South Lake Leelanau, 5,370 acres; North Lake Leelanau, 2,950 acres; Big Glen, 4,865 acres; and Little Glen, 1,400 acres.[9]

The name, Leelanau County, is believed to be derived from the words "lee" in English, French and Norse meaning protective shelter and 4(eau, " French for water; hence, Leelanau is land in the lee of the prevailing winds over the waters of Lake Michigan. However, as noted in Chapter

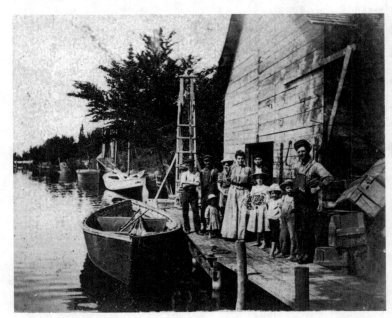

John LaRue, the first settler on the Leelanau mainland, established himself near the mouth of the Crystal River. This is how the river mouth looked at the turn of the century. (Marion Warnes)

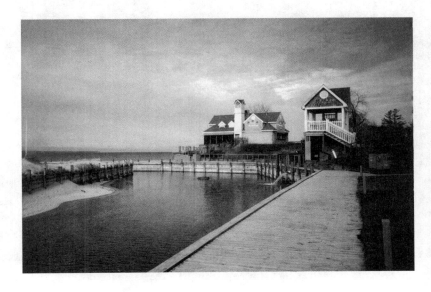

The river mouth in 2003 at the Homestead Resort.

(George Weeks)

This is how the former Grady Inn, which operated for much of the 20th century as the Sylvan Inn, looked after its 1987 restoration by Joe and Sue Williamson.
(Cottage Book Shop of Glen Arbor)

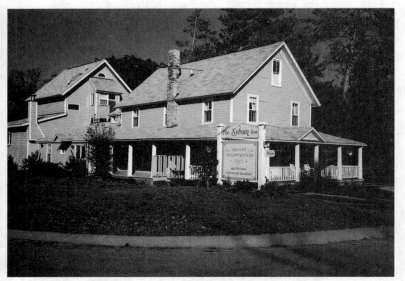

One, Leelanau was named in 1840 by Henry Rowe Schoolcraft, who said it meant "delight of life" as he chronicled in the Legend of Leelinau about an Indian maiden attracted to her sylvan land of delight. The modern day Leelanau Chamber of Commerce, adopting Schoolcraft's version, promotes Leelanau as "Land of Delight."

Glen Arbor—The Lakeshore's First Mainland Settlement

The first white settlement of Leelanau County arose on South Manitou Island by those who cut wood to fuel Lake Michigan steamships (see Chapter Seven). By 1840, W. N. Burton operated a wooding station there. In 1847, John LaRue, travelling to the island from Chicago, became the first European-American to establish a permanent residence on the lakeshore main-

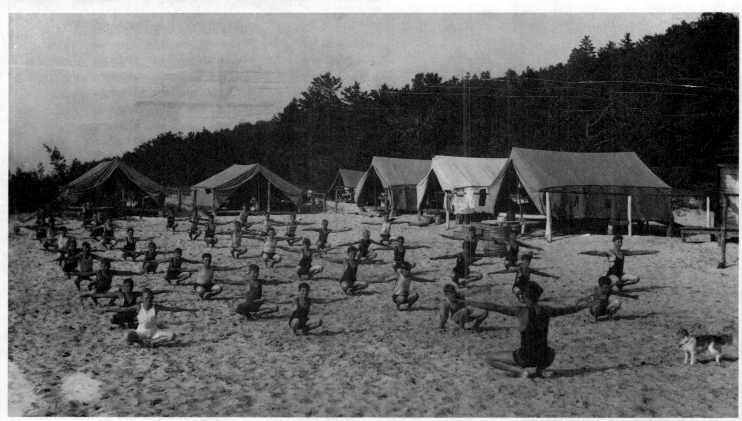

EXERCISING ON THE BEACH. *A Lake Michigan summer camp for boys was established near the mouth of the Crystal in the 1920s.* (The Homestead)

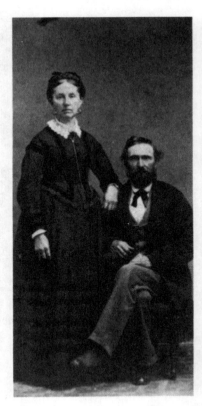

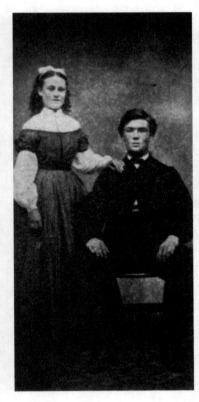

Few had a greater sustained impact in settling the Sleeping Bear area than John E. Fisher, who came from Wisconsin in 1854. Here he is with his wife Hariett, who is credited with naming Glen Arbor.
(Lake Street Studio of Glen Arbor)

Generations of Fishers remained in Leelanau, including son Charles, shown here with his wife Ettie in 1869.
(Lake Street Studio of Glen Arbor)

land where he opened a post for trading with Indians near the mouth of the Crystal River. This post was located in Glen Arbor Township, which was formally organized in 1856. Although the community has a business and government center, it did not incorporate as a village, and remains a township today. By 1867, the township had 200 people, four stores, two hotels, three boat docks on Sleeping Bear Bay, a blacksmith shop and a cooper shop.

LaRue was one of the "Three Johns" early pioneers of the Glen Arbor-Glen Lake area. John Dorsey, a Chicago barrel maker, was persuaded by LaRue to join his trading business in 1851. Dorsey, who sailed to Glen Arbor in his own sloop, operated a cooper shop, making kegs used to salt and ship fish that LaRue got from Indians. When Dorsey bought 108 acres of government land in 1859, the deed was signed in the name of President James Buchanan. Arriving in 1854 was John E. Fisher of Wisconsin, who bought 1,000 acres on the north side of Glen Lake (initially

called Bear Lake after the bears that prowled its shores), and in 1859 built a sawmill on the Crystal River.

Fisher, who became the township's first supervisor, had a more sustained impact on Glen Arbor than did LaRue, who later settled in Empire. Generations of Fishers followed, and his wife Harriet, inspired by sylvan beauty of arbors in a green glen, is credited with giving Glen Arbor its name.

Other early Glen Arbor settlers included William Walker, a doctor and friend of Fisher's who in 1856 bought 500 acres next to Fisher's property; George Ray of Ohio, Walker's brother-in-law, who became postmaster when a post office was established in 1857 and the same year completed the mainland's first wooding station at Glen Arbor's first dock; Thomas Kelderhouse, who in 1862 built another dock on Sleeping Bear Bay at Port Oneida; W. D. Burdick, who built a saw and grist mill on the east shore of Glen Lake and established the village of Burdickville; Carson Burfiend, a fisherman who took Fisher from South Manitou Island to the mainland and later settled Port Oneida, where he farmed; Erasmus Nutt, who arrived in Sleeping Bear Bay in 1855 aboard the chartered steamship *Saginaw* along with Ray, Burdick, eleven other persons and two cows.

The *Saginaw* was the first steamer to bring passengers to Glen Arbor. It originally landed its passengers by rowboat. Two years later, in 1857, Ray and Nutt built the bay's first of three docks, known initially as the Glen Arbor Dock. At other times it was called Central Dock since it was between the one built in 1862 to the east at Port Oneida and the one built in 1865 by C. C. McCarty (a brother-in-law of Fisher's) to the west at Glen Haven. The docks no longer exist.

Glen Arbor's importance—and that of its dock—was underscored in 1886 when Glen Arbor was designated as a U. S. port of entry in 1865–71. George Ray served as port inspector, headquartered at his own dock.

Just as Glen Arbor pioneer LaRue was the first white settler in mainland Leelanau County connected with its subsequent history, Glen Arbor itself reflects the rendezvous of yesterday and today in Sleeping Bear Country. Earlier it was a center for trading, lumbering and visitors, and today is a focal point for resorts, arts and crafts, shops, and recreation.

An example of tree-lined Glen Arbor's twin offering of history and hospitality can be seen within one block just west of the community's main intersection of M-109 and M-22. A turn-of-the century inn has been restored and is now a bed-and-breakfast. What once was an early Glen Arbor post office building is now a gift shop. Both are on the property originally deeded to William Walker in 1856.

Another example of the yesterday and today of Glen Arbor is the site where LaRue settled near the mouth of the Crystal River—a site that went from pioneer settlement, to summer camp, to school, to resort. The land once occupied by LaRue was purchased in 1921 by William "Skipper" Beals, a Missouri teacher who established a Lake Michigan summer camp there for boys. It became Camp Leelanau. By 1929, Skipper and

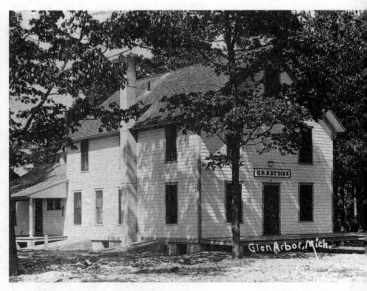

After sale of the Glen Arbor Lumber Company in 1907, George Grady turned this former quarters for lumberjacks into an inn. (Joe Williamson)

Cora, his wife, had a rambling farmhouse called "The Homestead," which included accommodations for the boys. That year, the Beals founded the Leelanau Schools, a private college preparatory school. The Homestead became a guest inn, which was part of a 900-acre campus run by Arthur S. Huey, who succeeded Beals as president of the Leelanau Schools and later sold much of the land.

In 1963, family control passed from the Hueys to a non-profit board, which by 1989, when the school celebrated its 60th anniversary, was functioning as the Leelanau Center for Education and operating what was called the Leelanau School on a 73-acre campus.

By 1990, the 220-acre Homestead Resort, which in 1972 became separate from the school, had 450 condominiums, 55 single-family home sites, 77 hotel rooms, a 12-run ski hill, and 36 kilometers of cross-country ski trails. It also had plans for a 270-acre golf course. Leelanau County also has Sugar Loaf Resort, which by 1990 had 150 hotel rooms, 60 townhouses, 18 condominiums, 22 downhill ski runs, 26 kilometers of cross-country ski trails and a 200-acre golf course.

Other Leelanau Settlements

Others prominent in initial settlement of Leelanau County included the Reverend George N. Smith, a Congregational minister who accompanied the Waukazoo band of Ottawas to present-day Northport in 1849 in order to avoid discord with Dutch immigrants in the Ottawa-Allegan area near Holland, and the Reverend Peter Dougherty, who in 1852 moved a Chippewa Presbyterian mission from Old Mission Peninsula to New Mission point near Omena.

Dougherty's mission was just north of a Catholic mission at Eagletown, formed by a band under Chief Pe-shaw-be that moved south from Harbor Springs. Eagletown became Peshawbestown, now center of the six-county Grand Traverse Band of Ottawa and Chippewa Indians, a federally recognized tribe that in 1980 became the political successor of the bands that signed a series of treaties with the federal government in the nineteenth century.

Roger L. Rosentreter of the Michigan Bureau of History wrote of Leelanau County: "An aggregation of beaches, forests, islands and sand dunes, Leelanau was first settled because of its natural beauty, isolation and pleasant climate. Although the isolation did not last long, the natural beauty and climate remained, allowing Leelanau to develop flourishing resort and fruit-producing industries."[10]

Empire

Empire's isolation ended in large part by the rippling effects of shipping. Steamers required wooding stations and spurred development of shoreline lumbering communities. One of the

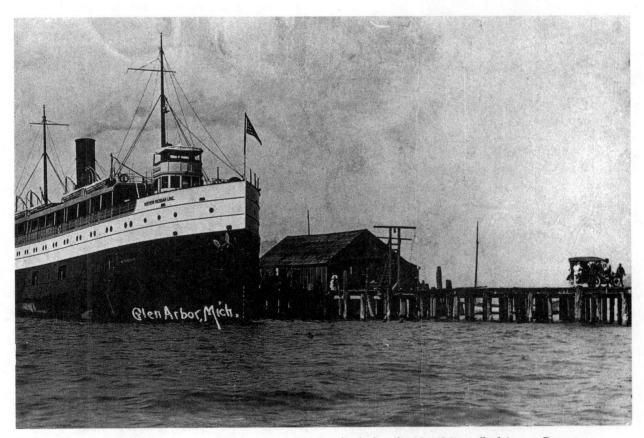

The steamer Missouri at the Glen Arbor dock about 1920. On the dock is the 1914 Maxwell of August Brammer, uncle of 1978–88 Glen Arbor Township Clerk Doris Brammer. (Glen Arbor Heritage Group)

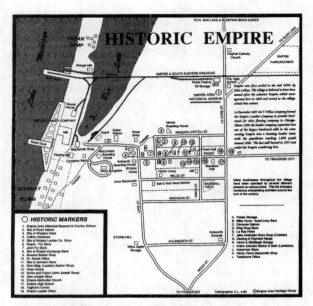

This was Empire at the time it was a booming lumber town. (Empire Area Heritage Group)t

county's largest lumbering operations was the Empire Lumber Company, which cut fifteen to twenty million board feet annually in the 1890s and early 1900s.[11] Destroyed by fire in 1906, the mill was quickly rebuilt. It burned again in 1917. With most of the area's virgin timber gone, the mill remained unrestored.

Two vessels of similar names are associated with the village of Empire. One is the steamship *Empire State,* which was deliberately and temporarily beached north of the community when it sprang a leak during a sudden and violent north, west gale 9 August 1849 while bound northward from Chicago with about 100 passengers.[12] In the winter of 1865 the schooner *Empire* became icebound off the settlement and temporarily served as the school for children of the few settlers.[13]

Empire Township was organized in 1871. The next year, George Aylsworth left his North Manitou Island wooding business for Empire, where he supplied steamships for 24 years. He built Empire's first dock, and established a grist and saw mill. Incorporated in 1895, the village reached a peak population of more than 1,000.

The community of Empire also reflects the yesterday and today of Sleeping Bear Country.

As the site of the Empire Area Museum and the Visitor Center of the Sleeping Bear Dunes National Lakeshore, Empire offers historical displays, as well as an introduction to today's attractions of the Lakeshore.

Empire, like Glen Arbor, is a community that survived the decline of lumbering and shoreline wooding stations. So did several communities outside the immediate Sleeping Bear area such as Leland, where Antoine Manseau came by canoe in 1852 in search of a site for a water-powered sawmill, and Suttons Bay, settled in 1854 by woodsman Harry C. Sutton and platted by him in 1867. Suttons Bay thrives today as a quaint waterfront village.

Suttons Bay, Leland, Northport, Empire and Glen Arbor are popular travel attractions on the M-22 loop from southern Benzie County to Traverse City. This route is considered one of the Midwest's most scenic drives. But in Leelanau County, as in Benzie, many of the early towns have disappeared.

Ghost Towns

Three of Leelanau's first settlements that became ghost towns are cited in Chapter Seven: Crescent on the west side of North Manitou and the village of North Manitou on the east side, and the village of South Manitou on South Manitou Island. Other ghost towns in the Lakeshore area included North Unity, Good Harbor and Port Oneida.

North Unity

North Unity on the Good Harbor Bay side of Pyramid Point was settled by Europeans who sailed north from Chicago in 1855 and built homes, a sawmill and a two-story store. Among these pioneers were members of the Kucera, Viskochil, Petertyl, and Kroupa families whose later generations became closely identified with the Leelanau-Grand Traverse area.

An insight into those hard times is provided by one of the settlers, Joseph Krubner, who said the settlement included thirty-two families. His vivid account was originally published by a

Chicago Bohemian newspaper and then in 1965 in English by Edmund M. Littell's *100 Years in Leelanau*. Krubner wrote:

> Some houses were all covered with hemlock branches, leaving small openings for windows. They looked more like bear huts instead of homes for humans. Some place they built the log house so low it was difficult for tall man to stand up in one.
>
> . . . For a while hungry wolf's (sic) were chased away from our doors. But with approaching spring, when the snow melted and the lake still frozen, no boats were able to reach us, potatoes and what ever we had was gone , hunger begins to strike again. By the time it reached its peak, we were saved, as a flock of wild pigeons came by. Everyone who had a gun and was able to use it, was shooting them. Few of small lakes helped to change our menu, as they were full of fish.[14]

Due to bad weather one late fall a sailing boat destined for North Unity stopped at South Manitou Island. "By the time the weather cleared, the captain and the crew were well liquored," wrote Leelanau County historian Julia Terry Dickinson. "They set sail for North Unity across Manitou Passage but during the short distance, they dumped all the food and provisions overboard, saving only the whiskey, which the crew themselves took care of." She noted that one settler, Joseph Shalda, walked more than twenty-five miles to Northport to get a sack of navy beans, which he carried to North Unity on his back.[15]

A North Unity post office was established in 1870, but a fire about 1871 and lack of income prompted families to move away. Shalda moved his family to what is now known as Shalda's Corners at the intersection of M-22 and Highway 669. For years, remains of a grist mill built at the outlet of Little Traverse Lake were visible. There

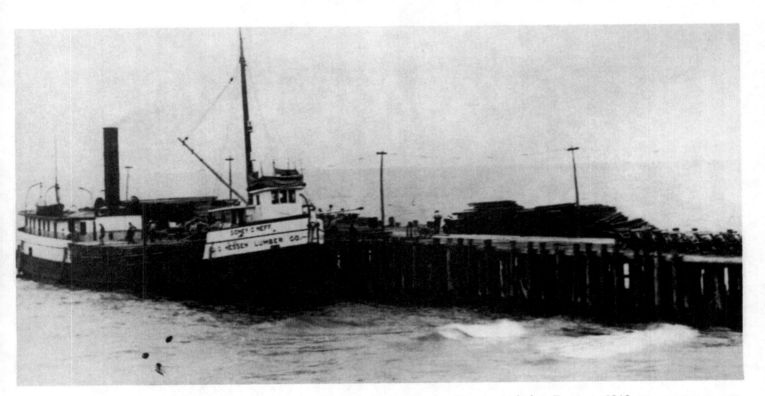

The Sidney O. Neff of the O.J. Nessen Lumber Co. at the Empire Lumber Company's dock in Empire in 1912. (National Park Service)

is little to remind today's visitors of those early days, other than Shalda's Corners and Shalda Creek, the stream that goes from Little Traverse Lake to Lake Michigan.

Good Harbor

Good Harbor on the Good Harbor Bay side of Pyramid Point flourished in the last quarter of the nineteenth century when 300 people were kept busy by its saw mill, cheese factory and wooding station. First settled in 1863 by H. D. Pheatt, Good Harbor was developed by three brothers, Richard, Otto and Henry Schomberg, who established the Schomberg Lumber Company and employed as many as 100 teams to haul logs. The town once had 18 houses, two general stores, a post office, boarding house, feed barn, and saloon. A Lutheran church established on higher ground near the village was rebuilt in 1919 and later expanded.

"When the mill burned down in 1906, the village lost its heart, and the inhabitants began to move away," said historian Dickinson.[16]

Today, there is little to mark the village, other than the nearby Lutheran Church and its adjoining cemetery, which are along M-22 where it intersects with Townline Road.

Port Oneida

The hardship of early settlement is underscored by the story of the pioneers of Port Oneida, on the Sleeping Bear Bay side of Pyramid Point. Fisherman-farmer Carson Burfiend, originally from Germany, and his wife Elizabeth, originally from, France, built a cabin near the shore in 1853—so near that it once was ravaged by a storm which scattered its contents on the beach. Three of their twelve children died young. The Burfiend home became the victim of occasional raids from Mormons from Beaver Island, who stole fishing nets and vandalized boats. On one occasion, they entered Burfiend's home while his wife and children huddled in fear upstairs, which they sealed by pushing a dresser over the trap door. They were unharmed, but the marauders pounded a hole in the bottom of a boat.[17]

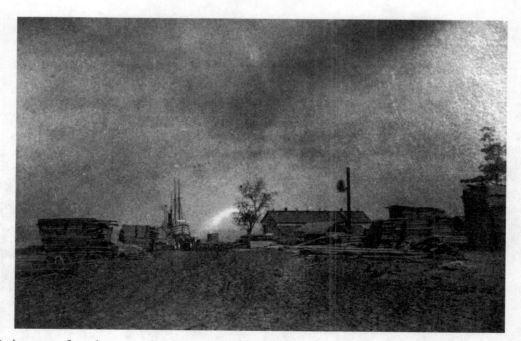

Good Harbor was a flourishing town for about 300 people around the time of this 1890 picture of its lumber dock on Lake Michigan. Its saloon and about everything else is gone, but a nearby church remains. (National Park Service)

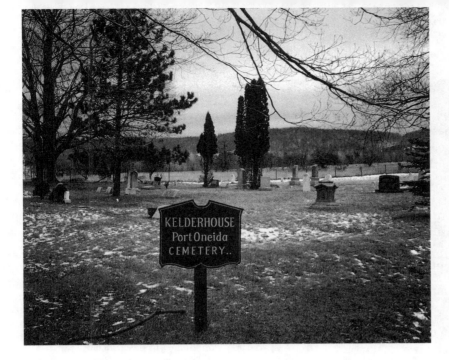

PIONEER PLOT. *This well-maintained cemetery was still used by their descendants more than a century after Thomas Kelderhouse and Carson Burfiend arrived to settle Port Oneida.*

(Cottage Book Shop of Glen Arbor)

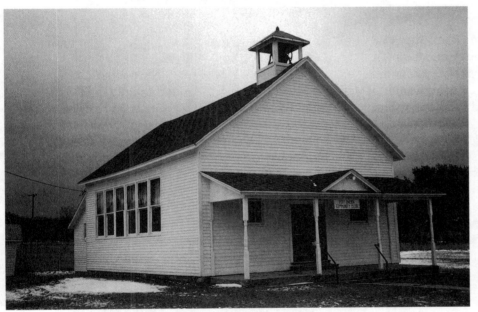

ONE-ROOM SCHOOL. *This is the sole remaining structure of the ghost town of Port Oneida, named after the first steamer that stopped there for wood.*

(Cottage Book Shop of Glen Arbor)

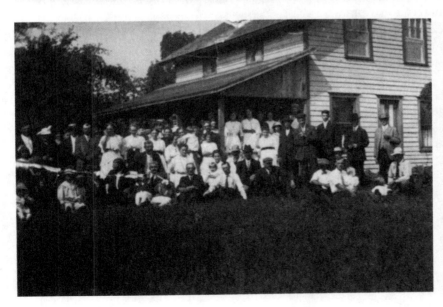

A gathering at Fred Baker's in Port Oneida. Circa 1910.

(Lucille Barratt)

Despite the adversity, the hardy Burfiend proved to be a successful fisherman and farmer, shipping out salted fish and berries. He moved inland from the shore, and ultimately acquired 302 acres from the United States government— at about $1.25 per acre. One of his deeds was signed in the name of President Franklin Pierce; another in the name of President Abraham Lincoln.

After surviving hardships of settlement and the hazards of unpredictable Lake Michigan, Burfiend died in his mid-sixties from a fall down stairs. Elizabeth Burfiend died at age eight-six. Many of their descendants remained in Leelanau County, including their great grandson, Jack Barratt, who lives within sight of where Burfiend's farm once stood.

Port Oneida got its name from the first steamer that stopped for wood at the dock built by Thomas Kelderhouse in 1862. Although waters off the point itself were shallow and treacherous, the dock was popular as a wooding station because it had a deep-water approach. Kelderhouse built a saw mill near the site where a one-room schoolhouse still stands. Although no longer used as a school, it has been used for community activities and still has the stove that once warmed its students.

The dock is gone, but a few pilings are visible. Gone are the saw mill, store and original houses of Port Oneida—much of their lumber having been used to build today's barns and other structures. Gone also is Port Oneida's place on the state map.

A Lutheran church and cemetery were established along what is now M-22. The church is gone, but the Kelderhouse Port Oneida Cemetery and the nearby school are today's reminders of yesterday's pioneers.

Port Oneida, where mail boxes were maintained in the store, was among at least twenty-six Leelanau County communities recorded to have had post offices. By 1990 there were only nine: Cedar, Empire, Glen Arbor, Lake Leelanau, Leland, Maple City, Northport, Omena and Suttons Bay.

Endnotes—Counties: Benzie and Leelanau

1. *Michigan County Maps and Outdoor Guide,* (Lansing, MI: Michigan United Conservation Clubs, n.d.), 14.
2. Sivert N. Glarum, Our Land and Lakes: *Michigan Benzie County Lower Hering Lake,* (Frankfort, MI: Sivert N. Glarum, 1983), 22.
3. Leonard Case, *Benzie County: A Bicentennial Reader,* (Benzonia, MI: Benzie County Bicentennial Commission, 1976), 20.
4. Charles M. Anderson, *Memos of Betsie Bay: A History of Frankfort,* (Manistee, MI: J. B. Publications, 1988), 6.
5. Roger L. Rosentreter, "Benzie County," *Michigan History Magazine.* Bureau of History, Michigan Department of State (November-December 1979), 8.
6. Theodore and Bonita Reuschel, The Story of Aral, Benzie County, Michigan. Reprint Lansing, MI, Benzie Area Historical Society with permission of the Bureau of History, Michigan Department of State, 9. (Leelanau)
7. Edmund M. Littell, *100 Years in Leelanau,* (Leland, MI: Leelanau Prospectors Club, 1965), 24.
8. Michigan County Maps and Outdoor Guide, 62.
9. Leelanau Enterprise, 1 May 1958 (Leland, MI).
10. Roger L. Rosentreter, "Leelanau County," *Michigan History Magazine* (September-October 1985), 8.
11. Littell, 67.
12. *Some Other Day (Remembering Empire),* (Empire, MI: Empire Area Heritage Group, 1974), vi.
13. Julia Terry Dickinson, *The Story of Leelanau,* (Omena, MI: Solle's Bookshop, 1951), 38.
14. Littell, 55–60.
15. Dickinson, 42.
16. Dickinson, 41–42.
17. Robert Dwight Rader, *Beautiful Glen Arbor Township,* (Glen Arbor, MI: Glen Arbor History Group, 1977), 27; Littell, 48; Dickinson, 43; and Jack Barratt of Glen Arbor, great grandson of Carson Burfiend, interview with the author, 1989.

See also: Charles Burmeister, "A Short History of Benzie County," Michigan Pioneer Collections, 18 (1892); W. L. Case, The Tragedy of Crystal Lake, Benzie Record (1922) and reprinted by the Benzie Area Historical Society; Pete Sandman, The Landmarks of Frankfort, Michigan, an undated 1980s pamphlet. Elvin L. Sprague and Mrs. George N. Smith, *History of Grand Traverse and Leelanaw Counties,* (B. F. Bowen, 1903) Reprinted (Traverse City, MI: Grand Traverse Historical Society, 1976); Roy L. Dodge, *Michigan Ghost Towns* (Oscoda, MI: Amateur Treasure Hunters Association, Inc., 1970); various nineteenth and twentieth century editions of the *Michigan Manual,* (Lansing, MI: State of Michigan), published every two years, lists populations, post offices and other information from all 83 counties in the state.

CHAPTER 6

Glen Haven Historic Village and King David of the North

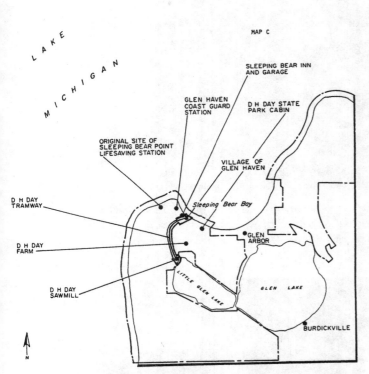

Significant sites in the Glen Haven Village Historical Area. (National Park Service)

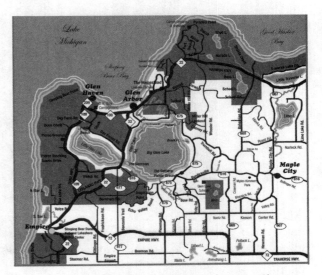

This map shows Glen Haven's location between Sleeping Bear Point and Glen Arbor. Shaded area is park land, although there are several pieces of private property within the boundaries.

(Glen Lake-Sleeping Bear Chamber of Commerce)

Glen Haven on Sleeping Bear Bay earned its place on the National Register of Historic Places as a turn-of-the-century company lumbering town by being perhaps the best preserved example of a frontier wooding station and steamboat stop on the Great Lakes-certainly on the eastern

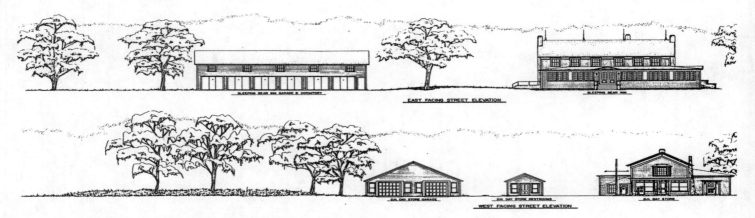

Glen Haven Historic Village (facing sides of the street)

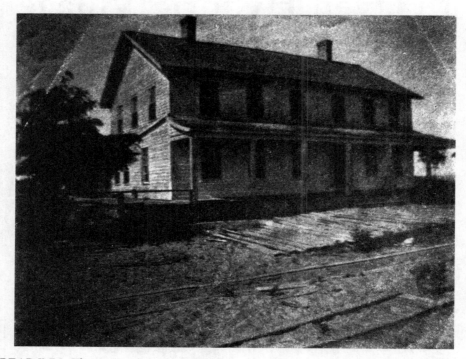

SLEEPING BEAR INN: This picture from the 1890s or earlier is believed to be one of the first of the inn built in Glen Haven in 1857. The tramway in front of the inn, which initially was called Sleeping Bear House, was built about 1870. About 1907, D. H. Day relocated the tramway behind the inn. (National Park Service/Bob Travis)

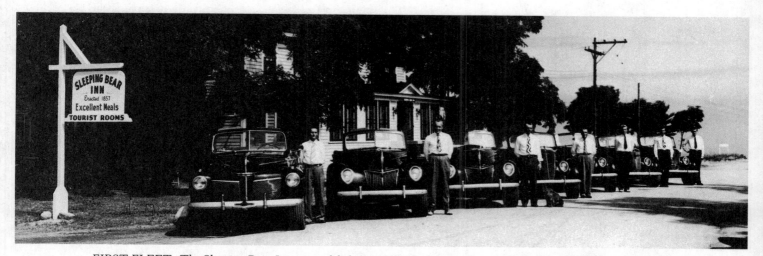

FIRST FLEET: The Sleeping Bear Inn, remodeled in 1928 to look basically as it does today, is the backdrop for this early 1940s picture of the first fleet of the Mercury and Fords of Sleeping Bear Dunesmobile Rides began in 1935 by Louis Warnes and his wife Marion, youngest daughter of D. H. Day. (Marion Warnes)

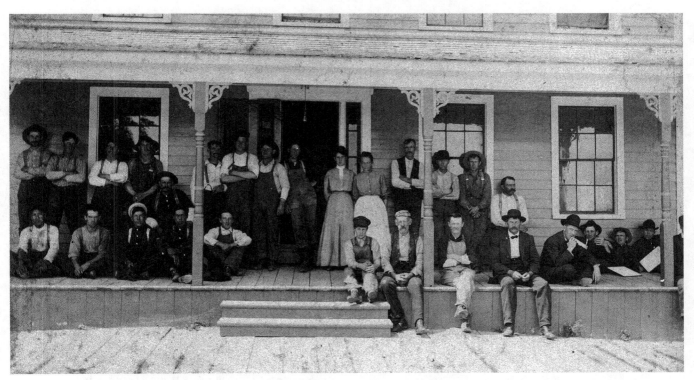

This is an early 1900s gathering of Glen Haven workers on the porch of the Sleeping Bear Inn. Sitting at the right on the edge of the porch with hat and bow tie is village blacksmith John Basch; sitting at left end of the porch with a cap and white shirt is John Westman, member of one of the Native American families that lived along Sleeping Bear Bay just east of the village. An area road is named after him. (D. H. Day III)

shore of Lake Michigan. It also earned a special place in Michigan history due in large part to David Henry Day.

When Day died in 1928 at age seventy-six, newspapers said Michigan had lost "King David of the North." While not really a king, he was a prince among pioneers. He came to Glen Haven by steamer in 1878 at age twenty-seven, and went on to diversified achievements in lumbering, shipping, forestry, conservation, road-building, tourism and growing and canning of cherries. He was the first chairman of the State Park Commission, and there was some talk of him as a possible Democratic candidate for governor of Michigan. Talk that he squelched.

On the day "King" David died, the *Traverse City Record-Eagle* said: "Few here had as great a part in the building of Northern Michigan as D. H. Day, and few in Northern Michigan were as well known elsewhere . . . D. H. Day did more

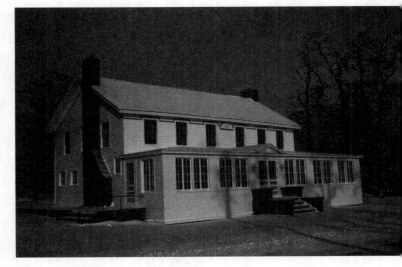

The inn in 2005. (Grace Dickinson)

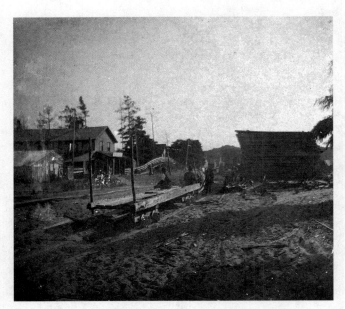

This circa 1897 picture, taken from in front of the inn looking toward the D. H. Day Store, shows a flatcar on the tramway. (Marion Warnes)

There already were Sleeping Bear Bay docks at Glen Arbor and Port Oneida, but Glen Haven, somewhat protected by Sleeping Bear Point, provided the most sheltered site and offered a deep-water approach at a time when adequate harbors were nearly non-existent along northwest lower Michigan.

McCarty also built a sawmill near the northwest shore of Little Glen Lake, using a tug to tow logs from various shoreline locations to the sawmill, where they were cut and hauled by wagon or sled to the Glen Haven dock. By about 1870, a tramway more than two miles long was built to haul the logs to the dock.

Frontier Steamship Stop

Glen Haven's development, initially slowed when early Michigan settlers left to fight in the Civil War, accelerated again through the Homestead Act of 1862. Among Union soldiers returning after the war was P. P. Smith, who became foreman for Northern Transit Company (NTC) at the Glen Haven cord wood station and later became Glen Haven postmaster.

than any other man to make Leelanau County the producer it is today."[1]

Day was not the founder of Glen Haven, nor the first to capitalize on its access to the relatively cheap and rapid transportation that the Great Lakes provided. In 1857, C. C. McCarty, a brother-in-law of Glen Arbor pioneer John E. Fisher, built a saw mill and inn on the beach west of Glen Arbor. He called his settlement Sleeping Bearville before changing it to Glen Haven. The inn initially was called Sleeping Bear House, and then Sleeping Bear Inn. (Documentation on the McCarty era is sketchy. Local history books have variously spelled his name McCarthy, McCartey and McCarty. The latter is correct, according to records of 1960s-1990s Postmaster Leo R. Buckler of the Glen Arbor Post Office, where McCarty was postmaster in 1859–61. National Park Service Historian Ron Cockrell also said "The year 1857 for the construction of the Sleeping Bear Inn should not be etched in stone even though most local history accounts and the Inn's National Register nomination claim this date.")

In 1865, McCarty built a dock at Glen Haven.

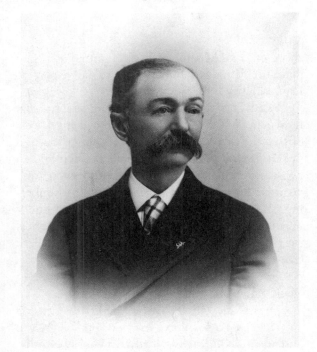

D. H. Day—a favorite family portrait provided by his grandson. (D. H. Day III)

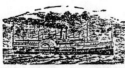

NORTHERN MICHIGAN
LINE.

1881   1881

≈ STEAMERS ≈

"Champlain"
—AND—
"Lawrence."

SATURDAY and *TUESDAY*, at 10 o'clock p. m.— FOR CHICAGO, MILWAUKEE.	*SUNDAY* and *THURSDAY*, at 5 o'clock a. m.— FOR LELAND, CHARLEVOIX, PETOSKEY, HARBOR SPRINGS, CROSS VILLAGE, Pt. St. IGNACE, MACKINAC, DUNCAN CITY, CHEBOYGAN.

These steamers have been finely fitted out, and Passengers and Freight will be carried for above ports at Reasonable Rates.

☞ Connections made at Cheboygan with steamers for Alpena, Rogers City, Crawford's Quarry, Port Huron, Detroit and Cleveland.

D. H. DAY & CO.,
AGENTS, GLEN HAVEN, MICH.

J. J. YOUNG, Agent, Chicago.—Wharf Foot North LaSalle St.
P. J. KLINE, Agent, Milwaukee.—Wharf Foot West Water St.

Tribune Print, Traverse City.

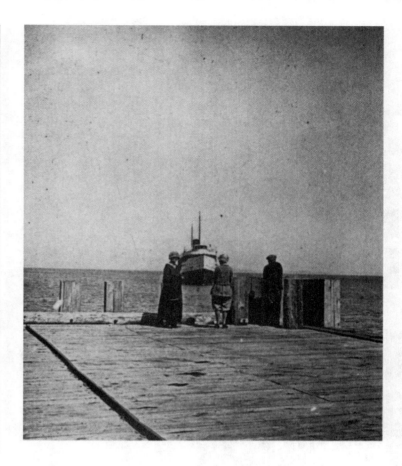

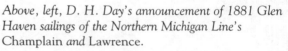

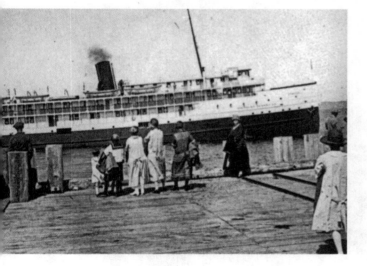

Above, left, D. H. Day's announcement of 1881 Glen Haven sailings of the Northern Michigan Line's Champlain *and* Lawrence.

         (Cottage Book Shop of Glen Arbor)

Above, right, the steamer Puritan *approaches the Glen Haven dock. Lulu Jones is in the dark dress. Circa 1925.* (Gary Jones)

Left, the steamer Puritan *off the Glen Haven dock. Circa 1925.*

Below, the steamship Manitou *made frequent stops at Glen Haven when it was the pride of Lake Michigan.*

         (Cottage Book Shop of Glen Arbor)

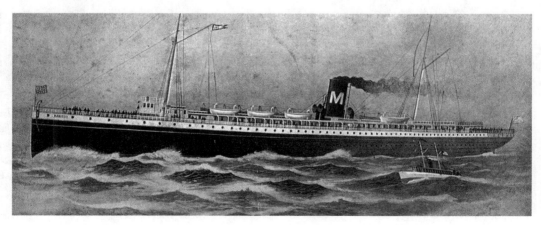

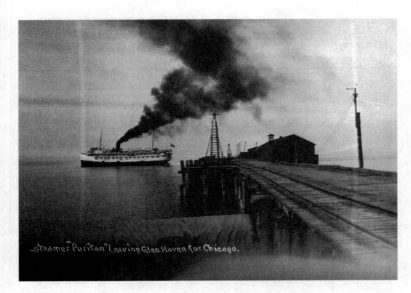

Steamer "Puritan" Leaving Glen Haven for Chicago.

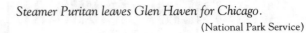

GLENHAVEN

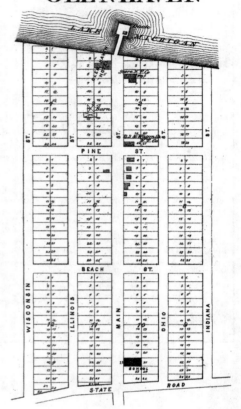

Plat map

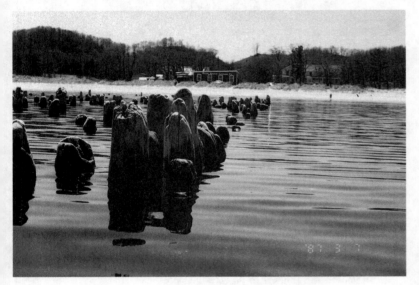

When Lake Michigan levels are low, as when this 1987 picture was ta[ken]
bleached pilings stand in testimony to a magnificent dock that was a bu[sy]
ramp on northern Michigan's water highway. (George Weeks)

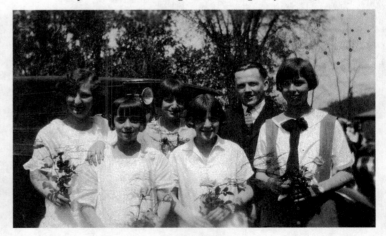

Glen Haven's one-room school, which had classes through the eighth grade, was located about where the northeast corner of the intersection of M-109 and M-209 is today.

(Marion Warnes)

The 1925 gradautes of the Glen Haven school. From left: Isabelle Nelson, Catherina Laird, Isabelle Lavance, Marion Day, Teacher Benhart Roen, and Nellie Smith, whose father at the time was in charge of the Sleeping Bear Point Coast Guard Station. Her brother, Willard, became commandant of the U. S. Coast Guard in 1966. (Marion Warnes)

In 1878, NTC President Philo Chamberlain acquired Glen Haven in order to assure a reliable supply of wood for a twenty four-vessel fleet providing service between Ogdensburg, New York, and Chicago and Milwaukee. A first class Ogdensburg-Chicago fare cost just twelve dollars. Glen Haven supplied about a quarter of the fuel for the fleet—an enormous undertaking considering that one steamer on a Great Lakes round trip could consume between 100 and 300 cords of wood.

To serve as NTC's agent in Glen Haven, Chamberlain picked D. H. Day, his sister-in-law's younger brother. Day had grown up in Ogdensburg, where his grandfather had moved in the early 1800s after the Day family emigrated from Wales to Vermont in the late 1700s. The job involved many responsibilities, including dockmaster when ships arrived at Glen Haven. The hazards of this duty are clearly described by National Park Service Research Historian Ron Cockrell:

> During Lake Michigan storms it was easy for a man to be swept away into the churning water. There were no lights between the NTC office in the general store and the end of the dock. In pitch blackness and during storms, the ships still had to be secured to the dock, or risk being run aground on the beach. The bridge of the dock began at the shore and extended into the bay approximately 150 feet where it widened to form a large platform where cordwood was stacked. A crude track of 2 x 4s ran the length of the dock and accommodated the horse-drawn carts which carried wood and supplies. In stormy weather, Day crawled on his hands and knees using the rails of the horse car track to guide him. He made his way cautiously along the tracks until he reached the huge lanterns which were hung at the end of the dock. He was then able to see and grab the vessel's deck lines to secure them.[2]

Before long, sometime dockmaster Day became master of all of Glen Haven. In 1881, Day bought most of NTC's properties, including the village of Glen Haven, using his savings and money borrowed from his friend Perry Hannah of

LOGS POSTER: D. H. Day announces prices he will pay for logs in the winter of 1895–96.

(Cottage Book Shop of Glen Arbor)

Traverse City's Hannah & Lay Lumber Company, where he served briefly as manager.

Day also announced that he and a silent partner had purchased the NTC steamers *Lawrence* and *Champlain* to form the Northern Michigan Line with freight and passenger service to Chicago, Milwaukee and a number of Michigan stops along Lakes Michigan and Huron. Northwest Michigan became a popular destination for vacationers, and steamer was a popular mode of travel.

In 1881, the Northern Michigan Line offered 10 P.M. departures for Chicago and Milwaukee on Saturday and Tuesday, and 5 A.M. departures on Sunday and Thursday for Leland, Charlevoix, Petoskey, Cross Village, Harbor Springs, St. Ignace, Mackinac Island, Cheboygan/Duncan City. Connections were made in Cheboygan for

D. H. Day Store in Three Centuries

It had occasional facelifts, but the D. H. Day Store throughout its operating days was always the center of Glen Haven activities. In 2003, the National Park Service opened the restored building as a 1920s general store-era attraction honoring D. H. Day.

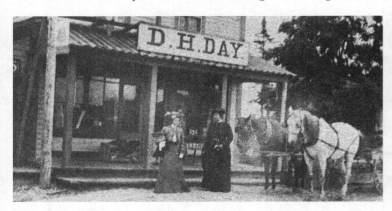

This picture, believed to be from the late 1800s, is one of the first of the store. (Glen Arbor History Group)

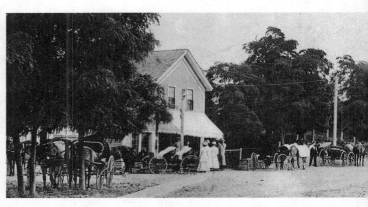

Carriages gather outside of store in 1905. (Travis Family Collection)

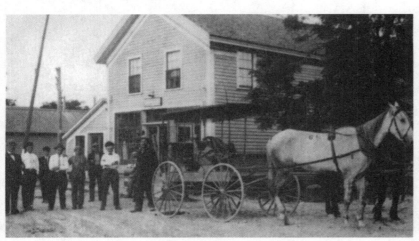

The store also served as Glen Haven's post office. Circa 1920.
(National Park Service)

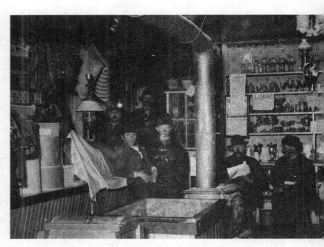

Interior of the store in the 1890s. (Glen Arbor History Group)

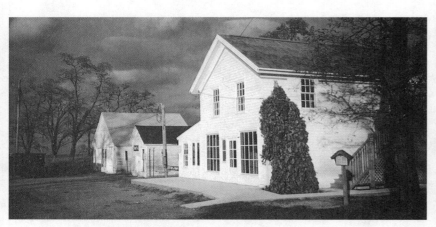

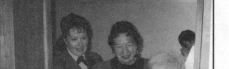
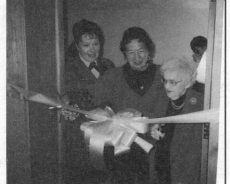

When motorists ordered gas from these circa 1930 pumps, the desired amount was pumped up into the glass containers, then released into the car. (National Park Service)

The store in 1999 as restored by the National Park Service, which preserved the Dutchman's-pipe climbing vine planted by D. H. Day as a tribute to his wife. (George Weeks)

Marion Warnes (right), daughter of D. H. Day, and Day granddaughter Pat Bennett (center) cut the ribbon for 2003 reopening of the store. Lakeshore Superintendent Dusty Shultz observes. (George Weeks)

Alpena, Rogers City/Crawford Quarry, Port Huron, Detroit and Cleveland.

Although Day was prominent in Glen Haven's maritime history, he fell far short of becoming a shipping tycoon himself. The *Lawrence* and *Champlain* went through a number of ownership changes in the 1880s, and the extent of his ownership in them has not been clearly established. He soon sold his interests in the Northern Michigan Line, which in 1894 merged with Seymour Transportation to form the Northern Michigan Transportation Company (NMTC).

NMTC operated four ships closely identified with Michigan's steamboat/resort heyday—the *Illinois*, *Puritan*, *Missouri* and *Manitou*. The *Manitou*, built in South Chicago in 1893, carried a crew of seventy five and up to 2,000 passengers. For a time, it was considered the finest passenger vessel on Lake Michigan. A 1901 flier for "The Palatial Steamship Manitou" touted "The Ideal Summer Trip" between Chicago and Mackinac Island, with "first class service in every way."

For about three decades, water was a far more pleasant way to travel than by road or rail. Many Chicago businessmen left their families in northern Michigan for summer vacations, joining them on Saturday mornings after an overnight trip from Chicago and then departing for Chicago Sunday night. The one-way fare: five dollars.

The Glen Haven beach and dock were popular meeting places, and arrival of steamers was a festive occasion, with area citizens often coming by small boat to watch the docking. Another event prompting the locals to get out on the beaches of Sleeping Bear Bay occurred when lumber was swept from ships and docks during storms. The wood was gathered to build many a home and barn.

When times were good for ship owners, the unloading of cargo at Glen Haven took twenty to thirty men about an hour. With expansion of trucking companies and improved highways, steamboat freight and passenger revenues fell sharply and NMTC was restructured. The Glen Arbor stop was eliminated around 1918 and the

pier allowed to deteriorate. Service continued to Glen Haven but by the late 1920s, there was little cargo and few passengers. Insolvency for operators of the steamships in 1931 brought the beginning of the end of Glen Haven's maritime role—and its massive dock.

Day's Kingdom

According to an 1881 plat map, Glen Haven had eleven buildings, including the inn, store, blacksmith shop, wagon shop and school. Day retained the deeds to all of the more than 100 lots in the village.

Day initially paid his lumberjacks 15 cents an hour, and dock hands 35 cents an hour. Pay was often in the form of coupons redeemable only at the D. H. Day Store, which also served as a telegraph office (Day built the telegraph line to Leland), a post office and a nerve center of the community. The second story of the store served as home for the Day family.

To the east of the store stood a granary and root cellar. To the north stood an icehouse where thick piles of sawdust kept as many as 5,000 blocks of ice weighing 150 pounds each frozen for summer use. The cutting of ice on Glen Lake was a major winter activity.

Glen Haven existed as an active recreation center for the Day family and neighbors, including the crew and families of the Sleeping Bear Point Lifesaving Service/Coast Guard Station. Back in Ogdensburg, Day's father, David Day, a vigorous athlete, bought ice skates for all of his children and insisted that they use them. D. H. Day did the same, building a covered, 150-by-50-foot ice-skating and curling rink in the village. A cherished call in the area came when Day's children phoned friends with the terse message: "rink's open tonight." Lights powered by a gasoline generator lit the rink, and skating halted promptly when Day, a strict disciplinarian, flashed the tights three times to signal bedtime. Day also built a tennis court, complete with bleachers.

Another popular pastime in the area was

catching a ride on the tramway that linked Day's dock with his sawmill near Glen Lake, riding on flatcars pulled by the locomotive that Day bought in 1907 from the J. 0. Nessen Mill that was dismantled at Glen Arbor. (After Day's locomotive was retired from service, it was on loan for a lumber industry display outside the Con Foster Museum in Traverse City's Clinch Park, and then was sold to Cedar Point amusement park in Ohio.) Day also entertained visitors on the Alice J. Day, a Glen Lake tug boat named after his oldest child and used primarily for towing logs.

Most of Day's employees were of Norwegian and Swedish descent, and some came from a small settlement of Indians just east of the village and west of what is now the D. H. Day Campground.

There were about a half dozen Indian families in the immediate area, totalling about thirty people. Most were related to each other and had last names of Westman and Jackson. Elizabeth Westman, a friend of the Day children, offered this recollection in 1975:

I was born in Glen Haven, the youngest of seven children and a member of the Ottawa tribe. We lived in a long building built by Mr. Day. The building was a short way from Sleeping Bear Inn. There was a slaughter house nearby and we got some meat from there. We used to cook in a three-legged iron kettle with

FAMILY PICNICS were favorite activities of the D. H. Day family. At this one, believed to have been after an 1895 ride on the tug Alice J. Day, Day is in the center of the picture with hat and cigar, holding his oldest child, Alice J. His brother, Rob Day, is standing at the rear holding his son, Larry. Rob's wife Corrine is on his right, in polka dots. To her right, is Eva Day, wife of D. H. Day. The happy fellow to Day's right was not identified, but the bearded man near Day is believed to be his father-in-law, William Farrant. (Travis Family Collection)

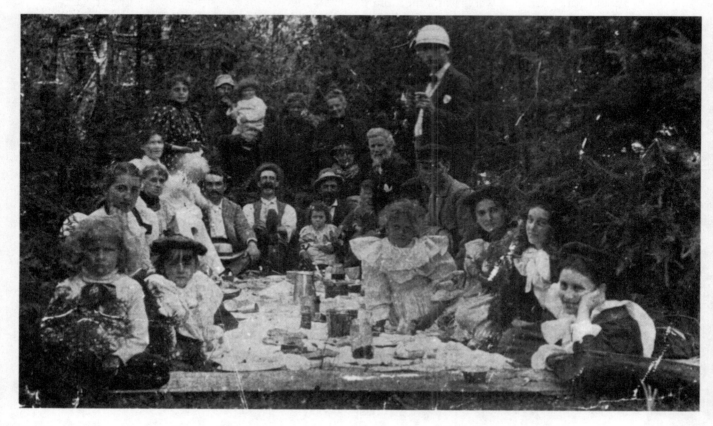

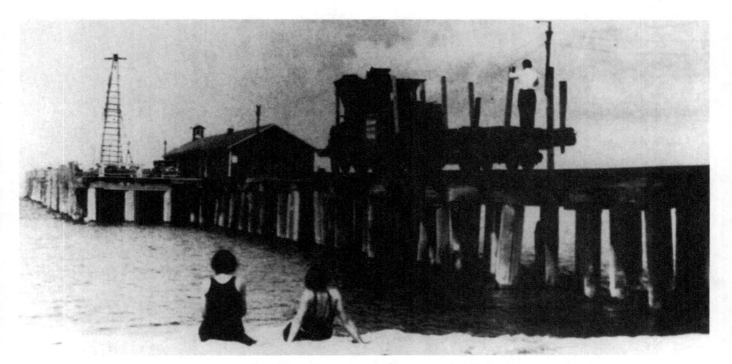

Even after decline of lumbering, D. H. Day's dock was used for shipping and his locomotive was a popular attraction. The historic, 50-foot Glen Haven Signal Tower, similar to those used at Sleeping Bear Point and South Manitou Island, can be seen on the dock. It was later moved ashore near the D. H. Day Store. (National Park Service)

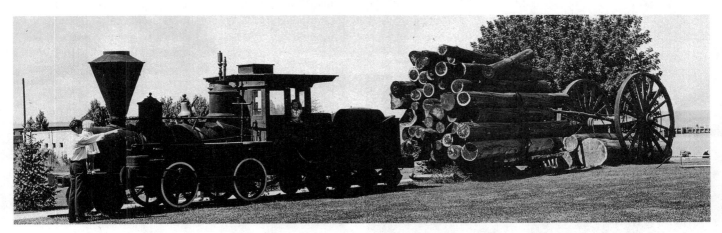

After D. H. Day's death, relatives loaned his locomotive to the City of Traverse City for this lumber industry display as it appeared in Clinch Park near the Con Foster Museum in 1939. It later was sold to the Cedar Point amusement park in Ohio. Then, after ownership by Greenfield Village in Dearborn, it was acquired by the Port Huron Museum. (The Detroit News)

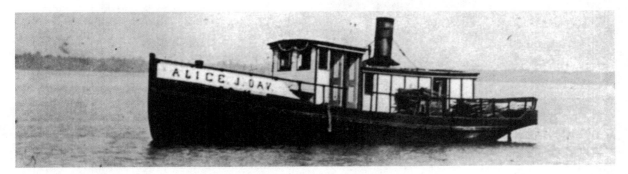

Tug Alice J. Day, named after Day's oldest child, on Glen Lake. (Marion Warnes)

no top on it. . . . We were share-croppers, too, so we had enough food. We were given brown stamps for shoes and green stamps for vegetables.[3]

The Day Family

As described by his sister, Margaret Thompson Day McFarland, Day was a "throwback to former generations, a bit feudal in his ideas and ambitions to found a family and estate that would carry on probably in the same locality for generations. He was wasted in a way; had he stayed out in the world he would have become a figure in either the financial or political world. In fact at one time he was approached by Party leaders (Democrats) to run for Governor of Michigan."[4]

Some of the best stories about Day's ambitions and zest for life are told in a 1968 letter that one of his daughters, Margaret Thompson Day Travis, wrote to her grandchildren passing on

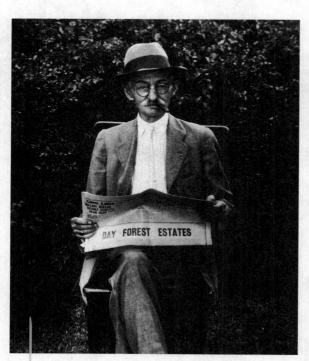

DAY WITH PROMO: *Real estate promotions said the Day Forest Estates could be "the most elaborate and exclusive resort in the United States." The Depression intervened.* (National Park Service)

stories "as I heard them from him." She described how his young friends in Ogdensburg were "a rather wild lot" so his family decided when he was about nineteen to send him to Milton Junction, Wisconsin, to work with an uncle who was a railroad man there. She said, "he arrived by train in Milton Junction walking on air and dressed to the teeth, complete with silk hat and cane—to find that the 'position' was wheeling freight on a handtruck! All he had was a one-way ticket and there was no escape, so he had to stay."[5]

After getting a job in Glen Haven, according to his daughter, Day found it "just too lonesome and dull" so he left for a period to go to Traverse City for his job with Hannah & Lay. In Traverse City, Day stayed at the Park Place Hotel, which was built in 1871, purchased by Hannah & Lay in 1879, and remains today the city's tallest and most familiar landmark. At the hotel, Day "and three other gay young blades shared a table in the dining room and had lots of fun together. One of their jinks was on a New Year's Day when they hired four horses and a very elegant sleigh and drove four-in-hand around town making New Year's calls."[6]

In his first year in Glen Haven, long before it became his kingdom, Day spotted a young princess and determined that she should one day be his wife. This is how Margaret Thompson Day Travis described "my father and mother's love story which is just as extraordinary as anything else in my father's history":

> When he first came to Glen Haven in his twenties he lived at what was the combined boarding house and hotel. It was the boarding house for the laborers and had a few better rooms for the steamship company officials and people who occasionally came and stayed. There he had a 2-room suite of bedroom and sitting room, which was his home for several years.
>
> The boarding house was run by Mr. & Mrs. William Farrant, a young French-Canadian couple who had come to the United States looking for free education for their children. They had a tiny son and a little daughter named Eva, about 5 years old. [It is believed she actually was nine or ten at the time.] By all accounts

she was a beautiful, charming child. My father loved children and made a companion of her from the start. She sat with him at his table in the dining room and he took her everywhere with him: in his 2-wheeled cart to the woods or the mill and fishing and frog-hunting, let her ride side-saddle on her mare, etc. As the years went on she had younger sisters and my father made much of them all, but it was she whom he took to his heart.

The story I have been told is that when his first Easter in Glen Haven came, he colored Easter eggs for her in the kitchen at the hotel and while he was doing this he told her mother that he was going to wait for Eva to grow up— and then marry her. And this he did.[7]

On 20 December 1889 David Henry Day, thirty-six years old, and Eva Ezilda Farrant, nineteen years old, were married. Over a span of twenty one years, they had nine children. A daughter died at birth in 1890 when Eva Day fell on stairs, forcing an early delivery. A son, Houston, died at age three in 1906. As late as 1989—

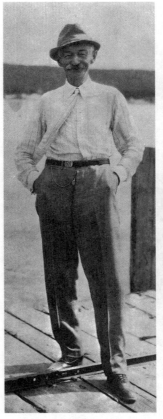

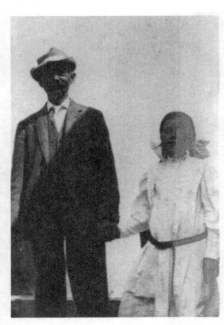

D. H. Day with daughter, Margaret.

D. H. Day astride a rail on his Glen Haven dock.
(Travis Family Collection)

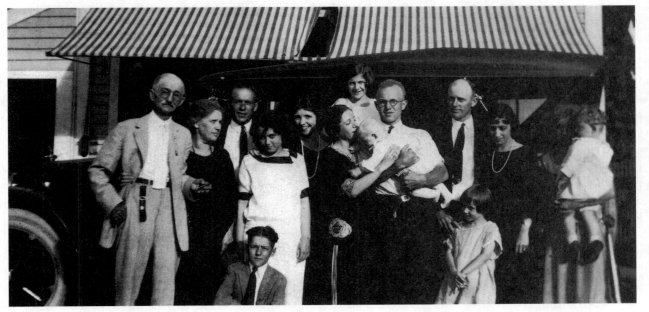

GLEN HAVEN'S FIRST FAMILY: *D. H. Day in front of his store and 1922 Nash with his wife and seven of their children and three grandchildren in 1923. Left to right: Day and wife Eva; son David; daughter Estelle (in white dress); son Bill (kneeling); Helen Day, wife of David (in black dress with pearls); daughter Marion (white dress in back) twin sister of Bill; daughter Margaret Thompson Day Travis (black dress); grandson Hugh Travis (baby); Fred Travis, husband of Margaret (white shirt, holding baby); Joe Leber (dark suit and tie); daughter Eva Day Leber (black dress); granddaughter Marion Rohns (child in front); daughter Alice Day Rohns (at far right), holding grandson Philip Rohns.* (Travis Family Collection)

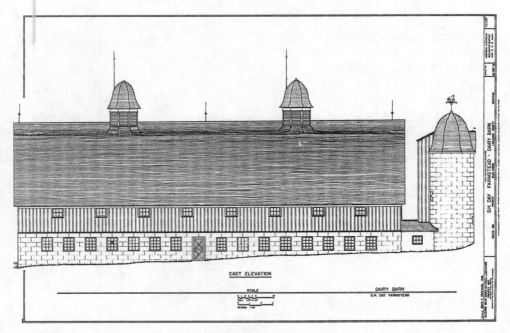

The D. H. Day Farm's dairy barn as it was submitted by the National Park Service for the Historic American Buildings Survey.

The Traverse City-based Western Michigan Development Bureau, whose longtime president was D. H. Day, published this picture of the barn in 191 (Vintage Views)

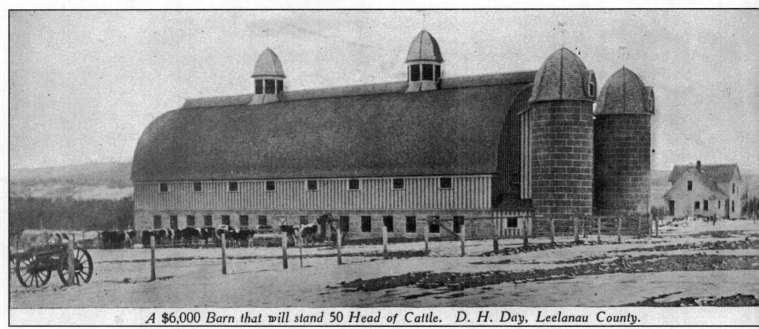

A $6,000 Barn that will stand 50 Head of Cattle. D. H. Day, Leelanau County.

the 100th anniversary of the marriage—a family torch of sorts still glowed in Glen Haven. That year, Marion Day Warnes, youngest daughter and last surviving of the nine children, planted a blue spruce tree on the knoll next to the D. H. Day Store and placed Christmas lights on it just as she had placed them on cut Christmas trees at the exact site—in fact, in the same hole—for about four decades.

A 1906 Christmas Pilgrimage to Traverse City

It was December 1906, and for a 10-year old girl living in northern Michigan, the season was touched with magic. As an adult, Margaret Thompson Day Travis wrote the following nostalgic account of her Christmas shopping trip from Glen Haven to the "fleshpots" of Traverse

City—an account that provides a graphic glimpse of travel by sleigh and train in early northwest Michigan:

> We didn't call it a pilgrimage then. To us it was a matter of course like Christmas itself—the whole family, seven strong, stepping out of our everyday frontier life and travelling forty winter miles for a two-day orgy of hotel luxury and glorious, prodigal shopping. Father was one of the early day lumbermen, whose business involved a great deal of shipping by water, and we lived in the tiny hamlet of Glen Haven, clustered around his docks on Lake Michigan. The Christmas shopping trip was our annual taste of the fleshpots.
>
> It would be mid-December and the snow already deep in that North Country. The journey began with an eight-mile sleighride to the nearest railroad at Empire. Father looked magnificent in a burly raccoon coat; Mother splendid in unaccustomed seal skin and Ostrich plumes; and of course, we children, under furskin robes swathed in mounds of coats, veils, and muffs, our nerve ends literally vibrating to the sweetness of the Russian harness chimes.
>
> Speeding across the snow between the black and white winter hardwoods, it was almost possible for us children to visualize that many-clappered music. In the narrow canyons of plowed-out logging roads, it rang out its imperious

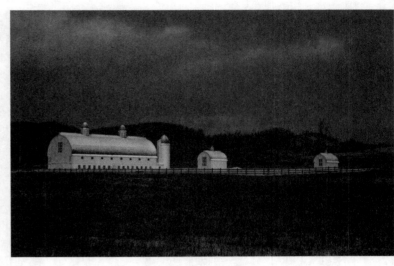

The south end of the barn as it appeared in 2005.

(Grace Dickinson)

CAR RALLY: *This circa 1941 gathering of cars in front of the inn was one of the "good roads" rallies brought to Glen Haven by D. H. Day. Lead car: Model T Ford.*

(Travis Family Collection)

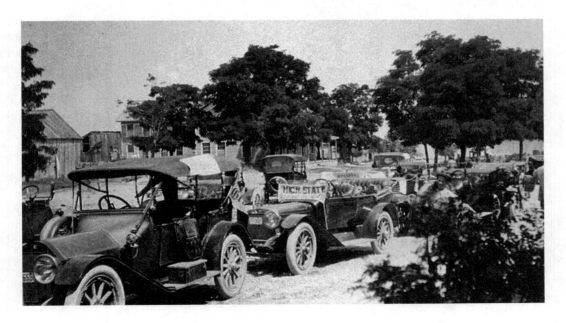

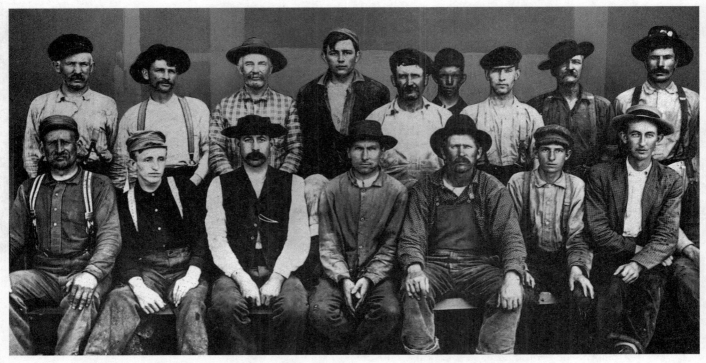

Turn-of-the-century lumbermen gather in Glen Haven. Many of their families remained in Leelanau County, including those of Archie Plowman, second from the right in the front row. The 1989 Empire-Maple City phone book had listings for five Plowman homes. (The Detroit News)

announcement of our arrival. The whole forest seemed to throb with a silver ecstasy.

At the railroad village, we caught a combination passenger-baggage-smoking car which had been hitched to the end of a long train. Logging railroads laced the country at that time. One rode them gratefully, perfectly willing to angle thirty or so miles in order to achieve what would have been twelve as the crow flies. We would change at various little junctions in the wood, moving from one coach or caboose to another; all equally gritty with coal dust, pitted from caulked boots, dirty with tobacco juice, and nauseating from the smell of coal gas.

We took the Empire & Southeastern at Empire; 12 miles later we were at Empire junction, the other end of the line. There, we transferred to the Manistee & Northeastern by means of a wooden plank extended between the two trains. The Manistee & Northeastern followed a circuitous route, first south, then east-

erly, then northeasterly to our destination, with several changes of trains, touching, among others, the villages of Honor and Interlochen.

As we travelled, past these grimy windows slid magic forests, and we children watched, enchanted, by the miles of evergreens knee deep in snow, draped and garlanded in snow—a million Christmas trees whispering to us with a million voices, whispering to us of Christmas delights. We began to be wrapped in Christmas as in a cloud.

Eventually, the logging rail roads merged with the main line. We would wait for three interminable hours at a dingy little station for the big train which would sweep us into Traverse City. The early winter darkness would fail while we waited, so that the train's incandescent eye rushed down on us out of the night. The trainmen swinging on and off the train were mysterious figures whose lanterns made dancing pools of light on the snow.

This train was clean, smooth-riding, and well-lighted. In it, Mother would be hooking furs, her fingers expertly working the difficult clasps of the period. Very quickly she would straighten curls and re-touch faces, while Father, his rustic raccoon coat replaced by a well-tailored overcoat and visored sealskin pill-box, arranged for "carriages" with the Traverse City transfer. Father was inordinately proud of his lively brood. Nothing tickled him more than the fact it took two carriages to transport us.

The carriages—closed hacks on runners—would be waiting for us under the station lights in Traverse City, waiting to gather us into their musty-smelling dark interiors. Slowly we would glide across the viaduct into the shopping district. Here it burst upon us at last, a fairyland of lighted plate glass windows, festooned with looped ropes of holly, filled with candy canes, life-sized dolls, mechanical trains, and ten-foot toboggans. What jeweler's windows, winking with diamonds and heavy yellow bracelets rich on purple satin; what Italian fruit stores, windows, glowing with deep red, yellow, and purple fruit, to say nothing of the great boxes of loose mistletoe and holly standing outside on the sidewalk! What throngs of people hurrying about on mysterious errands, their sleighs disappearing knowingly around corners while Salvation Army lassies rang bells beside kettles under street lamps!

Once at the hotel, there was much business of paying cab drivers and directing porters and marshalling us children en masse into the plushy mirrored parlors which smelled so excitingly worldly. There were smiling greetings from the proprietor and his wife, who were friends of Father and Mother. After which miles of labyrinthine hallways leading to walnut, marble and red-plush bedrooms where we hastily freshened up and hurried down to the big dining room with its gliding, black-uniformed waitresses, and then the supreme moment of ordering our own suppers from a printed menu. Fresh radishes with the soup, and crisp green parsley garnishing the meat, although snow lay deep outside the windows—could luxury go further?

Mother's methods with us were mass-production. Her first move the morning after we arrived was to run the whole flock of us through the hotel barbershop. Then she made group appointments for us with the dentist and the photographer. The necessities attended to, she turned us loose, each with a shopping list and the money we had been accumulating since July.

(Photo at top) As part of his economic diversification efforts, Day started this canning company in the 1920s.
(National Park Service)

(Photo at bottom) The canning company has been restored as part of the National Park Service's plan for Glen Haven. The pilings of the dock, shown here capped with snow in 1988, are protected as part of the Manitou Bottomland Preserve. To the left of the canning company there are picnic tables where lumber was once stacked.
(Cottage Book Shop of Glen Arbor)

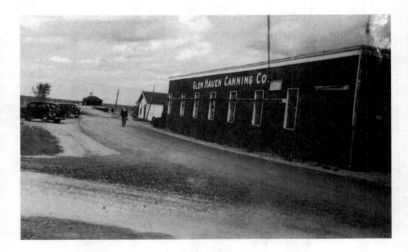

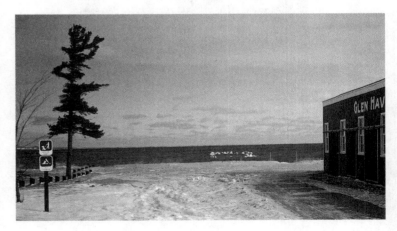

My older sisters, Alice and Eva, very prim and dignified, slipped away together quickly lest a younger one "tag along" with them. My brother, David, and I teamed up. That left Mother only baby Estelle to take with her while she shopped. In addition to the six of us, her list included gifts for her family scattered all over Canada, Father's family in upstate New York, and gifts for the maid at home and for sundry employees' families. We used to stumble upon her wherever we went, giving us a feeling of coziness in this strange vastness. She would be standing intently before a counter, or crossing the street half a block ahead of us, or sailing down the thick carpeted hotel corridor towards us when we would return to unload parcels. How her hazel eyes and her swinging diamond earrings sparkled against the soft darkness of her fur collar! How deliciously she rustled, how regally her village-made broadcloth skirt swept back when she walked! No world-famed Duchess would ever be half so chic.

Father had business at the bank, at the foundry, at the hardware stores, and harness

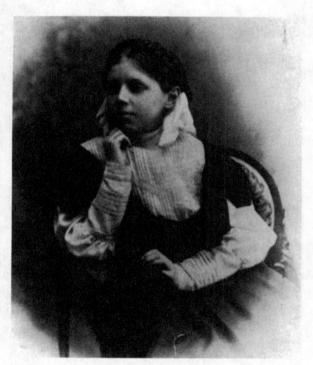

Margaret Thompson Day Travis in about 1910.
(Travis Family Collection)

shops. We saw him in the hotel at mealtimes, affable but elusive, and lost him immediately afterward to his concerns while we plunged back into the fairyland-musical carnival of the shopping district.

At night I would wake in the big bed and lie looking out through the opening between the window and the sill at the lights which pierced the city night, hearing the soft hotel stirrings going on all about me and the distant train whistles. The unaccustomed smell of coal smoke faintly nauseated me and I would lie there, vaguely disturbed by what seemed to my 10-year old mind a massive violation of the night, nostalgic for the limitless star-hung darkness of my experience, the reassuring pine fragrance coupled with the rhythmic pulse of Lake Michigan.

But the two days were a dream of delight. When David and I had bought all of the presents on our lists, we spent our time savoring city life. We went to all of the crepe-paper garlanded moving picture "palaces" and criticised them expertly. We tried all of the ice cream parlors and Kandy Kitchens. We bought exotic fruit and armfuls of holly and mistletoe. We began to see ourselves as pampered sophisticates, spending money, amusing only ourselves, eating delicious meals, and pressing buttons if we wanted anything.

On the third morning, all of this magnificence went into reverse. The mounting excitement of our arrival ran the other way. The hacks took us in daylight from hotel to train. The trains to which we changed grew progressively dingier. When we got off the last one, our waiting three-seated open sleigh looked cold and crude. The mound of coats were much more uncomfortable when donned in a cold station. Logging roads and snowy fields were dreary and commonplace after the splendor we had known.

But when the sleigh dipped into the snowy forest tunnels again, and the whole visible world rang with the silver clamor of the bells, our spirits stirred again. That music escaping into the forest trailed a Lorelei song back over its shoulder—a song which was at once a promise and a challenge.

"Tomorrow," David and I told each other, "we will go out into the woods—way back in the woods—way back in the woods and find a

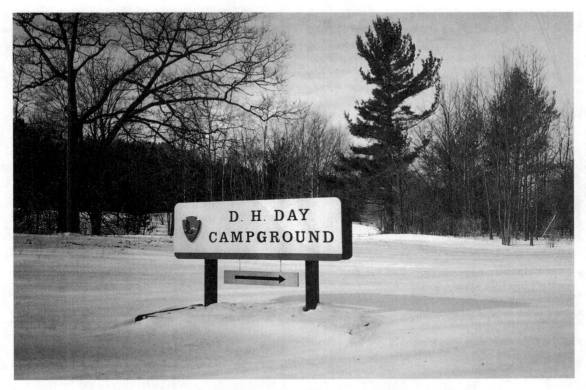

D. H. DAY CAMPGROUND: *The year-round D. H. Day Campground honors Michigan's first State Park Commission chairman. Day donated the land for the state park established between Glen Haven and Glen Arbor on M-109 that is now one of two campgrounds within the Sleeping Bear Dunes National Lakeshore.*

(Cottage Book Shop of Glen Arbor)

Christmas tree. We'll stay all day 'till we find a beautiful one, the most beautiful one we ever had—."[8]

Forest and Farm

Trees were important in the life of D.H. Day, who was the first president and one of the founders of the Michigan Hardwood Lumber Association. By 1910, he owned more than 5,000 forested acres and long before the reforestation movement came to northern Michigan he promoted it. The 1,400-acre Day Forest, with its huge second-growth trees, was viewed by government researchers as one of the best timber stands in the Midwest.

By the 1920s, Day also had more than 5,000 cherry and apple trees at the 400-acre D. H. Day Farm, which he called "Oswegatchi" after the New York community where his father was born and the Oswegatchi River on whose banks D. H. Day played.

Day grew hay and corn to feed his 400 hogs and prize herd of 200 Holsteins described as among the best in the state.[9] The farm, located just south of Glen Haven, has a massive white barn that stands today as a landmark of the heritage of Sleeping Bear Country. Day had the barn, house and three out-buildings built in the late 1880s and early 1890s. One outbuilding was the pig barn, one the creamery, and the third the bull barn. The farm is located on M-109, which joins M-22 to the south to link Glen Haven with

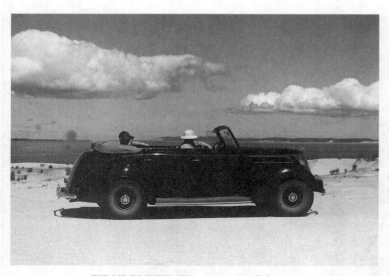

FIRST FLEET: *Wearing a sun helmet, Louis Warnes drives on the dunes in 1937 Ford from his first fleet.*
(Fred Dickinson)

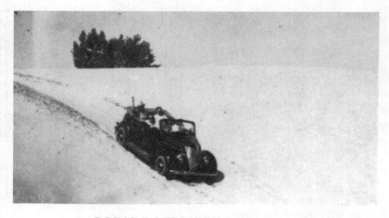

GOING DOWN "FOX DIP", *so named because the driver would say, "Look—there's a fox!" in order to distract riders just before the car took a dip that was one of the thrills of the tour. The woman in back is Mrs. Jack B. Jones. Circa 1940.* (Gary Jones)

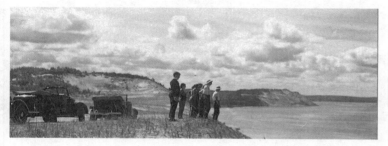

Viewing Lake Michigan from atop the dunes in the 1930s. (Fred Dickinson)

Empire. Day, a pioneer promoter of good roads in Michigan, played no small role in building the Glen Haven-Empire road. *The Traverse City Record-Eagle* reported: "Mr. Day planned the work, supervised it, and paid for the actual construction himself."[10]

Promotion of good roads became one of Day's objectives in his leadership roles in the Western Michigan Pike Association, which staged auto rallies in Glen Haven as part of its "good roads pike tours." As one founder of the Western Michigan Development Bureau in 1909, Day promoted road improvement throughout his nineteen-year tenure as its president. The bureau encouraged investors and settlers to come to the area and promoted development of west Michigan's agricultural and industrial potential. The bureau's slogan was "Every possible acre working all the time at that for which it is best adapted. "

Day had his own ideas for diversified use of every possible acre, His sawmill, which at its peak produced as much as 55,000 board feet of lumber a day, stayed in operation until 1923, beyond the end of the lumber boom.

During much of the boom from the Civil War until about 1900, Michigan was the national leader in lumber production. According to the Michigan Bureau of History, state loggers cut 161 billion board feet of pine logs and 50 billion board feet of hardwoods—equivalent to a half-mile wide, one-inch plank road from New York to San Francisco. In dollar value, Michigan lumber outvalued all the gold extracted from California by a billion dollars. In 1889, the year of greatest production, Michigan produced about 5.5 billion board feet. (A board foot, the standard unit of lumber measurement, is a piece of wood one foot long, one foot wide and an inch thick.)

As lumbering declined, Day planned for economic diversification—something that Michigan's economy has needed throughout its history of boom-and-bust cycles. In the early 1920s, he established the Glen Haven Canning Company on the shoreline near the dock and shipped cherries and other fruits to various Great Lakes cities.

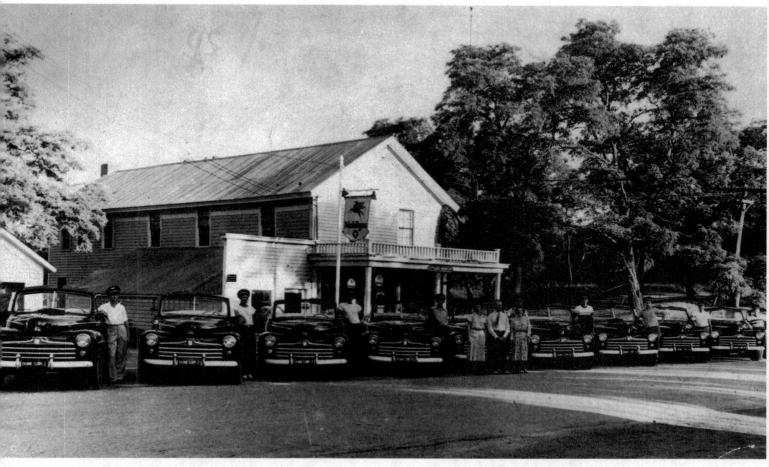

SECOND FLEET: *After World War 11, the fleet was formed with ten 1948 Fords, shown in front of the D. H. Day Store.* (Marion Warnes)

With improvement of roads, the Glen Haven dock faded in importance and fell victim to storms. Today, depending on Lake Michigan's fluctuating levels, pilings of the Glen Haven dock are in some years totally submerged, and in other years have their tops exposed as a reminder of Glen Haven's importance to the water highways of yesterday. The canning company building has been restored by the National Park Service and on occasion will house an exhibit of small craft used in the Manitou Passage.

Resort Development—"Adirondacks of Michigan"

A diversification project promoted by Day that was far bigger than the canning company

was resort development. According to National Park Service historian Cockrell, Day "wanted to harness the anticipated economic windfall of tourism to the full advantage of the region and Glen Haven village. His scheme was so grandiose that if successful, the Glen Haven/Glen Lake area would be transformed into the most elaborate and exclusive resort in the United States."[11] In large part because of the Depression, it was not successful. Here is what happened:

In 1922, Day sold a large portion of land, including reforested Alligator Hill between Lake Michigan and Glen Lake, for a real estate development that was called Day Forest Estates. Alligator Hill, so called because a portion of it resembles the silhouette of an alligator's snout, is a glacial deposit formed when two surrounding

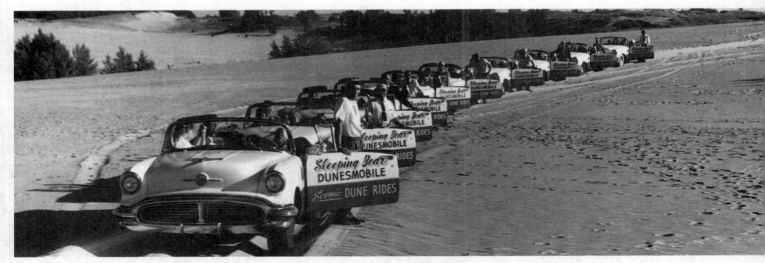

THIRD FLEET: *It began with ten 1956 Oldsmobiles, shown on the dunes. The lead driver is Tom Dean.*

(Marion Warnes)

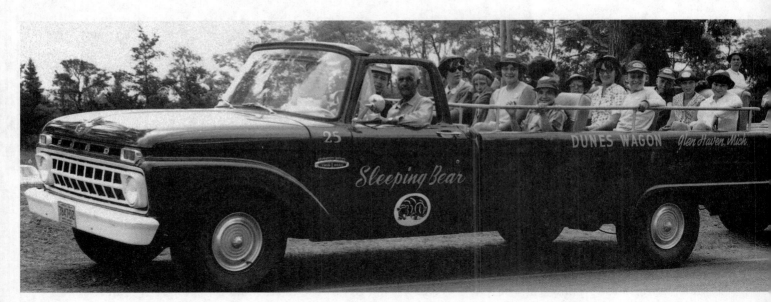

FOURTH FLEET: *Started with a 1965 Ford pickup, it consisted of 13 dunes wagons modified with a special stretch design by Louis Warnes. Vehicle 25 is shown with driver Bill Day, D. H. Day's youngest son and twin brother of Marion Warnes.* (Marion Warnes)

lobes of ice dumped their load of sand and rock into the area between the lobes. One real estate publication, calling the area the "Adirondacks of Michigan," proclaimed with a flourish:

"The project, deemed fit for the permanent Summer White House, can provide homes for residents of the Gold Coast of Chicago or Millionaire's Row of New York and leave nothing to

be desired that nature or men can provide. It will be a center of society."[12]

An 18-hole golf course was built, an air strip and clubhouse site were cleared, and access roads graded. A brochure about 1929 announced "the development of America's premier exclusive summer community."[13] The venture failed during the Depression, although the golf course

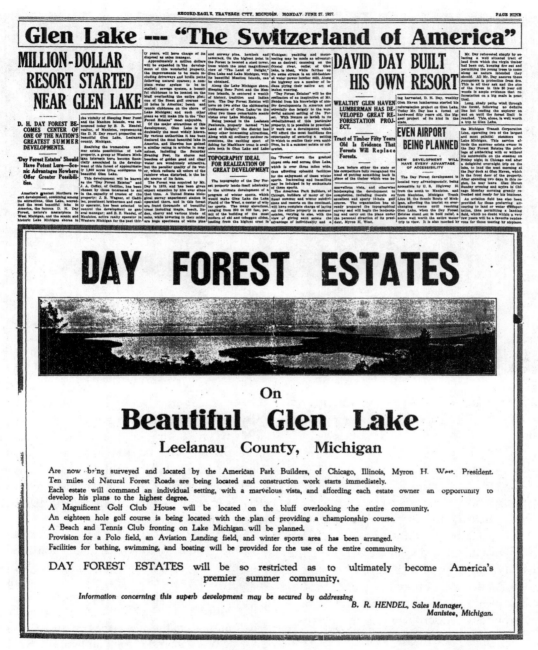

There was grandiose promotion for the Day Forest Estates, including touting it as "fit for the permanent Summer White House," but the Depression intervened and it was not developed. (Traverse City Record-Eagle, June 27, 1927)

operated for several years. One man who played it in the 1930s said "it was a great course, but if you went off the fairway, you were in a mighty deep, deep forest."[14]

Although the course is abandoned and over-grown, the outline of its fairways are evident today for those who use the National Park Service's Alligator Hill hiking and cross-country ski traits.

Day Forest Estates was not developed. But the

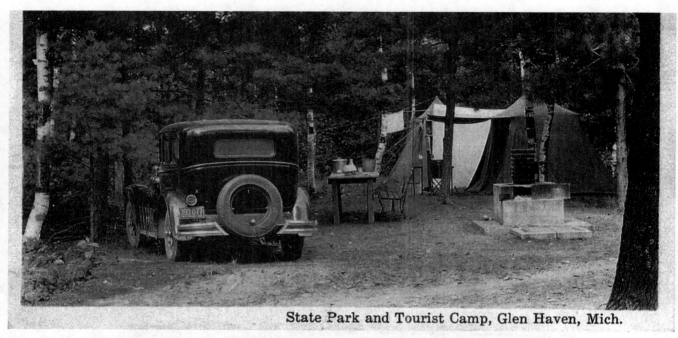

State Park and Tourist Camp, Glen Haven, Mich.

The D. H. Day State Park, shown here after its creation in 1920, later became the D. H. Day Campground within the Sleeping Bear Dunes National Lakeshore—one of the links of Sleeping Bear's yesterday and today. (D.H. Day III)

Glen Lake area, as D. H. Day anticipated, became a premier location for summer residents and visitors.

D. H. Day Campground

One of the most popular of Day's legacies in the Sleeping Bear Dunes National Lakeshore is the D. H. Day Campground on Lake Michigan between Glen Haven and Glen Arbor. Like the Platte River Campground in Benzie County, the campground is in an area previously used by pre-historic peoples and early settlers, and is now open year-round to modern day visitors on a first-come, first-served basis.

The campground is on a thirty two-acre site that Day donated 11 November 1920 to the State of Michigan. It became the D. H. Day State Park. Although described in many writings as Michigan's first state park, the Mackinac Island State Park, which the state acquired from the United States government in 1895, has that distinction. The Michilimackinac State Park at Mackinaw City was acquired in 1909. The Interlochen State Park, between Duck Lake and Green Lake in Grand Traverse County, was acquired when the state purchased 200 acres in 1917 to save a stand of virgin pine. But the D. H. Day State Park and the man who donated it deserve a special place in the history of Michigan parks, as described by a state historical marker that is in front of a log cabin built in 1923–24 on the campgrounds:

By the end of World War 1, with the rapid growth of the recreation industry in Michigan, a need for a statewide system of parks had arisen. In 1919, the State Park Commission was established. D. H. Day State Park, honoring the commission chairman, was the first park that it set up. When state parks were transferred to the Conservation Department in 1921, over 20 other sites had been acquired, most of them, like D. H. Day State Park, beautifully located on take shores.

Day's efforts on behalf of state parks helped enhance the reputation of Governor Albert E. Sleeper, who attended the commission's first meeting on 20 January 1920, as one of Michigan's leading conservation governors.

The Glen Haven area's recreational attraction

was expanded in 1931 when the Michigan Department of Conservation acquired 1,545 acres of the dune area from the federal government to create the Sleeping Bear Dunes State Park, which was later expanded to more than 2,000 acres. This, along with the D. H. Day State Park, became part of the Sleeping Bear Dunes National Lakeshore.

Dunes Rides

The Sleeping Bear Dunemobile Rides out of Glen Haven introduced thousands of people to the dunes during the mid-twentieth century. Throughout their forty-three years of operation, the rides were owned by Louis Warnes and his wife Marion, D.H. Day's youngest daughter. By this time, they owned the D. H. Day Store, and used it as base for the dunes rides.

The rides started in 1935 with a used 1934 Ford that took four people at a time, for a charge of 25 cents each, on a brief ride from Glen Haven to the crest of the dunes and back. By the time the rides ended in 1978, there were thirteen dunes wagons, each carrying as many as 14 passengers on a 12 mile, 35 minute excursion.

Glen Haven Today

By the mid-1970s, the National Park Service had purchased all of the village, although some residents retained occupancy rights for an extended period. In 1989, Carolyn Bumgardner, who grew up in the village as lumbering was dying out, was the only year-round resident. (Her grandfather, John Bumgardner, was the sawmill foreman in the early 1900s and her grandmother, Cynthia, cooked for lumberjacks. Their house, which no longer exists, was often occupied by mill or farm workers.) Some other residences were used periodically in the late 1980s, including the Dean house, owned by Tom Dean, a member of the last crew of the Sleeping Bear Point Coast Guard Station.

Commercial activity ceased. After 115 years of operation, the inn closed in 1972, but later became available for restoration and leasing by private interests. The D. H. Day Store closed in

1978 upon termination of the dunesmobile rides.

As an attraction in the Sleeping Bear Dunes National Lakeshore, Glen Haven will be interpreted for a number of maritime-related activities: cord wood station, freight shipping and receiving, passenger service, U. S. port of entry, frontier inn, fishing, hardwood lumber production and shipping, U. S. Weather Bureau Storm Signal Station, ferry boat service to South Manitou Island, fruit processing and shipping, steamboat/resort activities, and the nearby U. S. Life Saving Service/Coast Guard Station (See Chapter Nine), which was built in large part because of lobbying by D. H. Day. The dock site and nearby submerged wrecks are protected as part of the Manitou Bottomland Preserve, and are popular attractions for divers.

Most of the present towns of northern Michigan had their origins with the lumber industry, but few retain the look of those early days. Marie Scott of the Sleeping Bear Dune Preservation Committee said that Glen Haven "appears exceptional" within the Sleeping Bear Dunes National Lakeshore because it still exists, while such lumber-era sites as Aral, Port Oneida, Good Harbor and Crescent on North Manitou Island are ghost towns (See Chapter Five).[15] These towns were typical of the once-flourishing Great Lakes coastal lumber communities whose unprotected piers were abandoned and then destroyed by waves and ice after the lumber boom. These towns are gone. The frontier company town of Glen Haven remains. Most importantly, it still resembles the early shore facilities constructed at places that only rarely survived the intensive development of waterfront communities throughout the Great Lakes.

When Michigan gained statehood in 1837, what is now Glen Haven was a wilderness.

"Today, Glen Haven is the best preserved cord wood station on the eastern shore of Lake Michigan and perhaps the entire Great Lakes," according to the documentation for its place on the National Register of Historic Places. "The high degree of integrity of the historic setting makes an important contribution to the overall significance of the site. The general lack of modern intrusions within and adjacent to the village and along the shoreline, the broad reach of clear Lake Michigan water, the restored South Manitou Lighthouse and Sleeping Bear Point Coast Guard Station and the low base tones from the North Manitou Shoal Lighthouse combine to create a powerful historic landscape that echoes the feeling and associations of the period of significance."[16]

Glen Haven has another distinction. It is located on Michigan's shortest state highway, quarter-mile-long M-209.*

Endnotes—Glen Haven

1. Traverse City Record-Eagle (Traverse City, MI) 17 April 1928.
2. Ron Cockrell, *D. H. Day's Kingdom: A Special History Study of Glen Haven Village Historic District*, (Omaha, Neb.: National Park Service Midwest Regional Office, 1984), 11. 3.
3. Robert Dwight Rader, *Beautiful Glen Arbor Township*, (Glen Arbor, MI: Glen Arbor History Group, 1977), 73.
4. Margaret Thompson Day McFarland, in a letter that D. H. Day's daughter, Margaret Thompson Day Travis, wrote to her grandchildren in November of 1968. The letter was made available to the author by Margaret Thompson Day Travis' son, Robert F. Travis of Kala-mazoo and Glen Haven, from the Robert and Mary Travis Historical Collections.
5. Margaret Thompson Day Travis, in her 1968 letter to her grandchildren. She told them that in his family he was called by his middle name, "Henry." In high school, he was called "Hank." In Traverse City before his marriage his friends called him "Harry," and that is what his wife called him. Only friends made in later ears called him "David." He was also addressed as D. H. "
6. Travis.
7. Travis. (She said her grandfather's name was originally Guilliame de Pharand but it was changed when he became an American citizen and variously spelled in the family as Farant and Farrant.)
8. Slightly shorter variations of this account, provided to the author in 1985 by Robert F. Travis of Kalamazoo and Glen Haven, were published Dec. 22, 1985, in MICHIGAN, The Magazine of The Detroit News, and December 1986 by *Traverse, The Magazine*.
9. Traverse City Record-Eagle, 17 April 1928.
10. Traverse City Record-Eagle.
11. Cockrell, 33.
12. Clarence V. Smazel, "Michigan Has Won!" in *The Michigan Property Owner* (undated 1920s).
13. Rader, 89.
14. Thomas M. Farrell, information director for the Michigan Supreme Court, interview with the author, 1989.
15. Marie Scott, in a 7 April 1989 letter to Director Martha Bigelow of the Michigan Bureau of History.
16. Bill Herd, "Glen Haven Historic Village," a statement provided Sleeping Bear Dunes National Lakeshore staff.

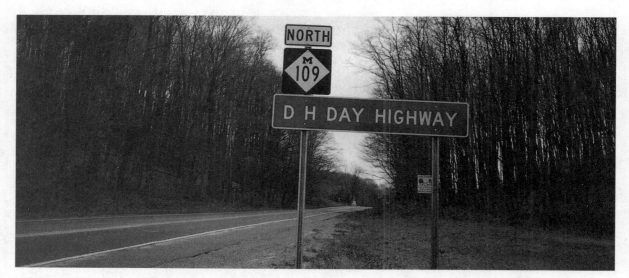

The M-209 name later was dropped and the short stretch was designated Glen Haven Road by Leelanau County. In 2001, the State of Michigan designated M-109 as D. H. Day Highway in honor of all that he did to promote good roads, tourism, conservation and the economy of northern Michigan. Behind the woods to the right of the sign at the southern entrance to the highway is the Maple Grove Cemetery where he was buried in 1928. (George Weeks)

CHAPTER 7

The Manitous:
Great Spirits of The Great Lakes

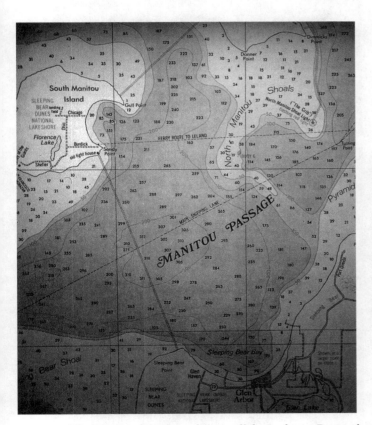

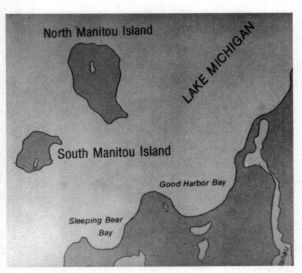

The Manitou Islands as they sit off the Leelanau Peninsula.(National Park Service)

The offshore jewels of the Sleeping Bear Dunes National Lakeshore were formed by glaciers, named by Indians, and settled by lumbermen and farmers. They were used as way-stations by the first settlers of the region, and by early mariners as beacons, havens and sources of fuel.

The islands of North Manitou and South Manitou are today much as they were in prehistoric days—attractions for seasonal visitors. The

81

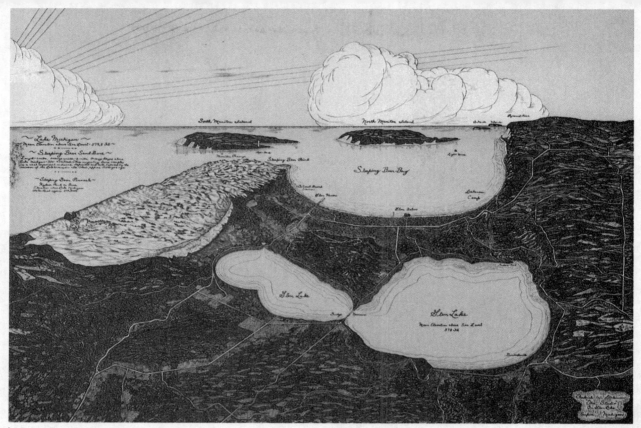

Manitou Passage - 1943   Frederick W. Dickinson

The Manitou Passage as drawn in 1943 by Leelanau County's Fred Dickinson.

first human inhabitants of the islands were migrating American Indians.

As recently as the 1970s, otherwise authoritative books on the Manitous suggested that Indians viewed the islands with "awe and foreboding hardly daring to cross the waters to explore them."[1] But archaeological evidence is that the islands were occupied by Native Americans in prehistoric days. Based on archaeological survey, Michigan State University's Charles E. Cleland concluded that North Manitou was probably inhabited by at least 1,000 B.C. and occupied again sometime between A.D. 1,000 and the coming of Europeans to the Lake Michigan basin.[2] Subsequent studies and discoveries raised the possibility of human activity on the islands as early as the Paleo-Indian period (11,000-plus B.C. to 8,000 B.C.).

North Manitou is one of the richest sources of archaeological discovery in the Lakeshore, especially along bluffs on the north end. Both islands have significant sites from the Late Woodland Period (600 B.C. to A.D. 1620), the most pronounced period of occupation and activity in Sleeping Bear's prehistoric period.

Regardless of how many years ago they first gazed upon the islands, the first people of the Manitous considered them embodiments of the dominating Great Spirit (see Chapter One). The Indian legend of the mother bear and her two cubs who fled a forest fire in Wisconsin by swimming across Lake Michigan concludes that the cubs never made it across. It said the Great Spirit Manitou created the Manitou Islands where the cubs perished. The importance of manitou to the first people of North America can be seen in the number of places that still carry its name.

In Canada, there are the province of Manitoba, the small town of Manitou and Manitoba Lake in southern Manitoba, Manito Lake and Manitou Beach in Saskatchewan, and Manitowang, Manitoulin District and Manitoulin Island in Ontario.

In the United States, there are the small towns of Manitou Springs in Colorado, Manito in Illinois, Manitou in Oklahoma, and Manitou Beach in Michigan's Lenawee County. Wisconsin has the county and city of Manitowoc, the Manitowoc River, and the small towns of Manitowish, Manitowish Waters and Manitowoc Rapids.

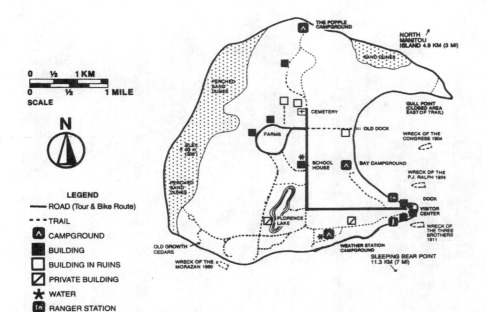

S. MANITOU HIKING
MAP: *This 2002 hiking map
shows the main features of
South Manitou.*
(National Park Service)

*By the time this 1982 aerial
Picture from a similar angle
was taken of the lighthouse and
life station, both had ceased
operations and the watchtower
was long gone.*
(Cottage Book Shop of Glen Arbor)

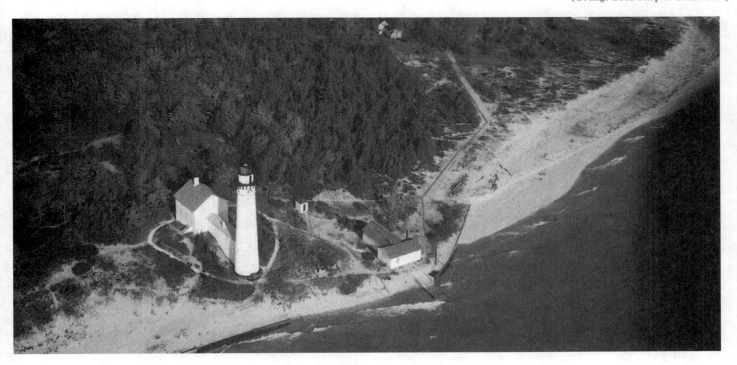

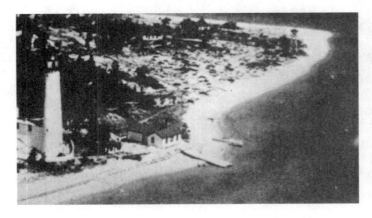

ISLAND VIGIL: *South Manitou's role as a
beacon and rescue station for Lake Michigan
shipping is reflected in this 1930s aerial view.
In the foreground is the 100-foot lighthouse
erected in 1871 to replace 35-foot tower built
in 1858 on a two-story brick building. The
original light was built in 1840 atop a wooden
house. At the point in this picture is the life
station's watchtower. To its right are the life
station and boat house.*
(National Park Service)

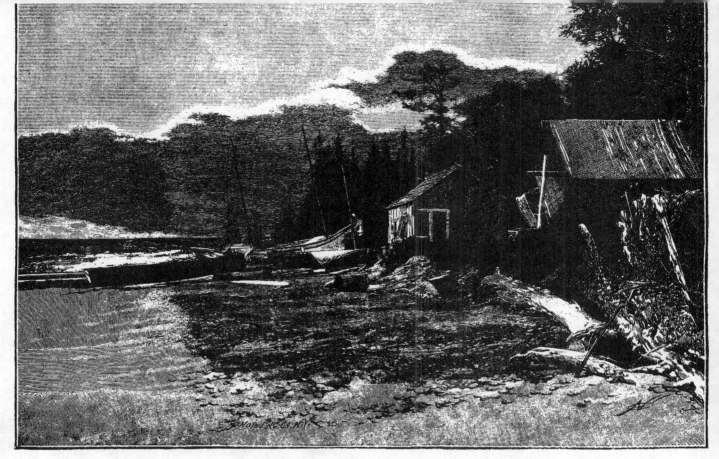

SOUTH MANITOU IN THE 1880s: *This 1880s U.S. Geological Survey lithograph shows a South Manitou fishing camp with boats, gill-nets on a reel and a shanty for cleaning fish.* (Courtesy Lewis Razek)

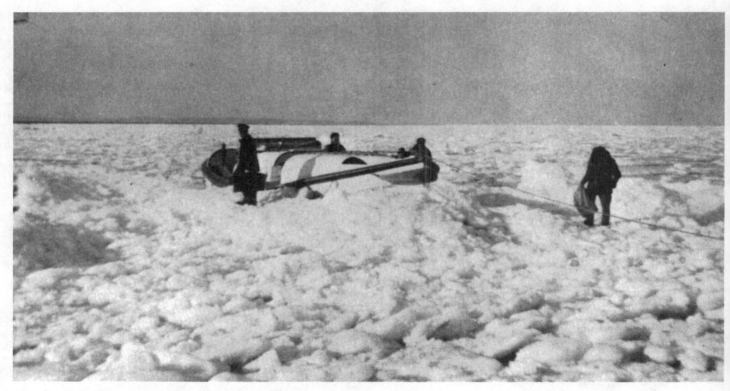

South Manitou was isolated duty for the Coast Guard in the winter, as shown by this picture of a 36-foot lifeboat transferring mail and crew between the island and mainland. (National Park Service)

The Manitou Islands of Leelanau County are not the only ones in the Great Lakes. In Lake Superior, there is a Manitou Island east of the tip of Michigan's Keweenaw Peninsula, and one among the Apostle Islands north of Ashland, Wisconsin.

A more scientific story of creation of the islands comes from geologists. They tell us the Manitous were left by the Wisconsin stage of the Great Ice Age. The islands are the south end of an archipelago that extends north to the Straits of Mackinac and includes (going northward) South Fox, North Fox, Beaver, High, Gull, Trout, Whiskey, Garden and Hog. The island

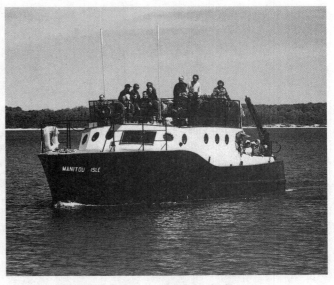

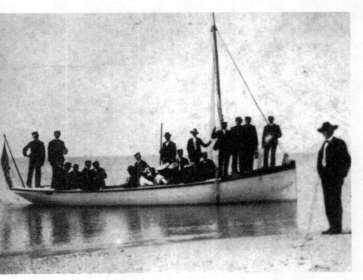

ISLAND TRANSIT: *For much of the 20th century, three generations of the Grosvenor family have provided ferry service to the Manitou Islands. George Tracy Grosvenor began service in 1918 with the Lawrence, which had been operated as an island ferry by John Paetchow. Grosvenor's son, George Firestone Grosvenor, assumed the business in the 1940s, and grandson Mike Grosvenor began taking over in the 1970s. By the late 1980s, the Grosvenor's Manitou Island Transit—the only public link with the islands— carried 6,000 to 8,000 visitors a year. By 1990, two vessels were used for the 1 1/2 hour trips: The Mishe Mokwa and the Manitou Isle.* (National Park Service)

MANITOU MUSIC: *This band from Glen Arbor came out to the Manitous for early 20th century performances.* (National Park Service/Sherwood Basch Collection)

chain represents the crest of a high ridge line formed by a tilted layer of limestone. The glaciers buried the ridge under a blanket of glacial debris. When glacial melt waters filled the Lake Michigan basin, the debris-covered tops of the ridge were exposed as islands.

In between prehistoric use of the island and the current use for Lakeshore visitors, both islands had a lively history.

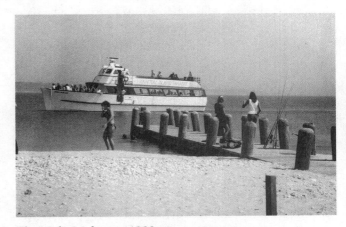

The Mishe Mokwa in 1983. (National Park Service)

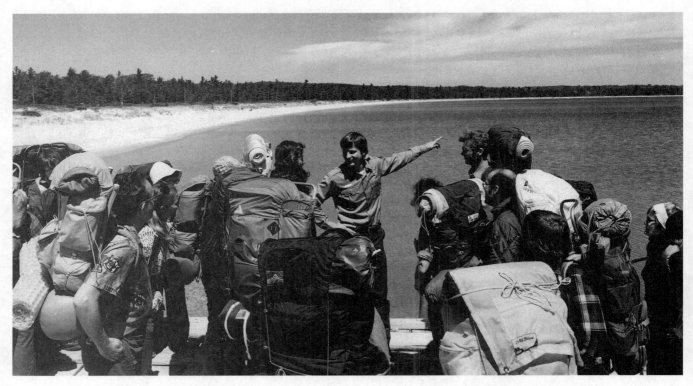

Backpackers are greeted by a National Park Service ranger upon arrival on the island in 1975. (Michigan Travel Bureau)

SOUTH MANITOU

This 5,260-acre island, eight miles square, is located seven and a half miles north of Sleeping Bear Point and 16 miles west of Leland. It was the site of the first settlement and some of the most bustling activity of the Sleeping Bear region in the mid 1800s.

YESTERDAY

As observed by South Manitou historian Myron H. Vent, it was only natural that the island, given its strategic location, became the first place of settlement and commerce in the region. It was the first island with a navigable harbor to be reached in the long voyage north from Chicago or Milwaukee to Buffalo. For southbound ships, it was the last natural harbor on the course to Chicago.[3]

The first settlers of the island served the early lake steamers, operating a wooding station and lighthouse. William N. Burton, originally from Vermont, and his family were the earliest recorded settlers on South Manitou. The date of their arrival is not clear but Vent concludes that it probably was 1835. By 1838 there was a house and steamboat landing that undoubtedly belonged to Burton, who operated a wooding station and became the first lighthouse keeper in 1840.[4]

An 1847 General Land Office Survey by Orange Risdon refers to "Burton's Wharf," a house, blacksmith shop, grocery store, barn and a wooden tamarack railroad track extending from "Burton's Harbor" inland "with branches for hauling steam boat wood—said in all to be between 3 and 4 miles." Risdon noted "timber all chopped off and burned over" near the north end of the island and near the harbor.[5]

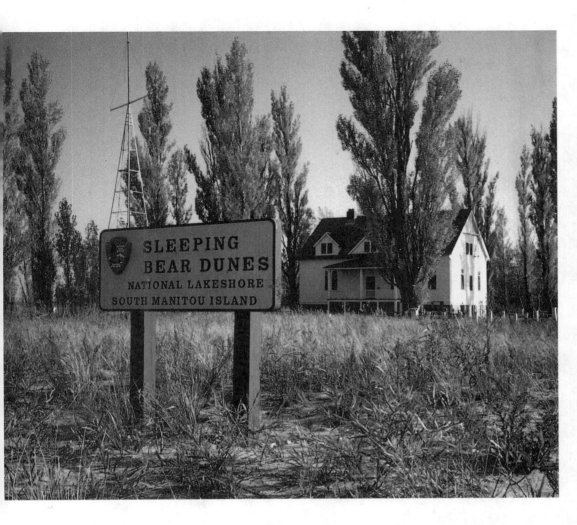

The Coast Guard Station, closed in 1958, is now the island's Ranger Station for the National Park Service.
(Cottage Book Shop of Glen Arbor)

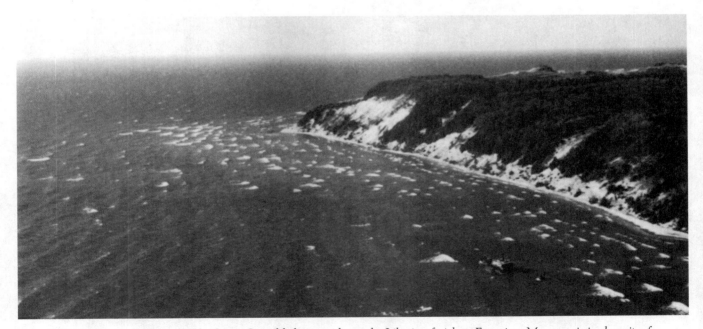

This 1989 picture from a U.S. Coast Guard helicopter shows the Liberian freighter Francisco Morazan is in the grip of the rugged southwestern tip of South Manitou where she stranded nearly three decades earlier. (Rich Brauer)

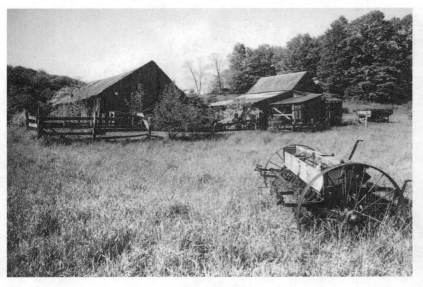

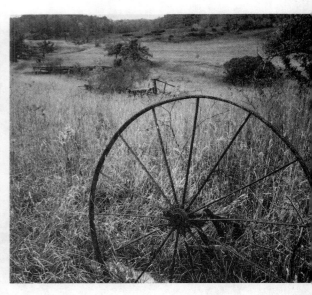

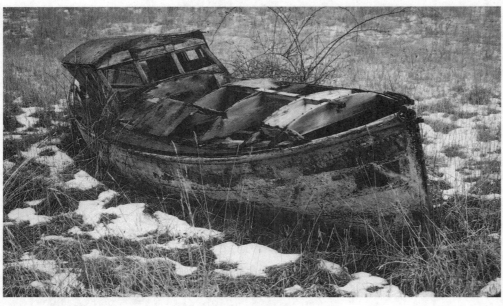

A reflection of yesterday can be seen today as South Manitou reclaims abandoned farms, boats, houses and cars.

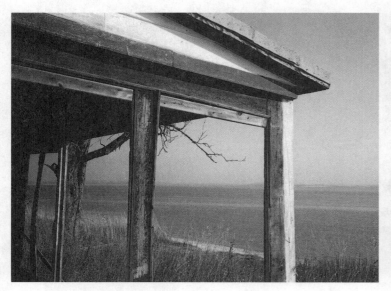

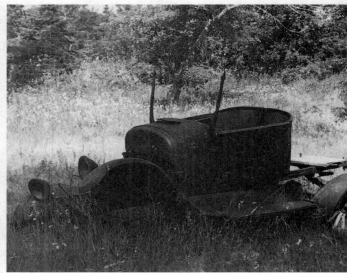

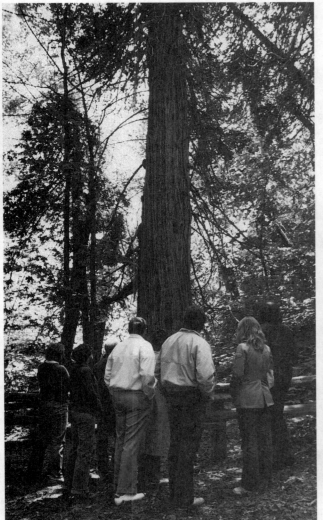

On the southwest corner of the island is the Valley of the Giants—a grove of virgin white cedar trees that escaped the lumbermen's ax. It includes the world record white cedar measuring 17.6 feet in circumference and more than 90 feet tall. On one of the fallen trees, growth rings were counted dating its existence prior to Columbus. Here, one of the giants has visitors in 1982.

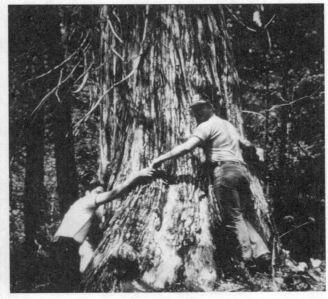

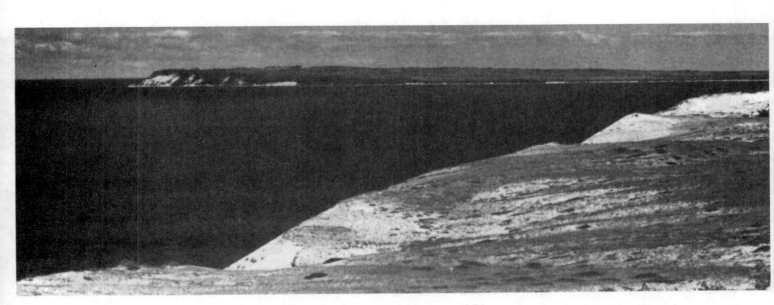

The southern end of South Manitou looking northwest from the Sleeping Bear Dunes in 1976. (All photos from Michigan Travel Bureau)

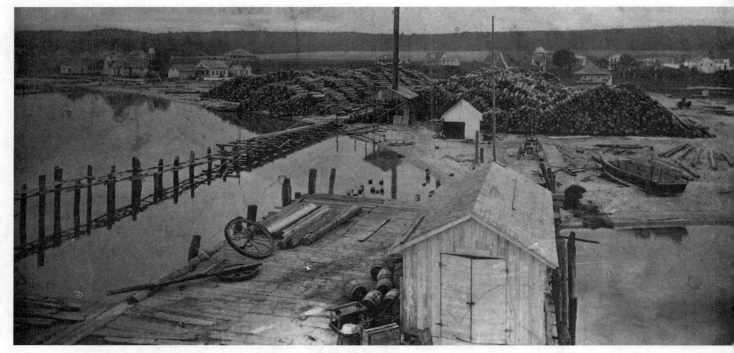

North Manitou, 1910. (Ed Beebe/National Park Service)

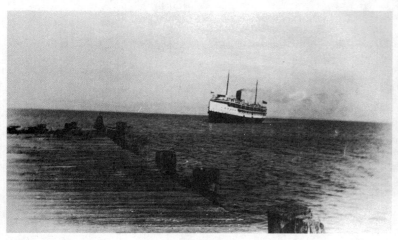

Passenger liner approaches North Manitou dock in 1916. (National Park Service)

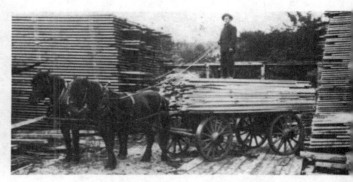

From an early 1900s postcard from Crescent. (National Park Service)

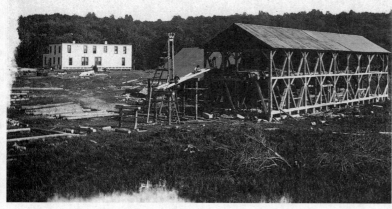

SAWMILL: *An early 1900s sawmill under construction on the west side of North Manitou, showing workers near a pile driver. In the background is the boarding house for mill workers. The town of Crescent was beyond the woods. Circa 1907.* (Courtesy Esther Morse)

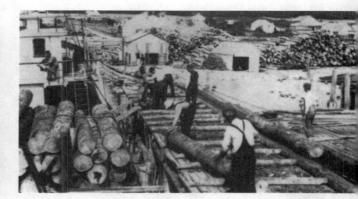

LOADING LOGS: *North Manitou's role as one of the largest lumbering sites in the Sleeping Bear area is illustrated in this early 1900s picture showing loading of a shipment of logs—with stacks more to go.* (National Park Service)

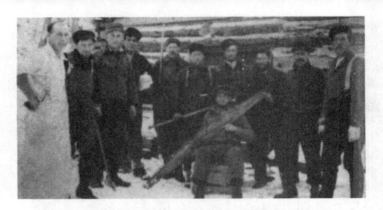

HEARTY DINERS: *Cook and lumberjacks at their North Manitou camp. Circa 1910.*
(Leelanau County Historical Museum)

MAPLE SYRUP: *Making it on North Manitou.*
(National Park Service)

LOCOMOTIVE: *A steam engine used by the Smith & Hull Company of Traverse City, which had extensive operations on North Manitou for nearly a decade. Circa 1909.*
(National Park Service)

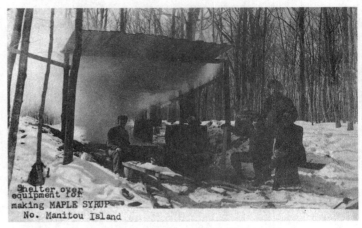

Despite all of this activity, Vent noted that the earliest record of title to a tract of land on the island appears to be fifty acres to Burton in 1849. Cutting of wood without title on government land was not unusual in those days.[6]

John LaRue, who came from Chicago to the Manitous in 1847 and began trading with Indians, moved to the mainland in 1848 to what is now Glen Arbor. As early as the 1883 publication of *History of the Grand Traverse Region*, LaRue has been widely described as the first white inhabitant of Leelanau County.[7] He was the first white settler on the mainland of what is now Leelanau County. At the time early writers referred to LaRue as Leelanau's first settler,

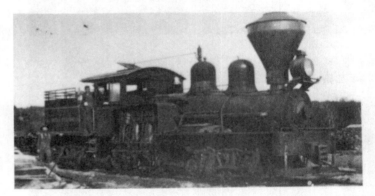

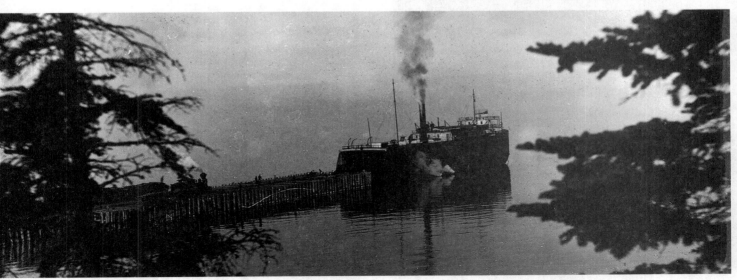

STEAM POWER: *A steam ferry backs into the dock on the west side of North Manitou. A steam locomotive, passing between piles of timber, approaches the ferry. The dock and the nearby town of Crescent were part of one of the largest lumbering operations in the Sleeping Bear Dunes area. After operations ceased, the dock and town were abandoned, and eventually reclaimed by nature. Circa 1907.* (Courtesy Esther Morse)

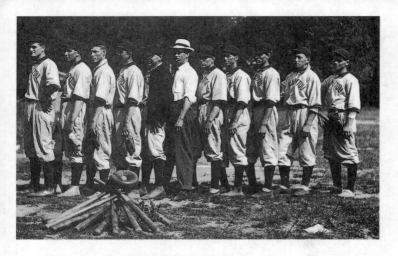

BASEBALL: *North Manitou's coach (in white hat) assembles his team for a picture taken by Nell Ferris White, wife of catcher James C. White, who is at the extreme left. White and his father, A. J. White, operated a sawmill on the island in the early 1920s. Circa 1907.* (Courtesy Esther Morse)

South Manitou was not part of Leelanau. It was in Manitou County, which was established in 1855 and dissolved in 1894.

In 1862, Congress passed the Homestead Act, which made public lands in the West available to settlers without payment to be used as farms. This prompted George Johann Hutzler, who had arrived on South Manitou in 1856 at age forty-two to work for Burton, to walk to Traverse City to file claim as the island's first homesteader.[8]

Farming and lumbering, along with tending to the lighthouse, brought the island's year-round population to ninety-eight in the 1880 census. Among the pioneer families were the Becks, who

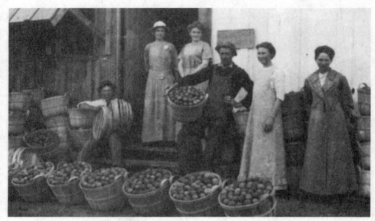

PACKING HOUSE: *At the peak of farming, about 1,000 of North Manitou's 15,000 acres were cultivated. General farming dominated until the turn of the century when fruit production took the lead. Here, apples are displayed at island's packing house. Circa 1915.* (Cottage Book Shop of Glen Arbor)

MAIL & MUNCHIES: *The early 1900s U.S. Post Office near Stormer Dock on the east side of North Manitou was in a building that did more than handle mail. One sign advertised "Cracker Jack" and another offered "Fine Tailoring." Circa 1910.* (National Park Service/ Michigan State University Archives)

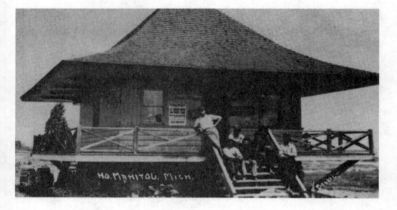

VILLAGE DOCK: *This dock served the village on the east side of North Manitou. To the left is the lifesaving station complex that was established in 1874 and phased out about 1940.* (National Park Service)

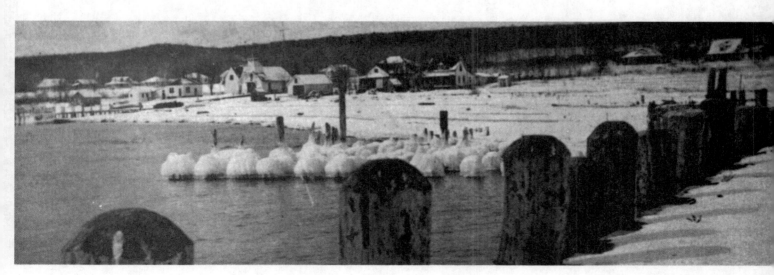

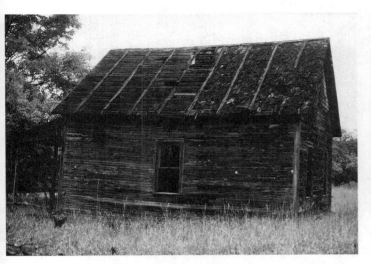

Abandoned farmhouse in 1979. (National Park Service)

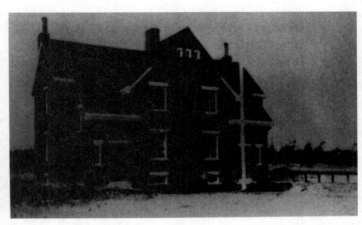

KEEPERS DWELLING: This was the longest surviving structure in the lighthouse complex at Dimmick's Point on the southeastern tip of North Manitou. Only ruins of the residence remain today. Circa 1900. (National Park Service/Berry Kramer)

arrived in the 1860s from Germany. In 1988 at age 101, Irwin Beck, who was born on the island in 1887, recalled attending the island school, which only went through the eighth grade. As was common at that time, he went by schooner to Chicago to finish high school.[9]

Also attending the island school was Admiral Willard J. Smith, who was the 1966–70 commandant of the U.S. Coast Guard. He grew up on the island after his father was assigned to the Life-Saving Service there in 1916. Smith told the *Leelanau Enterprise* the island children "broke our own path to the school in the winter months. . . . There was an iron stove in the middle of the classroom and the eighth grade boys would have to get to school early to start the fire and check to see if the pump had frozen."[10]

The Chicago fire of 1871 affected the island. Much of the sand and gravel used in building more permanent structures was supplied by the Garden City Sand Company of Chicago. It bought land on, and brought barges to, South Manitou for excavation.

For a period in the twentieth century, the island evolved into a central point for maneuvers of the Great Lakes Naval Reserve Fleet. "The area in the vicinity is still used for target

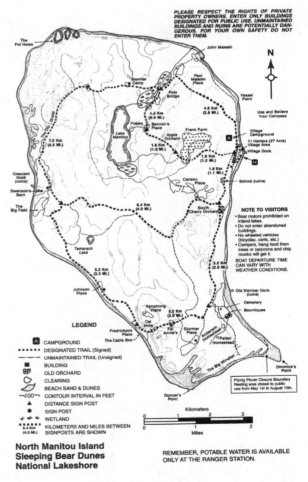

**North Manitou Island
Sleeping Bear Dunes
National Lakeshore**

Visitor map for North Manitou Island.

(National Park Service)

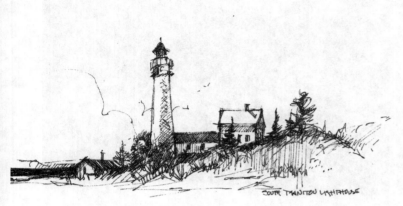

South Manitou Lighthouse.
(Sketch by Glen Arbor artist Suzanne Wilson)

practice by the fleet and boat traffic is cautioned to remain clear of a specified area," according to Leelanau author Edmund M. Littell.[11] There even was occasional submarine "warfare" in Lake Michigan. An Atlantic Fleet submarine would enter the lake in the summer months, hiding in its depths to give the reservists practice in finding it. For years, the aging destroyer escort USS *Daniel A.* Joy served as the flagship of the fleet, known as the Midwest's "Corn Belt Fleet. "

In 1974, the last year-around residents, Ed and Esther Riker, left the island after the National Park Service bought the part of the island where they had worked for 20 years as caretaker- tenant farmers. For much of the twentieth century, three generations of the Grosvenor family provided ferry service to the Manitou Islands. George Tracy Grosvenor began service in 1918 with the *Lawrence*, which had been operated as an island ferry by John Paetchow. Grosvenor's son, George Firestone Grosvenor, assumed the business in the 1940s, and his son, Mike Grosvenor, began taking over in the 1970s. By the late 1980s, Grosvenor's Manitou Island Transit—the only public link with the islands—carried 6,000 to 8,000 visitors a year under a concession with the National Park Service. By 1990, two vessels were used for the 1½-hour trips: the *Mishe Mokwa* and the *Manitou Isle*.

TODAY

South Manitou, with its protected harbor and better docking and other visitor facilities, receives the most visitors. It is maintained by the National Park Service for hiking, low-impact wilderness camping, exploring and viewing of such historic sites as the school house. Among its attractions are:

Visitor Center, formerly the Island Post Office in the center of the village, houses exhibits that tell the human and natural history of the island.

Coast Guard Station, originally established in 1901 as a U.S. Life-Saving Service station, it along with the Service became part of the Coast Guard in 1915. Rescues from the station, which had a six-man crew, were made by either shooting a line to the wreck and hauling the victims to the shore in a breeches buoy, or rowing a surf boat to the scene.

Lighthouse, first built in 1840 and replaced by a higher tower in 1871, it was abandoned in 1958. It has been restored and is available for ranger-led tours.

Wreck of the *Francisco Morazan* is a Liberian freighter which ran aground about 300 yards off the southwest shore of the island in a snowstorm 29 November 1960. It hit rocks at the site of the 4 November 1903 wreck of the freighter *Walter L. Frost*.

Florence Lake is named for Florence Haas, who took over the job as mail carrier from Glen Haven to South Manitou after the 1912 drowning of her husband Joseph, son of nineteenth century island pioneers. She has been described as the Great Lakes' first licensed female captain.[12] Described as a "Sparkling jewel, cuddled deep in the bosom of her mother Isle," by Gerald E. Crowner, a 1926–1928 surfman at the South Manitou Station, Florence Lake was always "Alive and dancing when caressed by summer breezes that send countless wavelets shoreward, to lap softly on her sandy shore. . . . Dear to my memory are her countless moods, ever changing with the passing seasons . . . "[13]

Farms, especially the historic Hutzler and Beck farmsteads, are among abandoned sites.

Abandoned machinery also is present. By 1870, most islanders farmed land. By 1920, 20 percent of the island was cultivated. Isolated from the outside world half the year, the farms were self-sufficient. By 1948, only two active farms remained—but they too are now abandoned.

The Valley of the Giants, located in the southwest corner of the island, is a grove of virgin white cedar trees, including the world record white cedar measuring 17.6 feet in circumference and more than 90 feet tall. Some of the trees are more than 500 years old, growing since before the time of Columbus, and escaped the lumberjack axe, presumably because of their size and location (see page 89).

Dunes, located on bluffs on the west side, are accessible by trails and are covered by sand dunes perched high above Lake Michigan.

NORTH MANITOU

This 15,000-acre island, with 20 miles of shoreline, is 7¾ miles long by 4½ miles and about

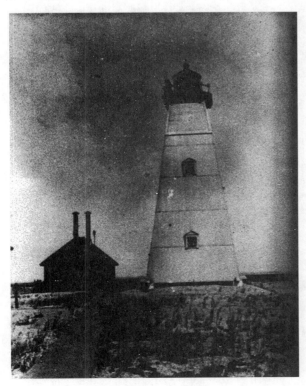

North Manitou Light. (National Park Service)

12 miles by boat from Leland. Its highest point is in the northwest corner, 1,001 feet above sea level and 421 feet above Lake Michigan. Its widely varying topography includes Lake Manitou (elevation 675 feet); rugged, wooded bluffs; low, sandy open dune land; and high sand hills and blowout dunes such as Old Baldy on the southwest side.

YESTERDAY

Logging was the major factor in history of the island, which, like South Manitou, was a strategically-located source of wood for early steamers. It also had thriving sawmills, some farming, hunting and summer homes.

Much of the first recorded history centers on wood dealer Nicholas Pickard, a New Yorker who came to the island in the 1844–1846 period and by 1857 evolved into the biggest landowner on North Manitou.[14] He built wooding docks at various locations, including on the west side where the now-ghost town of Crescent developed.

Other woodcutters were on the island earlier but not for sustained settlement. Joseph Oliver, a native of Pennsylvania credited with being the first settler in Benzie County, was described in one 1892 account as having "removed to Manitou Island" in 1820 for trapping and fishing.[15] Another described him as being on "Manitou, without saying which one, with his wife in 1848.[16]

North Manitou's earliest recorded landowner, Neil McFadyen of Erie County, Pennsylvania, bought about 45 acres in 1848.[17] The first real land mogul was Albert W. Bacon of Grand Traverse County, who during the 1860s acquired 6,765.9 acres for later resale.[18]

Much of the early story of North Manitou is the story of big landowners. It "almost always was owned by one or a very few large landowners," reported historian David L. Fritz, who in 1986 prepared for the National Park Service the island's most thoroughly-documented history data.[19] After Bacon, there was a series of major landowners, including the Smith & Hull Lumber Company (Frank H. Smith and W. Cary Hull) of

Traverse City, which Fritz described as doing "probably the most detrimental cutting of hardwoods on the island" between 1909 and 1917.[20] Yet it was not detrimental to the economy of nearby Traverse City, as Smith & Hull supplied the city's Oval Wood Dish Company, proclaimed to be the largest of its kind in the world, and provided year-round jobs for 350 workers who produced dishes, clothespins, washboards and finished lumber.

William R. Angell, under aegis of the Detroit Trust Company, bought up much of the island in 1926 and "became the single greatest owner of land for all time on North Manitou."[21] After his death in 1950, the Angell Foundation through the Manitou Island Association continued to manage resort and logging operations, and annual deer hunts. By the time the National Park Service acquired the island in 1984, only 21.8 acres involved owners other than the foundation.

When a year-around population of 269 was reported on the island in the 1860 Census, half of the heads of household were foreign-born, predominately German.

TODAY

The National Park Service manages the island to provide a primitive experience emphasizing solitude, a feeling of self-reliance, and a sense of exploration. The primary visitor activities are primitive camping, hiking, backpacking, and hunting. "North Manitou becomes the ultimate wilderness experience within the Lakeshore," said John Abbett, the Lakeshore's assistant superintendent in the late 1980s.[22]

Little evidence remains of the island's lumbering heydays. The once-booming town of Crescent is now an open field with one old barn. In the village area on the east side of the island, however, one of the most significant sawmills in Michigan is located. Even though the sawmill was built at a late date, possibly as late as 1927, it was built using the traditional technology. The engine and equipment date from 1875, and the method of construction and style of layout are typical of sawmills of that era.

Bill Herd, ranger and historian for the Sleeping Bear Dunes National Lakeshore, indicates that "it is significant because steam powered sawmills of this type, once common, are now rare. . . . It is as though workmen built one last mill to be a memorial to their trade."[23]

One center of attraction is the old Coast Guard complex. A life-saving station was established in 1874; a watchtower in 1877; more dwellings in 1897 and a lighthouse and fog signal house on the southeast tip of the island between 1896 and 1898. The lighthouse was abandoned in 1935 and destroyed by a storm in 1941.

The island has one of the few nesting areas in the Great Lakes for the piping plover, a diminutive, beach-nesting shorebird that is an endangered species.

Endnotes—The Manitous

1. Myron H. Vent, *South Manitou Island: From Pioneer Community to National Park,* (Nassau, Del.: Manitou Publications, 1973), 8.
2. Charles E. Cleland, "A Preliminary Report on the Prehistoric Resources of North Manitou Island, submit red to William R. Angel Foundation, Detroit, 1967, 1, 11.
3. Vent, 40.
4. Vent, 32.
5. Joseph Rogers, "South Manitou Island: A Field Trip Sourcebook and Guide," Northwestern Michigan College, Traverse City, MI, 1966. Excerpts from Orange Risdon's survey are on p. 29.
6. Vent, 32.
7. M.L. Leach, *A History of the Grand Traverse Region,* Grand Traverse Herald, Traverse City MI, 1883, p. 66.
8. Vent, 28.
9. *Leelanau Enterprise,* (Leland, MI), 9 June 1988. Article by Sarah McDaniels.
10. *Leelanau Enterprise,* 19 January 1989. Article by Amy Hubbell.
11. Edmund L. Littell, *100 Years in Leelanau,* (Leland, MI: Leelanau County Prospectors Club, 1965), 19.
12. Robert Carey, "Quiet South Manitou not typical island getaway," *Detroit Free Press,* 7 May 1989.
13. Gerald E. Crowner, *The South Manitou Story,* (Mio, MI: Gerald E. Crowner, 1982), 54.
14. David L. Fitz, "History Data Report on North Manitou Island," National Park Service, 1986, 4.
15. Charles Burmeister, "A Short History of Benzie County," *Michigan Pioneer Collections,* 18 (1892), 503.
16. Sivert N. Glarum, *Our Land and Lakes,* (Frankfort, MI: Sivert N. Glarum, 1983), 22.
17. Fritz, 7.

18. Fritz, iv.
19. Fritz,
20. Fritz, i.
21. Fritz, iv.
22. Stephen E. Yancho, "North Manitou Island: Its Splendor Revealed," *Traverse, The Magazine,* (August 1986), 35.
23. Bill Herd, statement to the author, 1990. See also:

Charles M. Anderson, *Isle of View: A History of South Manitou Island,* (Frankfort, MI: Charles M. and Selma O. Anderson, 1979).

"South Manitou Island," and "North Manitou Island," National Park Service brochures produced in cooperation with Manitou Island Transitcruises operated by Mike and George Grosvenor, Leland, MI.

CHAPTER 8

Lights of the Passage: The Beacons of Sleeping Bear

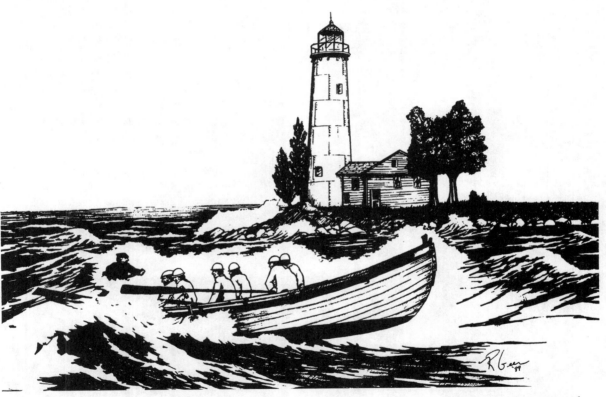

This generic scene by Richard Geer of the Michigan Bureau of History was the logo for the 1989–90 "Beacons and Bravery" exhibit at the Michigan Historical Museum that included extensive displays of the lighthouses and life-saving stations of Benzie and Leelanau counties. (Michigan Historical Museum)

Although the navigational utility of yesterday's lighthouses has been diminished by the automated beacons of today, four lighthouses of the Manitou Passage remain, and with a future as bright as the guiding lights their beacons once emitted. After decades of steering vessels from

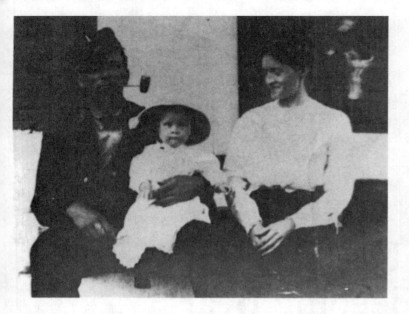

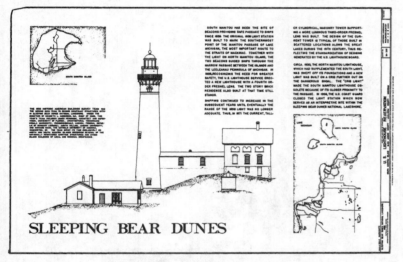

SLEEPING BEAR DUNES

Drawings of South Manitou lighthouse submitted in 1988 by the National Park Service for the Historic American Buildings Survey.

treacherous shoals, the majestic guardians are themselves protected by government agencies and citizens who believe their heritage is worth preserving.

Hundreds of lighthouses throughout the United States have been lost. Only 750 remain of an estimated 1,400.[1] Several were sold as surplus in the 1930s; some keepers' quarters were actually razed by the U.S. Coast Guard.

The North Manitou lighthouse, built in 1896, was closed in 1935 and succumbed to shoreline erosion in October of 1942. Only four Manitou Passage lighthouses remain:

Grand Traverse lighthouse, closed in 1972, is a museum operated by the Grand Traverse Lighthouse Foundation. Though not within the Manitou Passage, this lighthouse has long been associated with the other lights of the passage because it guides ships in and out of the narrow

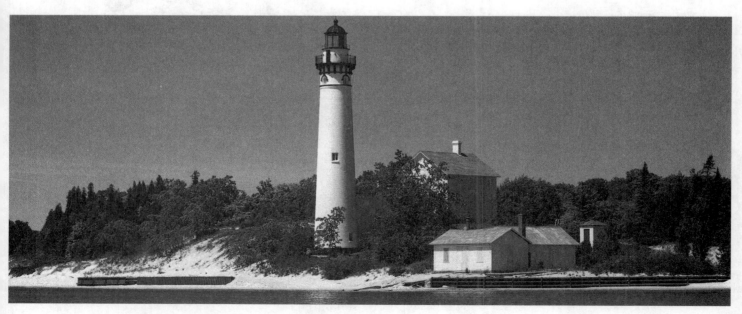

South Manitou Lighthouse in 1982. (Michigan Travel Bureau)

shipping lane between the Manitou Islands and the Leelanau County mainland. The entrance to Grand Traverse Bay is now marked by an automated light atop a steel tower on the shore near the lighthouse.

North Manitou Shoal Light, also known as the "Crib," is fully automated and maintained by the Coast Guard. It marks a shoal in the Manitou Passage between the Manitou Islands and Leland.

South Manitou Island lighthouse, abandoned by the Coast Guard in 1958, is part of the Sleeping Bear Dunes National Lakeshore. It is maintained by the National Park Service and open to the public for tours.

Point Betsie lighthouse, fully automated in 1983. The lighthouse was transferred in 2004 from the U.S. government to Benzie County, to be maintained by friends of Point Betsie Lighthouse.

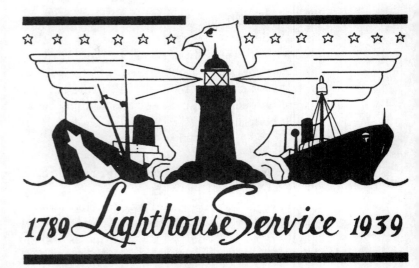

The logo of the U.S. Lighthouse Service.

(U.S. Coast Guard)

The United States Lighthouse Service was enacted by the first Congress, and officially created with President George Washington's signature 7 August 1789. Long before this, though, the first lighthouse in the colonies was built in Boston Harbor in 1716. The first Great Lakes lighthouse was built in 1818 at Fort Niagara, New York.[2]

Shipping on the Great Lakes increased along with the region's population and commerce, especially after completion of the Erie Canal in 1825 and the opening of the locks in Sault Ste. Marie in 1855. Keeping pace with the growth in shipping, lighthouses marked the more prominent points and shoals along the shipping lanes.

The centerpiece of any lighthouse is the lens which magnifies the light for passing ships. Early lighthouses used a reflecting system known as the Winslow Lewis patent system. The parabolic reflectors were easily bent, though, and their silver coating was rubbed off with repeated polishing. A superior method of refracting light was developed in 1822 by French physicist Augustin Jean Fresnel. The Fresnel lens uses many panels of polished glass surrounding a light source to refract the light and focus it toward the horizon. United States lighthouses did not start using Fresnel lenses until 1852.[3]

The source of the light which was reflected and refracted changed over the years, too. Early lights were produced by burning wood or coal, but the resulting soot soiled the lenses. Whale oil burned cleaner, but it became expensive. Various vegetable oils were tried, and by the 1860s, lard oil became the standard. Kerosene was widely used by the 1880s. Acetylene lamps, which did not require wicks, gained popularity by the 1920s. This allowed the first step toward lighthouse automation, with the development of a "sun valve" which shut off the flow of fuel during daylight hours. Today's electric lamps use line current, diesel generators or solar-charged batteries.[4]

The Coast Guard's Lighthouse Automation Program (LAMP) began in 1968 and was completed in 1990, ending more than 200 years of manned lighthouse operation in this country. The last manned Great Lakes lighthouse, at Sherwood Point, Wisconsin, was finally automated in 1983.

Though there was no radio communication with passing ships in the early days, ships' pilots and lighthouse keepers used signals to exchange greetings. Ships would blow a salute with their whistles; lighthouse keepers would flash back a hello.

Each lighthouse looked and sounded unique. With different colored roofs and towers, they could be distinguished during the day. At night, pilots would know each lighthouse by the pattern and color of its light signals. Even the foghorns were unique, varying the pitch and duration of their blasts.

GRAND TRAVERSE LIGHTHOUSE

This lighthouse, located north of Northport at the tip of the Leelanau Peninsula, has a history fairly typical of Great Lakes lighthouses. Abandoned by the Coast Guard in 1972, it passed among government agencies which had no use for it. Its location within the staffed Leelanau State Park is probably the biggest single factor sparing it from the vandalism which has plagued so many other obsolete lighthouses.

Now owned by the State of Michigan, it is leased to the Grand Traverse Lighthouse Foundation, a non-profit, volunteer organization restoring the house and grounds for the enjoyment and education of the public. Part of the house is a museum which relates the area's shipping history.

The first light tower and separate keeper's house built on Cat's Head Point (now known as

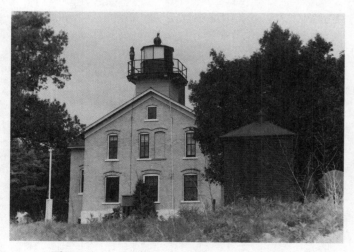

This picture was taken in 1940 of the Grand Traverse Lighthouse, which closed in 1972 and in 2003 was conveyed to the Michigan Department of Natural Resources to be part of the Leelanau State Park. (Fred Dickinson)

Cathead Point) were completed in 1853. The present building, a combination residence and lighthouse, was built in 1864, its foundation made of bricks salvaged from the original building. The cupola which housed the light perches on the peak of the roof, putting the light 47 feet above lake level. The building was last remodeled in 1916.[5]

The point may have been marked for ship pilots even before the first tower was erected. A pile of stones has been discovered in the woods a short distance from the present lighthouse on which a lard-oil beacon probably burned to guide ships while the tower was being built.[6]

The foundation chose one of its founding members as the museum's first live-in caretaker. Douglass McCormick said it felt like being home again.[7] He lived here in the 1920s and 1930s as a teenager, along with his ten brothers and sisters, when his father was lighthouse keeper.

On display in the museum is a fourth order Fresnel tens (first order being the largest), similar to the one which surrounded a kerosene-burning wick and threw its light 12 to 17 miles offshore. Later, the light was powered by electricity. The lens is on loan from the Coast Guard, which will not allow it to be displayed in the cupola for fear that it would be too tempting a target for sharpshooting vandals. McCormick suspects that the original lens from this lighthouse has become someone's coffee table.[8]

McCormick said the job of a lighthouse keeper was a hard one, with never a dull moment. "A lightkeeper never has idle time. It was a hard life, but we were all quite happy."[9]

In addition to lighting the light at dusk and extinguishing it at dawn (along with pulling curtains around the tower so the lens wouldn't magnify sunlight and start fires), tending a lighthouse required constant maintenance, cleaning and polishing. The lighthouse keeper or his assistant had to be on watch at all times.

In foggy weather, a fire needed to be started and stoked for the steam-driven foghorn. McCormick especially remembers this chore, recalling it was like a game to run from the house to the signal building to keep the fire going. If he could not make the run in the thirty to forty-five seconds between blasts, he says he would "stand there and shake" because the horn was so loud.[10]

The signal building remains, but today's pilots get audible warnings about the point from an automated foghorn eight miles offshore. Daytime navigation is aided by red and white diamond-shaped markers on a steel tower erected on the shore near the lighthouse in 1972. Atop this tower is an automated beacon which warns nighttime sailors of the rocky point at the north end of the Manitou Passage.

NORTH MANITOU SHOAL LIGHT

Built in 1935 to mark a shoal just 20 feet below the surface of the water, the North Manitou Shoal Light replaced a succession of beacons aboard anchored vessels that warned passing ships of the reef since 1910.

A nickname given it during construction has stuck. For a while, passing ship pilots called it "The Crib" because it was built on a square concrete foundation, or crib.

Much of the structure was actually constructed in Frankfort, then transported to the shoal on two barges and sunk onto its crib. The main deck is about 20 feet above the water. Diesel generators which supplied electricity for the light and the crewmen worked on this level.

The next level contains the three bedrooms, kitchen, dining room and bathrooms which comprised the living quarters for the three crewmen who staffed the Crib at any one time during the shipping season. The red blinking light is about 75 feet above the water.[11]

Any lighthouse duty is somewhat isolated, but offshore duty was especially so. The crewmen, who spent two weeks on duty with one week off, were busy during their shifts, but had very limited recreational opportunities between shifts. They watched television, read books and magazines, played board games, sunbathed and chatted by radio with passing ship captains. They also looked forward to deliveries from the supply boat from Leland or the occasional pleasure boat that tied up for a visit. Some crewmen

pursued hobbies, like puzzles or ham radio. At least one Coast Guardsman used to perfect his rapelling techniques by lowering himself from the tower to the deck on ropes as if he were descending a mountain.

The Crib was the last manned offshore light station in the Great Lakes when it was automated by the Coast Guard in 1980. The beacon and fog signal are now powered by electricity supplied by underwater cable from the mainland.

The lightship that the Crib replaced also has been preserved. The North Manitou Shoal Lightship became Huron Station Lightship in 1935, and later was berthed for ultimate use for public visits.

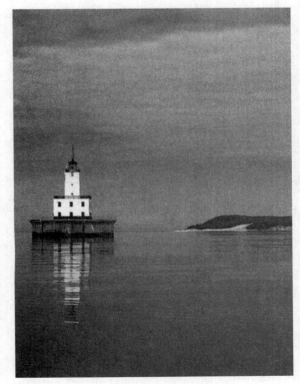

North Manitou Shoal Light—the "Crib."

(Grace Dickinson)

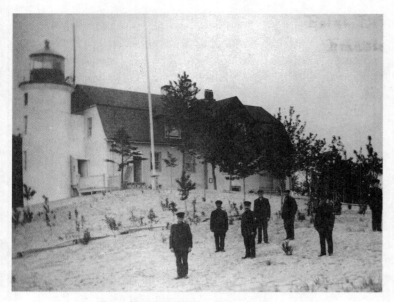

An early crew of Point Betsie Light.
(Institute for Great Lakes Research/Michigan Historical Museum)

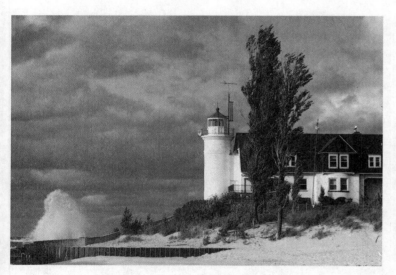

Point Betsie Light in 1996. (Jerry Decker)

SOUTH MANITOU ISLAND LIGHTHOUSE

South Manitou Island provides the only natural harbor in the 220 miles between Chicago and the Sleeping Bear area. Since it also served as a fuel stop for wood-burning nineteenth century steamers, South Manitou became an essential destination for many early ship captains.

The island's first lighthouse was modest. This small wooden house with a light on top was completed in 1840. The island's fog signal was a 1000-pound bell. In 1858, a larger lighthouse keeper's dwelling was built, and a steady white beacon inside a fourth order Fresnel lens was perched atop a 35-foot wooden tower on its roof.[12]

As shipping traffic increased, even this improved light proved inadequate. In making a case for a new tower and light for the island, an 1869 report emphasized the importance of this location:

> Through the channel between South Manitou Island and the mainland, the principal commerce of the lake passes, guided by this light which should have a lens of higher order, with greater elevation and a characteristic distinction not readily mistaken. It is also a guide to a harbor of refuge which is probably more used than any other on the entire chain of lakes, and it is frequently impossible to distinguish the present light from those on board vessels at anchor.[13]

The 100-foot tower built in 1871 was one of the highest on the Great Lakes. The new light consisted of three wicks fueled by kerosene and surrounded by a third order Fresnel lens. In 1875 the first steam-driven fog signal on Lake Michigan was installed in the separate fog signal building. Two wood-burning boilers produced the steam to blow the whistle every two minutes in foggy weather.[14]

Abandoned by the Coast Guard in 1958, the lighthouse has been stabilized and partially restored by the National Park Service. Tours of the tower and keeper's dwelling are conducted daily during the summer.

POINT BETSIE LIGHTHOUSE

Though many lighthouses throughout the nation have been given new life as parks, museums, restaurants, inns, schools and homes, the Point Betsie lighthouse into the last decade of the twentieth century remained useful to the

Coast Guard. The automated light marks a prominent point just north of Frankfort; the keeper's quarters currently house Coast Guard personnel from the Frankfort life-saving station.

Completed in 1858 on what was then called Point Aux Bec Scies (sawed beak point), this last manned light station on the eastern shore of Lake Michigan was automated in the spring of 1983. The ten-sided cast-iron dome at the top of the 27 foot tower contains a fourth order Fresnel lens.[15] The lamp originally burned coal oil. It was later fueled by kerosene; now the automated light is electric.[16]

The first keeper, Dr. Alonzo Slyfield, came from the South Manitou lighthouse. He and his two sons served for twenty-two years as keepers of the Point Betsie lighthouse.[17]—Don Weeks

Endnotes—Lighthouses

1. *Lansing State Journal*, 1 November 1987. (Article by Norris Ingells).

2. 1989 *Lighthouses of Michigan Calendar*. (Great Lakes Lighthouse Keepers Association and Michigan United Conservation Clubs. 1989).

3. Mike Van Hoey, "Preserving the Lights of the Straits," *Michigan History Magazine*, (Sept./Oct., 1986), 24.

4. Van Hoey, 24.

5. Informational brochure prepared by the Grand Traverse Lighthouse Foundation.

6. Grand Traverse Lighthouse Foundation brochure.

7. Douglass McCormick, interview with the author in Northport, MI., August 1986.

8. McCormick interview.

9. McCormick interview.

10. McCormick interview.

11. *The Traverse City Record-Eagle*, 18 November 1980. (Article by John L. Russell).

12. National Park Service, "Lights of the Passage," (U.S. Department of the Interior, 1989).

13. Myron H. Vent, *South Manitou Island: From Pioneer Settlement to National Park*, (Myron H. Vent, 1973), 47.

14. "Lights of the Passage."

15. "Lights of the Passage."

16. "Michigan's Lighthouses," (Lansing, MI: Michigan Department of Transportation).

17. "Lights of the Passage."

CHAPTER 9

Heroes of the Storm—
The U.S. Life-Saving Service
and U.S. Coast Guard

Semper Paratus—"Always Ready"

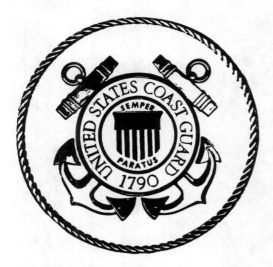
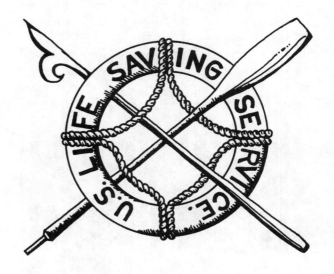

Coast Guard and USLSS emblems

If there is one building that represents the activity of yesterday and today along the Sleeping Bear Dunes National Lakeshore, it is the Sleeping Bear Point Coast Guard Station Maritime Museum.

It is a centerpiece of the rich heritage of the Manitou Passage, the major and narrowest passage along the Lake Michigan coast for shipping between Chicago and the Straits of Mackinac, and the magnet for the first settlement of Sleeping Bear. Now, as a museum, the station is a major attraction for visitors to the Lakeshore.

This two-story building was built at the point in 1901 for the United States Life-Saving Ser-

107

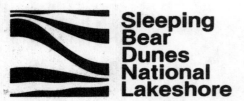

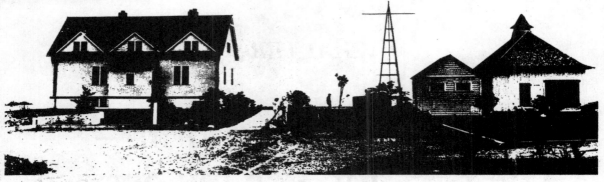

SLEEPING BEAR POINT
COAST GUARD STATION
MARITIME MUSEUM

vice (U.S.L.S.S.), the government agency responsible for shore rescues before being merged in 1915 with the Revenue Cutter Service to create the U.S. Coast Guard.

Long before the modern Coast Guard, with its highly-visible helicopters and rescue boats that patrol by air and sea, the Great Lakes' Heroes of the Storm were surfmen who stood watch on remote shorelines and risked their lives rowing on raging seas in open boats.

The Sleeping Bear Point station possessed two means of rescue. Either surfboats that could carry eight to ten passengers in addition to their own crews, or a beach apparatus that involved either a "breeches buoy" or a "life-car." One of the boats was a twenty-three foot monomoy craft that was relatively light, about 1,000 pounds. It could be launched by rail or hauled on a horsedrawn cart down the beach when a

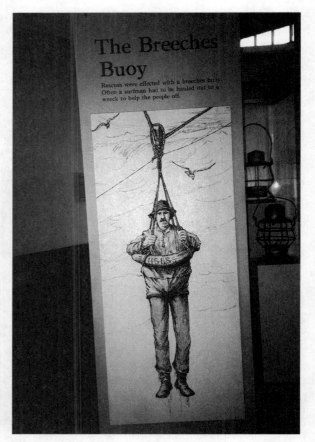

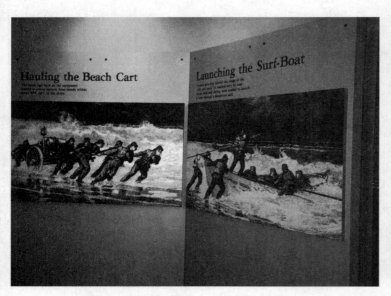

These drawings, which originally appeared in Scribner's Magazine in 1880, are part of the Life-Saving Service exhibit at the Sleeping Bear Point Coast Guard Station Maritime Museum.

108

wreck was some distance away from the station. It had a shallow draft, a center board, a sail, and a design that made it maneuverable in a heavy surf. A twenty-four foot version of this boat also was in use at the station.

The other basic design was a twenty-six foot Beebe-McLellan surfboat, launched off a rail extending from the station's boathouse to the water. It also could be moved on a beach cart. It was the boat of choice when the wreck was farther offshore, beyond the breaking surf. Air tanks under the deck, along both sides and in the bow and stern made it extremely buoyant. It also was a good sailing boat, with a centerboard and mast. It was self-bailing. Water that came in the boat would flow into tubes and then out through valves along both sides that opened downward by pressure of any water in the boat and closed when pressure ceased. A thirty gallon tank below deck could be filled with water to provide ballast.

Despite their special design features, it was dangerous to take the boats out in a storm. The preferred method of rescue was the breeches buoy—so called because it had a pair of canvas pants, or breeches, sewed to a life ring.

The beach apparatus, kept in a mortar cart that could be pulled by men or a horse, included a small cannon known as a "Lyle gun"—the only cannon ever invented by the Army in order to save lives rather than take them.[1] The gun was designed in 1877 by David A. Lyle, an Army Ordnance officer, after the War Department was asked to research means of reaching ships stranded or wrecked off the coasts of the United States.

A small bag of black powder provided the force to hurl a 19-pound steel projectile from the shore. Tied to a loop in the end of the projectile was a light line that fell across the ship. By pulling a series of successively heavier lines, the crew on the ship was able to rig the breeches buoy so it could be pulled back and forth between the beach and the wreck. One by one, those aboard would ride ashore in the buoy.

Another rescue device that could be pulled back and forth from shore was the boat-like life,

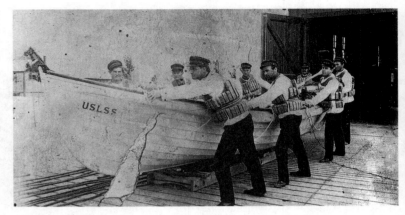

Crew and surfboat at the point. Circa 1905. (National Park Service)

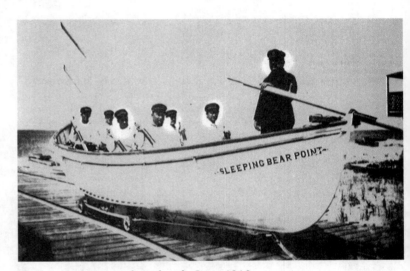

Surfboat and crew on launch rail. Circa 1910. (National Park Service)

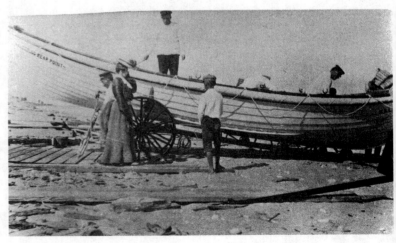

Self-bailing surfboat on boat wagon at the point (National Park Service)

109

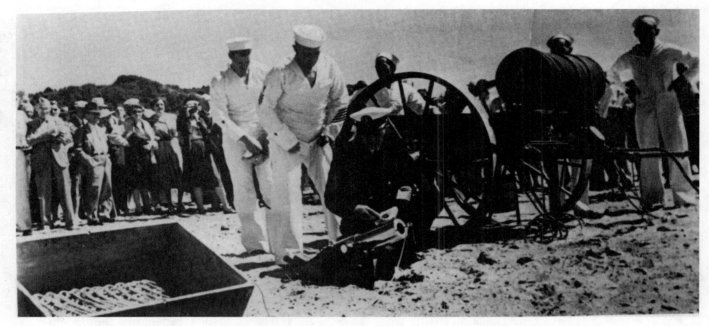

Keeper William Fisher prepares to fire the line-throwing Lyle Gun during a 1926 beach rescue demonstration on South Manitou. (National Park Service)

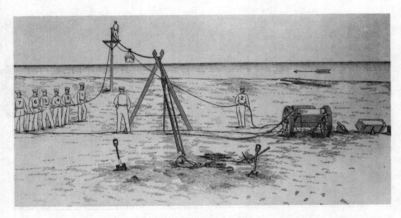

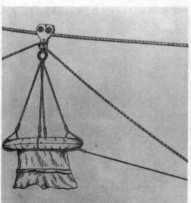

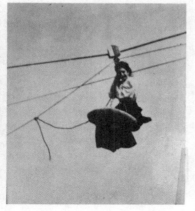

or surf, car, a metal pod that could hold several passengers who would crawl in through a hatch that would be bolted shut for the harrowing trip to shore. How harrowing was described by a nineteenth century article in *Harper's Magazine:*

> To be shut up in this manner in so dark and gloomy a receptacle, for the purpose of being drawn, perhaps at midnight, through a surf of such terrific violence that no boat can live in it, can not be a very agreeable alternative; but the emergencies in which the use of the life-car is

(Left center) This illustration from a Life-Saving Service drill manual shows the setup of the beach apparatus and crew Position for the practice sessions that were held every Thursday for beach rescue using the breeches buoy.

(Bottom left) The breeches buoy—a pair of canvas pants sewed to a life ring—allowed one person at a time to be pulled to the beach from a wrecked ship.

(Bottom right) A keeper's daughter riding in the breeches buoy during a practice drill.

(National Park Service)

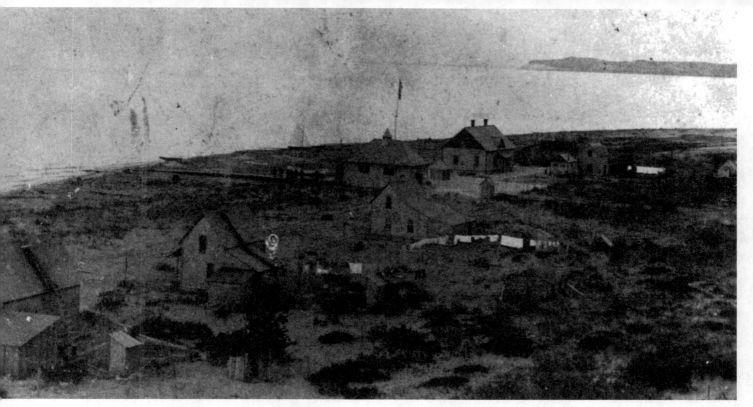

Above is where the original Sleeping Bear Point station was located, but as the 1920 picture (below) shows, the dune that now dominates the point began to engulf the station and forced its move to its present location. (National Park Service)

called for, are such as do not admit of hesitation or delay.[2]

Although the beach techniques were effective only within about 350 yards from shore, beach rescues remained frequently possible since most shipwrecks occurred close to shore. For one thing, early mariners, lacking modern navigational aids, often had trouble keeping track of their location and therefore used a "coasting" technique, following the coastline within sight of landmarks. Furthermore, ships often steered for shore when in danger. By far, most Sleeping Bear wrecks resulted from ships being driven aground or ashore.

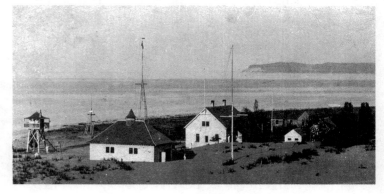

(National Park Service)

The Sleeping Bear Point station, and those on South and North Manitou islands, were typical of the many life-saving stations along the Great Lakes and the Atlantic. The South Manitou station also was built in 1901. It closed in 1958. The North Manitou station began operating in 1887 and became inactive in the 1930s.

The three Manitou Passage stations, along with the Point Betsie station that began operation in 1876 just north of Frankfort and 19 miles

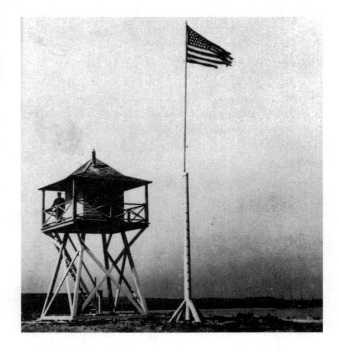

South Manitou watchtower. Note schooner in harbor.
(Ethel First Stormer/Michigan Historical Museum)

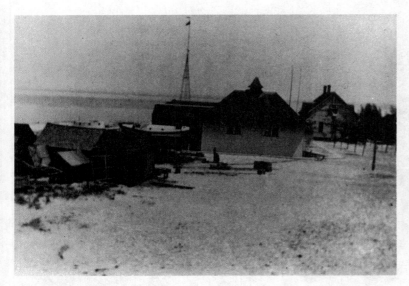

The South Manitou Island Life-Saving Station was built in 1901 and closed in 1958. (National Park Service)

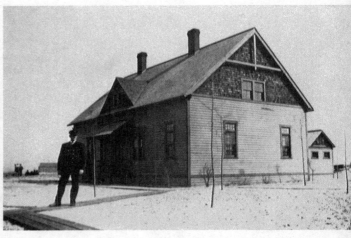

Keeper Gus B. Lofberg in front of the South Manitou Life-Saving Stati *built in 1901 and closed in 1958. Circa 1902.* (National Park Service)

southwest of Sleeping Bear Point, were among about 60 U.S.L.S.S. stations along the Great Lakes. Lake Michigan had 31. By state: Michigan, 17; Wisconsin, 9; Illinois, 4; and Indiana, 1. (The first U.S. lifeboat station was erected by the Massachusetts Humane Society at Cohasset, south of Boston, in 1807, long before inception of the U.S.L.S.S in 1871. In its 44 years, the Service rescued more than 178,000 people.)

The keeper (informally called "captain" or "skipper") and crew had daily routines standardized throughout the service. The primary responsibility was to be on constant watch for ships in danger and to keep a record of passing vessels. On clear days, from sunrise to sunset, a surfman on Day Watch always manned the lookout tower. At night and on foggy days, the men walked beach patrol, lighting a coston signal flare to warn off ships that strayed too close to shore. The signal also was a means of signaling distressed vessels that help was on the way.

Gerald E. Crowner, surfman at the South Manitou station in 1926–1928, wrote:

> I can't recall an instance when a beach patrol was ever aborted because of foul weather. I have made patrols in blizzards and driving rain and sleet storms when gale winds drove ice water

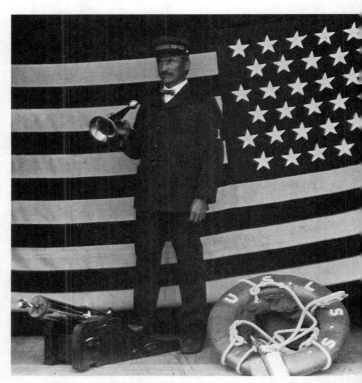

Charles Robinson was 1910–1914 captain, or keeper, of the Sleeping Point Life-Saving Station. Here, he poses in front of the boathouse w horn, Lyle Gun, flag and breeches buoy. (Lyle Robinson/National Park S

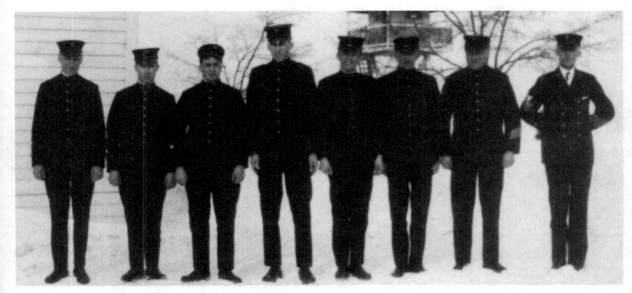

Keeper Fred J., Marsh (right) and crew in the 1920s when the station was still at the point. Next to him is John Basch, whose family had generations of life-saving service and included Oscar Smith, who was keeper at both Sleeping Bear Point and South Manitou, and Willard J. Smith, 1966–70 commandant of the U.S. Coast Guard.

(National Park Service)

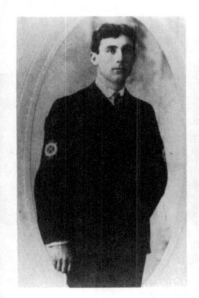

Fred J. Marsh, here a No. 4 surfman, rose to become keeper of the Sleeping Bear Point Station from 1926 to 1936, a span that included the 1931 move of the station. He also served at the Point Betsie Station during his 30-year career.
(Helen O'Neil/National Park Service)

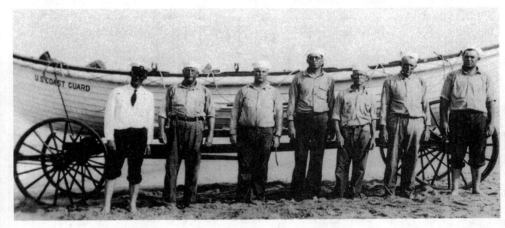

Most days, the crew wore snappy uniforms when posing for pictures. This day was an exception.
(National Park Service)

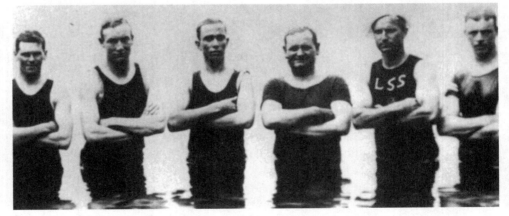

Surfmen in surf attire. Circa 1910. The picture was provided by the family of Benhart Brammer, who is second from the left. (Glen Arbor History Group/National Park Service)

113

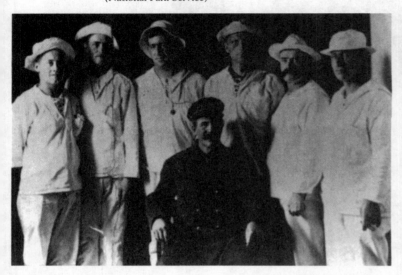 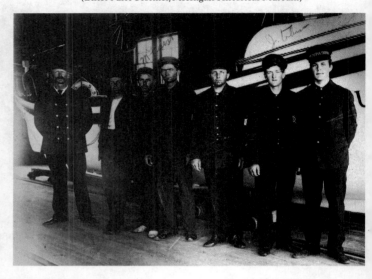

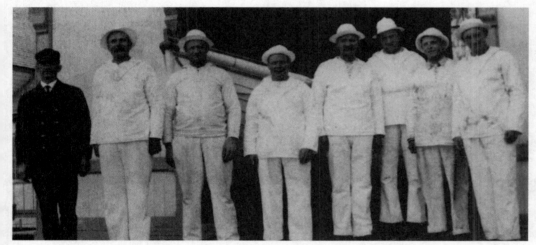

The Point Betsie crew in 1915 (top left).

South Manitou's 1906 U.S. Life-Saving crew. From right: Capt. Jacob Van Weelden, and surfmen George L. Haas, Martin Furst, James Mikula, George Kelderhouse, John K. Tobin, and Harold Barnard (top right).

This was the North Manitou crew about 1915. From right: Keeper Sammet, Abraham Anderson, Tom Laird, Lewis Dustin, Hans Halseth, John Basch, Charlie McCauley, and Roy Vert.
(Sherwood Basch/National Park Service)

down one's neck. Many times, too, I encountered severe electrical storms that came ashore with severe wind squalls during the summer months. The patrolman faced the storms of all seasons and many times the going was extremely difficult, but go we did in fair or foul weather.[3]

Crowner also described how men on night duty at the three stations would share moments on telephone calls carried over a submerged cable that came out from the mainland:

> One of the crewmen on North Island played the mouth organ, and he played it beautifully. Quite often he would call me when I had the midnight to two watch and play songs for me. . . . Many times I would call Sleeping Bear lookout and he would call the operator at Maple City and all of us would enjoy his music, and carry on a four-way conversation. . . . Several times our operator at M.C. would interrupt our music and conversations, and say, 'hold it boys, I have a call.' Then, after the call was completed she would cut in, and say, 'O. K. fellows let's have some more music.'[4]

The first keeper of the Sleeping Bear Point station was Capt. William Walker of Grand Haven. He brought along a six-man crew, as well as his mother, step-father, two sisters and a small

This scene, looking toward the back of the North Manitou station complex, was on an Oct. 16, 1906 postcard mailed from the island to Suttons Bay by Oscar Smith, then a member of the crew.
(Sherwood Basch/ National Park Service)

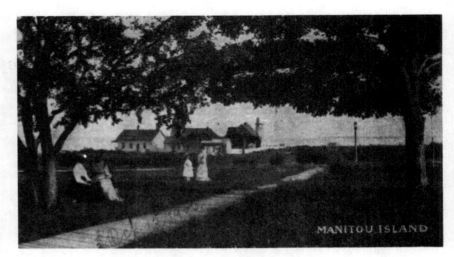

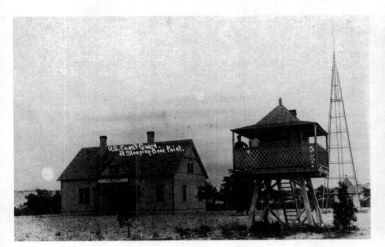

Sleeping Bear Station and Watchtower. (National Park Service)

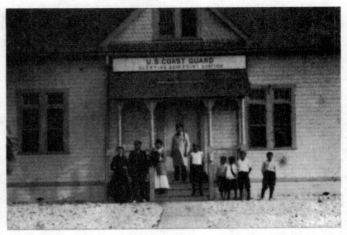

A pet dog, held by woman in white skirt, joins this 1920's family scene on the station porch.

(National Park Service)

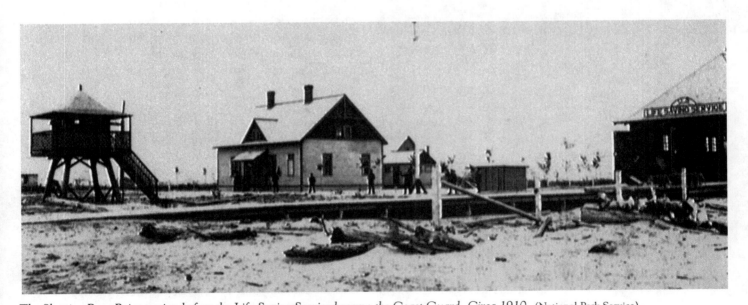

The Sleeping Bear Point station before the Life-Saving Service became the Coast Guard. Circa 1910. (National Park Service)

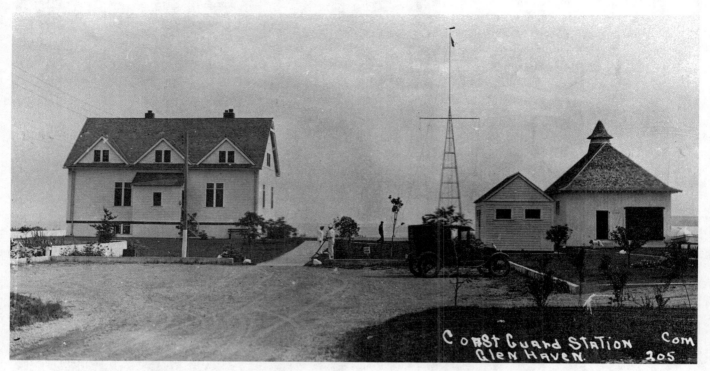

Looking toward the shore, the Sleeping Bear point Coast Guard Station shortly after its 1931 move from the point to near Glen Haven. (National Park Service)

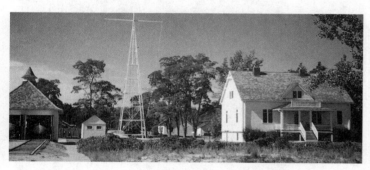

Looking from the shore in 2003, the station and its boathouse, constituting the Maritime Museum complex. (George Weeks)

homes near the station and moved their families there.

"The influx of so many people made a pleasant addition to the social life of Glen Arbor Township," according to Ida Farrant, member of Glen Haven's most prominent pioneer family. " . . . there was much exchange of hospitality in the way of parties and social activities. Every Thursday morning at 9 o'clock, an exhibition was given in boat drills, breeches buoy rescue, drowning resuscitation, wig-wag signaling, etc. This provided one of the favorite pastimes for summer guests."[5]

In the U.S.L.S.S., each day of the week except Sunday was set aside for a specific activity. The usual routine: Monday, clean and polish equipment and wash floors and windows; Tuesday, boat drills; Wednesday, signal drills; Thursday, beach rescue drill; Friday, practice resuscitation, the system of artificial respiration to revive apparent victims of drowning; Saturday, wash day for clothing, bedding and some station equipment. With substantial time set aside for scrubbing, it is small wonder most stations were spic-and-span.

The station at Sleeping Bear Point included the station house (which had living quarters for the keeper as well as a bunk room, living room and kitchen-mess room for the crew), a boathouse, outbuilding, lookout tower, signal tower, and small homes for the families of the surfmen. A married crewman could stay with his family on his day off, but was required to sleep at the station during the rest of the week.

To accommodate a 34-foot lifeboat that required deeper water for launching, a second boathouse was built on a wharf in Sleeping Bear Bay, about a mile east of the station.

Precarious Point

The location at the point proved to be a precarious one. According to Ida Farrant, in the summer of 1903 "a terrific electrical storm destroyed the lookout building," killing a surfman who was on watch at the time.[6] That could happen at any location, and complications caused by fluctuating lake levels were encountered by other stations on Lake Michigan. But there were decidedly unique problems at Sleeping Bear Point, which was far more exposed than the station at South Manitou. "It was so exposed, you really couldn't get a decent launch when there was much of a wind—you really had to manhandle the boat into the water," according to retired Admiral Willard J. Smith, the 1966–1970 commandant of the U.S. Coast Guard who lived at both the South Manitou and Sleeping Bear Point stations when his father was the keeper there.[7]

Periodically, Sleeping Bear Point becomes precarious when wind and shoreline currents extend it out over what becomes a steeply sloping, unstable platform in deep water. In December 1914, about 20 acres of land at Sleeping Bear Point slumped into Lake Michigan, the same thing that happened again in the landslide of 1971. The slump changed the shoreline and made boat launching all the more difficult in heavy surf. Despite all of this, the biggest prob-

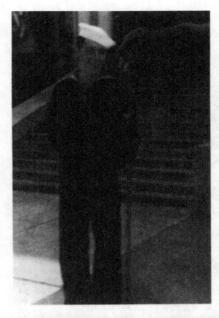

Machinist's Mate Thomas G. (Diz) Dean put the padlock on the door when the Sleeping Bear Point Coast Guard Station closed in May of 1944. (Dean Family Collection)

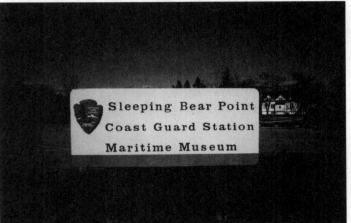

With its displays and demonstrations, the Maritime Museum is one of the most popular attractions of the Sleeping Bear Dunes National Lakeshore. (George Weeks)

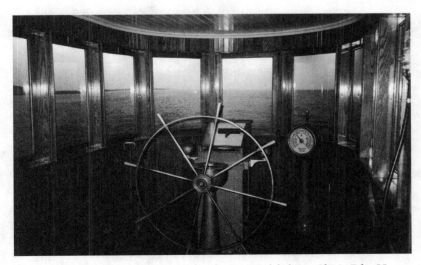

The keeper's bedroom of the station has been remodeled as a Ship's Pilot House. (George Weeks)

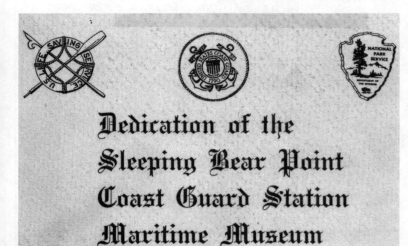

Dedication of the Sleeping Bear Point Coast Guard Station Maritime Museum

Saturday, August 4, 1984
2:00 p.m.

lem for the station at the point was drifting sand which threatened to bury it and its buildings. In 1931, the station and other buildings were moved eastward to their present location near Glen Haven. Horses pulled them over a system of rollers, track and cables. The signal tower also was moved, but the lookout tower remained at the point on a dune that provided the best visibility of the Manitou Passage.

End of an Era

Over the years, the need for life-saving stations lessened. The number of Great Lakes cargo-carrying ships had reached a peak of about 1, 700 in the mid-nineteenth century.[8] As power replaced sail, there was less danger of vessels

Below, Superintendent Richard R. Peterson of the Sleeping Bear Dunes National Lakeshore was master of ceremonies when the Sleeping Bear Point Coast Guard Maritime Museum was dedicated August 4, 1984. On the porch of the station at the ceremonies were, left to right: Glen Arbor Township Supervisor John Depuy; Chairman John Daugherty of the Sleeping Bear Dunes Advisory Commission; Preservation Director Kathryn Eckert of the Michigan Bureau of History; Peterson; Adm. Willard J. Smith (Ret.), Former commandant of the U.S. Coast Guard whose father once was keeper of the stations at the point and South Manitou; and Randall Pope, deputy director of the Midwest Region of the National Park Service. (National Park Service)

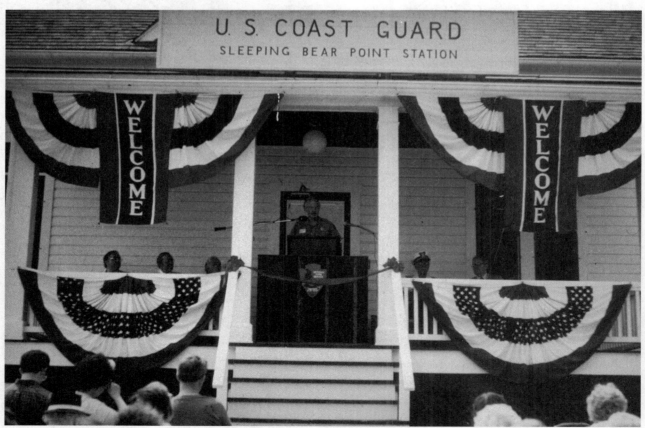

being driven upon the Lake Michigan shoreline. Radio, radar and other technological developments gave ships better means of avoiding danger. Radio beams helped guide ships though the Manitou Passage. Furthermore, the U.S.L.S.S. and its surf rescues evolved into the U.S. Coast Guard and its mission of search and rescue.

"Adding power was the most dramatic change," said Admiral Smith.[9] Motors gave rescue boats greater range than those with only oars and sails. Later, airplanes gave the Coast Guard enormous range for search, and introduction of helicopters provided improved capability for search *and* rescue. The mostly shore-bound rescuers evolved into a wide-ranging air-sea force.

In 1938, the Coast Guard stationed a detachment at the Traverse City Airport with one plane and crew. It was discontinued in World War 11. In 1946, the Traverse City Coast Guard Air Station was activated, with Willard Smith as its first commanding officer. By 1989, the station had 15 pilots and covered a territory that included all of Lake Superior and the northern half of lakes Michigan and Huron. Among its fleet were three HH-3F "Pelican" helicopters, with a top speed of 130 knots and a range of 600

to 700 miles. Also of continuing importance to the Manitou Passage are rescue boats from the Coast Guard station at Frankfort, which has responsibility up to North Manitou Island. To the north, there is a station at Charlevoix.

After its move, the Sleeping Bear Point Coast Guard Station became essentially an "eyes and ears" operation, providing shore patrols and relaying communications while leaving rescues to a motorized boat stationed at South Manitou.

During World War II, the station closed. In

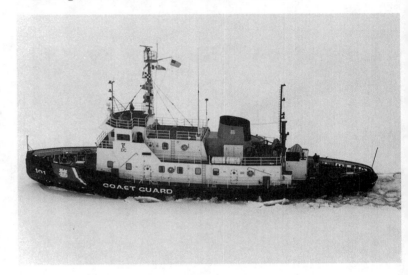

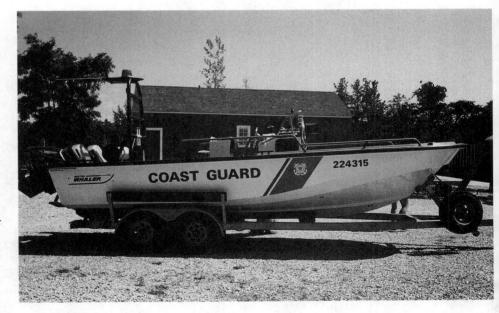

Large Coast Guard vessels such as these come through the Manitou Passage occasionally but most rescue work is by smaller, Frankfort-based power boats and Traverse City-based helicopters.
(U.S. Coast Guard)

This Frankfort-based Boston Whaler, on display at the Sleeping Bear Point Coast Guard Station Maritime Museum in 1989, is dispatched for rescue with considerably more speed than the first surf boats and beach carts of the Manitou Passage.
(Cottage Book Shop of Glen Arbor)

1943, most of the station's crew left to go to the South Pacific to help land troops. In its final days, the station had a three-man crew. First Class Petty Officer James W. Fitzgerald was in charge. Others were Second Class Petty Officer-Machinist's Mate Thomas G. ("Diz") Dean and Second Class Petty Officer-Seaman Roy P. Burns. They did little more than meet the boat from South Manitou Island, relay phone calls, and maintain their required marksmanship with

the sixteen guns that by then had been assigned to the station. "They kept shipping us ammunition like you wouldn't believe," recalled Dean.[10]

The Sleeping Bear Point Coast Guard Station was retired from active service when, on a bright spring day in May 1944, Diz Dean put a padlock on the door and walked away from what in its heyday was headquarters for some of Michigan's fabled "Heroes of the Storm."

TODAY

Owned by the Coast Guard until its transfer to the General Services Administration in 1958, the station remained idle until 1971 when it served briefly as the visitor center for the newly-established Sleeping Bear Dunes National Lakeshore.

Historic restoration in 1982 and 1983 returned the buildings and grounds to their 1931 appearance, except for the interior of the boathouse and the crew's bedroom which were restored to the way they looked in the early 1900s. Exhibits and furnishings were installed, and the National Park Service re-opened the station as a maritime museum. It was officially dedicated on, appropriately, Coast Guard Day, 4 August 1984.

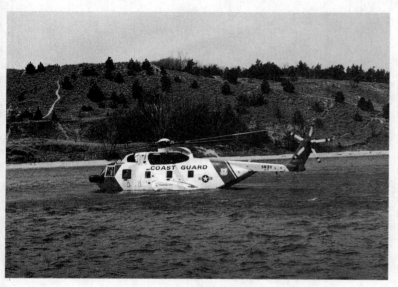

Helicopter rescues can involve a landing on water.
(U.S. Coast Guard)

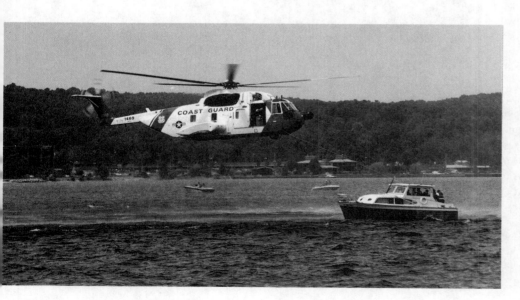

Or lowering of a rescue device from the air.
(U.S. Coast Guard)

The exhibits include displays on such ship-wrecks as the freighter *Francisco Morazan*, which ran aground off South Manitou Island in 1960, and the steamer *Rising Sun*, wrecked off Pyramid Point in 1917.

Among the artifacts are nautical equipment, a Manby mortar, forerunner to the Lyle gun, and a Fresnel lens from a lighthouse beacon. An entire room is devoted to a simulation of a pilot house of a Great Lakes ship, providing a panoramic view of the Manitou Passage.

The boathouse is restored to the first decade of the 1900s. It has two surfboats, one of them an original built in the mid-1880s for a lifesaving station in Wisconsin. The other is a replica Beebe-McLellan built especially for the museum. The boathouse also has a fully-equipped beach cart, and a variety of other items used in rescues. Tracks leading from the boat house toward the water aided in launching the surfboats.

Endnotes—Heroes of the Storm

1. "Lyle Line-Throwing Gun," (Empire, MI: Sleeping Bear Dunes National Lakeshore, 1989).

2. Jacob Abbott, *Harper's Magazine*, 1851. Reprinted in *The United States Life-Saving Service*—1880, (Golden, Colo.: Outbooks, 1981), 34.

3. Gerald E. Crowner, *The South Manitou Story*, (Mio., MI: Gerald E. Crowner, 1982), 78.

4. Crowner, 38.

5. Ida Farrant, in a 1940s handwritten history of the Sleeping Bear Station provided by the Day and Travis Historical Collections. She was the daughter of William Farrant, a French Canadian who operated the village inn at Glen Haven. Her sister, Eva, married Glen Haven's most prominent citizen, D. H. Day.

6. Ibid.

7. Adm. (ret.) Willard J. Smith, interview with the author, 16 August 1989. Smith was born in Suttons Bay, MI, May 14, 1910, lived briefly on North Manitou Island before his father was transferred to South Manitou and then Sleeping Bear Point, and attended high school in Charlevoix. He had a variety of Great Lakes assignments, including command of the Traverse City Air Station, before becoming Commandant of the U.S. Coast Guard in 1966 until his retirement in 1970.

8. Ibid.

9. Smith, in a 1984 interview with National Park Service Ranger-Historian Bill Herd of the Sleeping Bear Dunes National Lakeshore. A recording of the interview is available to visitors at the Sleeping Bear Point Coast Guard Station Maritime Museum.

10. Thomas G. Dean, interview with the author, 6 August 1989.

CHAPTER 10

Shipwrecks of Sleeping Bear and the Manitou Passage

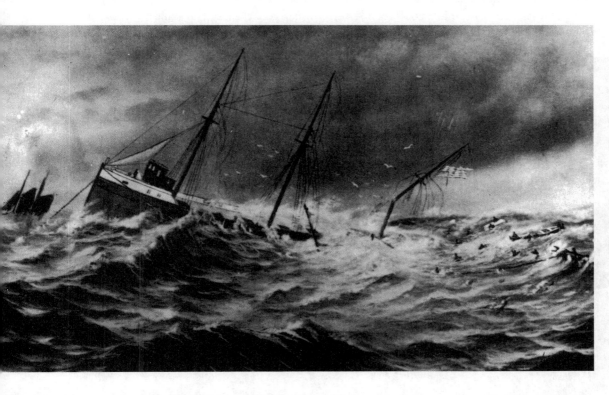

This painting shows the schooner Driver *helping victims of the 1883 sinking of the H.C. Akely off Saugatuck. In 1907,* Driver *herself wrecked off Sleeping Bear.*
(State Archives of Michigan)

dismasting blasts as direful as any that lash the salted wave . . . have drowned many a midnight ship with all its shrieking crew

—Herman Melville on the Great Lakes[1]

For early Great Lakes ships, the Sleeping Bear lakeshore was both a haven and a graveyard. The narrow Manitou Passage had protected harbors and treacherous shoals. Thousands of ships passed by safely. Those that did not include some of the most storied wrecks of the Lakes. Some are ghost ships that "went missing"—simply disappeared. Some are on the list of Great Lakes maritime mysteries that began in 1679 with disappearance of the *Griffin*, the first commercial vessel on the Lakes. Conjectured sites of its demise include islands about 40 miles northwest of the Manitou Islands. (The 65-foot, 45-ton *Griffin*—also spelled Griffon—was the first European trade vessel to sail between Lakes Huron and Michigan and within about four months of its launching became the first Great Lakes shipwreck. It was built for Rene-Robert Cavelier, Sieur de La Salle, as part of his plan for direct trade with Indians near the Straits of Mackinac and his longrange hope for involvement in French colonization of the interior of North America. With a load of furs from Wisconsin, the *Griffin* left Green Bay 18 September 1679 for the Straits and was never seen again. The Janu-

ary/February 1980 issue of *Michigan History* magazine said "it is generally assumed that it was lost during a storm near either Summer, Rock, or Washington islands in northern Lake Michigan" off Wisconsin. But Harrison John MacLean, author of The Fate of the Griffon, wrote in 1974 that he believed he discovered her remains in an island cove near Tobermory, Ontario, in Lake Huron's Georgian Bay.)

French naturalist Francis Count de Castlenau, who travelled the Manitou Passage in 1838, described how "we were a plaything of the giant waves that pushed us toward the immense bank of sand" of Sleeping Bear. He wrote of Lake Michigan: "I have seen the storms of the Channel, those of the Ocean, the squalls off the banks of Newfoundland, those on the coasts of Amer-

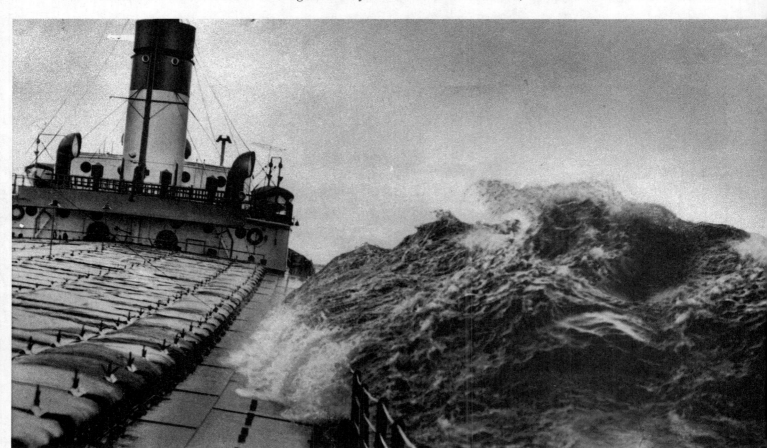

The waves on the Lakes have a different motion: they jump and tumble rather than roll and swell. This comment by shipwreck author William Ratigan is illustrated by this 1961 picture of the James A. Farrell *riding a Lake Superior storm.* (The Detroit News)

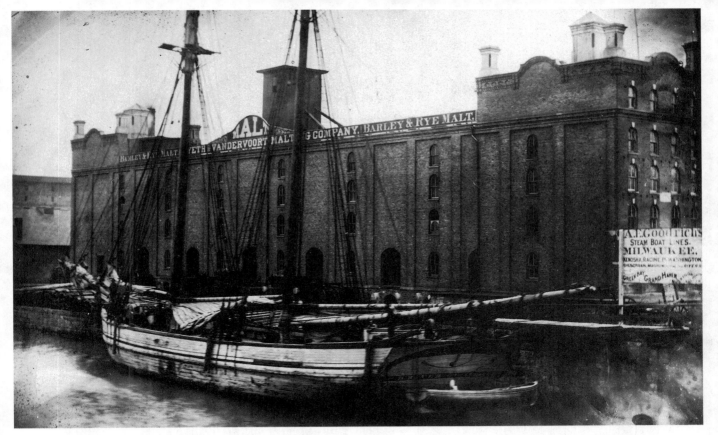

In all of her 55 years, the Josephine Dresden was in Lake Michigan lumber trade and a familiar sight in the Manitou Passage. She is shown here in 1906 after becoming one of the first schooners on the lake to be fitted with a gasoline engine. In September of 1907, she helped salvage the wreck of the H.D. Moore off South Manitou. Two months later, Dresden herself wrecked at North Manitou Island. (Northwest Michigan Maritime Museum)

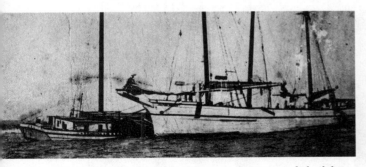

Josephine Dresden *salvaging H.D. Moore, after it stranded while trying to enter South Manitou harbor in a fierce thunderstorm September 1907.* (Northwest Michigan Maritime Museum)

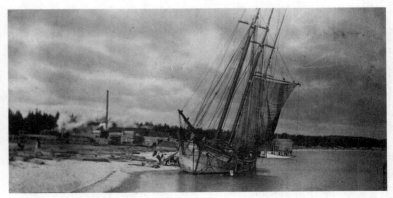

Schooner Margaret Dall, built in 1867, wrecked on South Manitou Nov. 16, 1906. She dragged anchor and stranded in a southeast gale.
(Northwest Michigan Martime Museum)

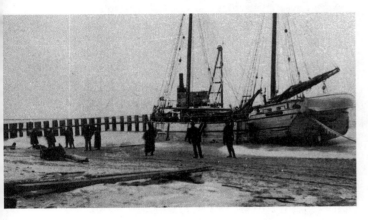

Josephine Dresden *wrecked November of 1907, hard aground by Crescent dock on the west side of North Manitou Island. She had been anchored near the beach when a sudden wind shift drove her to the beach. Although much of the cargo was saved, the ship was a total loss.*
(Nothwest Michigan Maritime Museum)

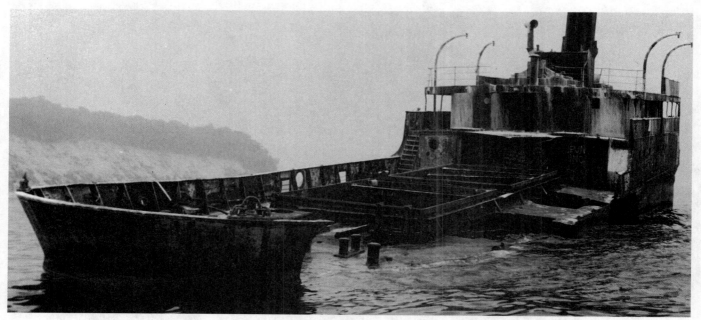

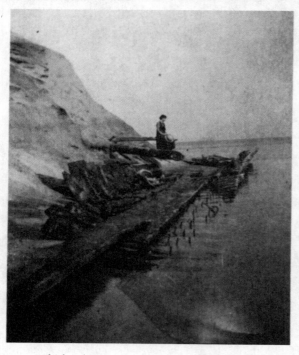

William Ratigan, author of *Great Lakes Shipwrecks & Survivals*, provides one answer:

These great ships sail Great Lakes that can swallow them in one black moment without a trace. Storms exploding across hundreds of miles of open water pile up mountainous seas that strike swifter, and more often, than the deadliest waves on any ocean. Before the ship has a chance to recover from the last blow, the next is upon her. The Lakes captain has no sea room in which to maneuver; unlike his saltwater counterpart he must stay the course throughout the storm; he must weather the teeth of the gale. . . . The waves on the Lakes have a different motion; they jump and tumble rather than

ica, and the hurricanes of the Gulf of Mexico. Nowhere have I witnessed the fury of the elements comparable to that found on this fresh water sea."[2]

That was in the nineteenth century. What about now in an era when sailing vessels and early steamers have yielded to ore and grain carriers longer than a football field—vessels equipped with the most modern navigational aids and supplied with sophisticated weather forecasts?

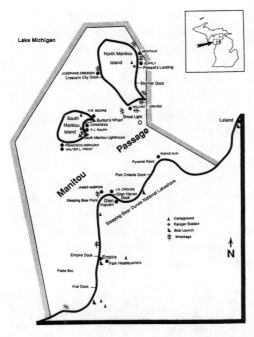

(Driver's Guide to Michigan)

roll and swell. . . . (they) strike quicker in comparison to the more lethargic ocean waves because they are less dense.[3]

Each lake has its own character, and its special danger. Ratigan said sailing masters pay the utmost respect to Lake Michigan, and not only because of its long history of sudden disaster. On one hand, it has prevailing winds that sweep its length "to roll up backbreaking seas." On the other, it has few natural harbors or even man-made places of refuge for large lakers. And then there is "the crowning fact that it is the trickiest of the Lakes to keep a course on, due to currents caused by a flow around the Straits of Mackinac when the wind shifts."[4]

When Dana Thomas Bowen published a 1952 list of the twelve worst ship disasters in Great Lakes history, based on the number of lives lost, five of them were in Lake Michigan, more than on any other lake.[5] He put things in perspective by suggesting that "life aboard Great Lakes vessels is probably safer than being abroad on the streets of a great city, or on a teeming crosscountry highway."[6]

Nonetheless, as the Great Lakes go, Lake Michigan has its particular hazards. As Milo M. Quaife states in his book, *Lake Michigan*, "Probably the most constant single cause of disasters on Lake Michigan throughout the centuries has been the tempests which often develop suddenly and rage with appalling fury." Such an arising tempest, according to a legend cited by Quaife, once caused 500 braves of the Wisconsin Winnebago to perish after they set off by canoe to battle Foxes on the Michigan side of the lake.[7]

Referring specifically to the Manitou Passage, Great Lakes maritime writer Dwight Boyer called it "fearful . . . dangerous. . . . Shipmasters caught in fog or foul weather while navigating Manitou Passage breathe a sigh of relief when South Manitou is astern. Her rocky shores and offshore reefs hold the bones of many sail and steam vessels that came upon her in fog or snow, or sought her lee for shelter." He said ninety-six wrecks were logged by keepers of the South Manitou Light. (Some presumably were salvaged to sail again.) Boyer called the disemboweled Liberian freighter *Francisco Morazan*, visible off the island's southern shore decades after its 1960 wreck, "a grim, gray reminder of South Manitou's infamous heritage of tragedy."[8]

While there is no discounting that heritage, as of early 1990, nearly three decades have passed since there was a shipwreck in the Manitou Passage.

During the era of more frequent shipwrecks, the Manitou Passage on one hand could be treacherous to steamers as well as schooners. On the other, for those captains able to maneuver into it, South Manitou Island provided the first navigable harbor to be reached in the long voyage north from Chicago or Milwaukee enroute to the Mackinac Straits. For southbound ships, it was the last natural harbor on the course to Chicago.

South Manitou's natural harbor has been a haven during some of the great storms of the Great Lakes. During one of the worst, the one in 1913 that sank twelve ships, the steamer *Illinois* nudged its bow on the island sand and kept its engine going for about a day until the storm eased. The ship was then able to back off and resume its journey to Chicago from Mackinac Island.

While it is not a harbor, Sleeping Bear Bay also provides relative shelter and was—as it is today—used as a haven from Lake Michigan storms. The Bay's historic village of Glen Haven was aptly named. Steve Harold, author of *Shipwrecks of the Sleeping Bear*, has observed: "We have the combination of a narrow and dangerous passage and the best protection in 200 miles of Lake. Although thousands of vessels have reached this protection, a small number have met disaster in the protected Passage."[9]

How many? Estimates vary, and Harold warns: "Most shipwreck books and charts seem to be written from hearsay. Firsthand accounts make fascinating reading but everyone's memory fades and dims with the passage of time. Consequently, there is little accurate information about wrecks." He also warns that the term shipwreck carries a number of meanings, and that some ships listed as wrecks were later salvaged and returned to service.[10]

A marker outside the Sleeping Bear Point Coast Guard Station Maritime Museum puts the number of shipwrecks "in the Sleeping Bear area" at about eighty. The Maritime Heritage Alliance of Northern Lake Michigan, in a December 1988 report on state designation of the Manitou Passage Bottomland Preserve, referred to "70 known shipwrecks in the vicinity of the Manitou

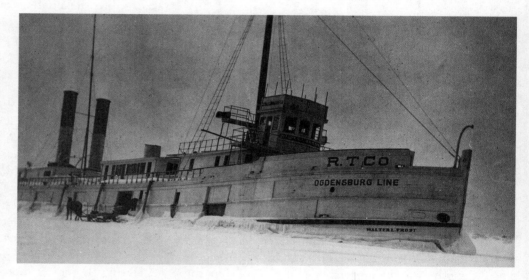

At the same site of the Morazan *wreck, the steamer* Walter L. Frost *went aground in 1903.*
(Northwest Michigan Maritime Musem)

Submerged remains of the Frost *can be seen near the* Morazan *in this 1980s picture.*
(Northwest Michigan Maritime Musem)

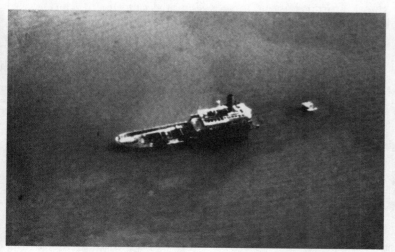

Islands." The Northwest Michigan Maritime Museum (NWMMM) in Frankfort published a chart of forty-nine shipwrecks of the Manitou Passage in 1988 but began revising it in 1989 as its researchers obtained further information and divers organized by Museum Director Jed Jaworski mapped wreck sites as part of a project funded by local businesses and a Coastal Zone Management grant.

Much depends on the parameters established for study. The NWMMM study focuses on the 282 square miles of the preserve. For an expanded area beginning at the northeast edge of Grand Traverse Bay and extending southward, a

1957 chart by A.C. and L.F. Frederickson of "lost ships and cargoes" cites 200 wrecks in 200 miles.[11] Harold's book, the most authoritative on Sleeping Bear shipwrecks, was limited to the mainland side of the Manitou Passage in an area stretching from the Platte River to Grand Traverse Point.

The Bottomland Preserve includes the Manitou islands and waters on all sides of them. As of 1990, it was one of seven Michigan preserves encompassing 1,650 square miles of Great Lakes bottomland. The other preserves are the Straits of Mackinac; Alger and Whitefish Point in Lake Superior; and Thumb Area, Thunder Bay and Sanilac Shores in Lake Huron. Anyone disturbing wrecks in preserves is subject to fines of up to $500, six months in prison and seizure of their boats and equipment.

While the Manitou preserve goes no farther north than Good Harbor Bay, many of the ships traversing the Manitou Passage were wrecked farther north along the Leelanau Peninsula, including Leland and Cathead Bay. This chapter, updated with results from 1989 surveys, includes wrecks around the Manitou Islands and along the mainland from Benzie County's Platte River to Grand Traverse Point at the northern tip of Leelanau County.

Lost Vessels of Sleeping Bear

The earliest reported wreck in the preserve was the *Free Trader*, lost in 1835. The most recent wreck at this writing is the *Morazan*, which went aground in 1960 off South Manitou Island at the site of the 1903 wreck of the freighter *Walter L. Frost*. Significant new discoveries of wrecks were made in the late 1980s after the Manitou Passage became Michigan's newest bottomland preserve.

The shipwrecks of Sleeping Bear and the Manitou Passage are compiled in the chart on pages 139–141. Following is a representative selection of those wrecks, selected by such factors as their historical significance, lore they may reflect, shoreline rescues and accessibility to divers:

Free Trader—This schooner was possibly the first shipwreck of Sleeping Bear. Both the Northwest Michigan Maritime Museum and maritime historian Harold list it as the earliest.

British writer Harriet Martineau, reporting on an 1836 voyage through the Manitou Passage, wrote of the Sleeping Bear shoreline: "Just here, Mr. D. pointed out a schooner of his which was wrecked in a snow storm the preceding November."[12] Harold said the reference was to a

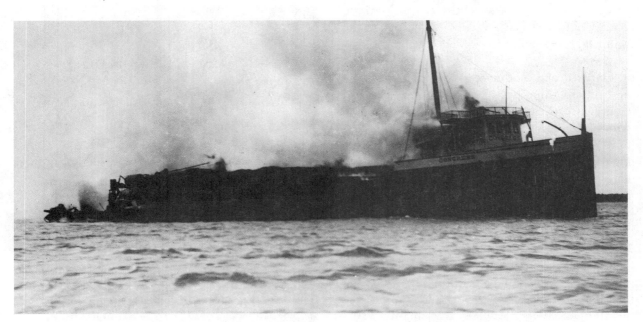

Steamer Congress *burning off South Manitou in 1904.* (Northwest Michigan Maritime Museum)

Michael Dousman, who had the *Free Trader* built at St. Ignace in 1829. Since final disposition of other vessels owned by Dousman was known, Harold concluded: "By a process of deduction, it can be reasoned (Free Trader) was the vessel lost at Sleeping Bear."[13]

Francisco Morazan—Deduction is not needed about this wreck. The U. S. Coast Guard was called out when this Liberian freighter ran aground off South Manitou 29 November 1960 on the same shoal where the *Frost* wrecked fifty-seven years earlier. The thirteen member crew and the captain's wife were saved, as was some of the cargo that included 335 tons of lard, 159 tons of hides, 95 tons of canned chicken, 26 tons of coin-operated vending machines, 3 tons of baled hair, 2 tons of bottle caps, and a ton of toys. In 1990, much of the *Morazan* was still above water.

Walter L. Frost—Carrying grain, this steamer ran aground off South Manitou 4 November 1903. It was a total loss but all twenty-one aboard were saved. Like the *Morazan*, much of it remained above water after the wreck, but now is a ghostly skeleton whose submerged bones can be seen in about 25 feet of water about 100 yards south of the *Morazan*.

Congress—About a year after the *Frost* wrecked, this 267-foot steamer caught fire while being loaded with wood at the South Manitou dock. Cut loose to save the dock, it burned to the water line and sank in 160 feet of water 4 October 1904.

Onward and ***Skidmore***—Both met the same end on the same day at about the same place. Otherwise, they were not particularly notable wrecks but are included here because they are 1885 examples of how vulnerable vessels were even when unloading at docks along Lake Michigan's eastern shore. Furthermore, a contemporary account is available on these wrecks from a nearby newspaper published three days after the 21 September 1885 wreck. This is how the losses were reported by the *Leelanau Enterprise*:

> Two vessels, the Onward and the Skidmore, both of Milwaukee, are complete wrecks, the former at Gill's Pier on Lake Michigan, and the latter about two miles south of Gill's Pier.

Both vessels were loading wood at the pier Monday when a strong southwest wind warned them to take shelter elsewhere. The Skidmore had completed her load and was endeavoring to make away when it was discovered she had sprung a leak. The wind had hauled around to the northwest and was blowing a gale.

The seas were driving with great strength almost defying an antagonist, and the captain deemed it advisable to run the Skidmore ashore, which he did, and no sooner had she touched ground whan her hull broke midships, Tuesday's storm making a finish of her.

The Onward being only partially loaded and having hopes of being able to get away was scuttled at the pier, and subsequently went to pieces where she lay.

The respective crews are all safe, no one being injured and they are busy "stripping the slain." We understand there is no insurance on either vessel, and they were quite old.[14]

J. Young Scammon—This 1854 wreck is cited not because it was a major maritime event, but rather as a vignette on early maritime life and improvised means of ship-to-shore communication involved in rescue of crew and passengers.

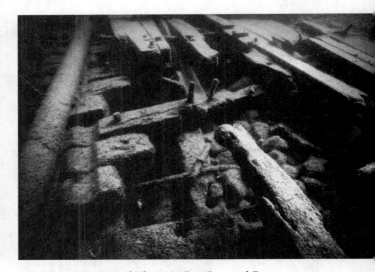

The Rising Sun *wrecked in 1917 at Pyramid Point while downbound with 32 people and a cargo of potatoes, rutabagas and lumber. It now is one of the popular Sleeping Bear area dive sites and on a clear day can be seen from the bluffs.* (Media Vision)

The brig, owned by Hannah & Lay Company of Traverse City, encountered a northeast gale on 8 June and was driven toward South Manitou Island. Seeing the vessel in trouble, South Manitou Lighthouse Keeper Alonzo Slyfield, who had become keeper nine months earlier, signaled to the crew to send him a buoy attached to a rope. After it reached shore, Slyfield attached a bottle to the rope with a note advising the crew to "send word by bottle" on how he could be of assistance. He was told of difficulties with the ship's anchor chains, and asked to "look out for us ashore."

Slyfield patrolled the beach until, an hour later, the ship came broadside to the shore. A spare spar was launched over the rail, with one end resting in shoal water. The survivors, including four women, slid down the spar. Slyfield took them to the lighthouse, where "we found that during my absence I had been blessed with the arrival of an eight-pound, blue-eyed boy, and there was indeed a feeling of happiness in the station that night, and I felt satisfied that I had accomplished more that day than on any other day of my previous life."[15]

This depicts mid-nineteenth century life during days of settlement in Sleeping Bear County and infancy of Lakes shipping. Slyfield went on to accomplish more in his later life. Keeper Slyfield in the above account is the same Slyfield in Chapter Five who, as a 1860s physician in Benzie County, waded the icy Platte River eighteen times on a winter's day while making his rounds,

Rising Sun—This could be called the story of the many lives and death of *Minnie M.* She was launched at Detroit in 1884 as *Minnie M.*, a 133-foot passenger and package freight steamer. She began service out of Escanaba's Little Bay de Noc, and then moved to Cheboygan. She had a variety of assignments, including service between Mackinac Island and Sault St. Marie, until about 1900, when she was sold to the Algoma Central Railway and became Canadian *Minnie M.* Two sales later, she became property of the House of David of Benton Harbor and renamed the *Rising Sun*.

In October 1917, the *Rising Sun* went to High

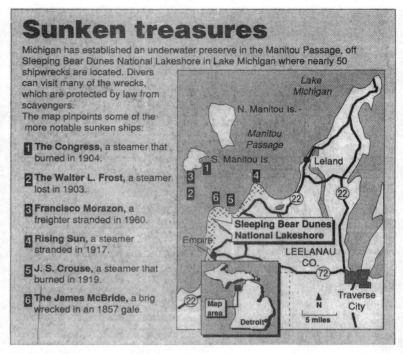

Sunken treasures

Michigan has established an underwater preserve in the Manitou Passage, off Sleeping Bear Dunes National Lakeshore in Lake Michigan where nearly 50 shipwrecks are located. Divers can visit many of the wrecks, which are protected by law from scavengers.
The map pinpoints some of the more notable sunken ships:

1. **The Congress**, a steamer that burned in 1904.

2. **The Walter L. Frost**, a steamer lost in 1903.

3. **Francisco Morazon**, a freighter stranded in 1960.

4. **Rising Sun**, a steamer stranded in 1917.

5. **J. S. Crouse**, a steamer that burned in 1919.

6. **The James McBride**, a brig wrecked in an 1857 gale.

Sunken treasures map. (The Detroit News)

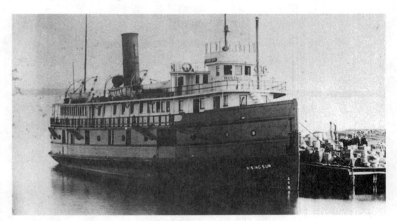

The Rising Sun, originally the Minnie M., before its 1817 wreck. (National Park Service)

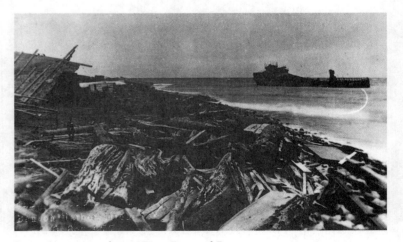

Rising Sun aground in 1871 at Pyramid Point. (National Park Service)

Island to get potatoes, rutabagas and lumber to take to Benton Harbor. On 29 October, in one of the early-season snowstorms that sweep the Lakes, the Rising Sun went aground at Pyramid Point. Lifeboats were launched and all thirty-two people aboard eventually saved.

As was often the case with Great Lakes wrecks, shoreline residents, not the U.S. Coast Guard, were the first to provide assistance. In this case, Fred Baker, summoned in the night by survivors pounding at the door of his home atop the Port Oneida bluff, was the first to respond. He hastened to his barn, quickly unloaded 60 bushels of potatoes that were on his wagon, hitched his team, and went down to the beach. The survivors, including a woman found unconscious on the beach, were brought to Baker's house. (By the 1990s, Baker's daughter, Lucille, who was four years old at the time of the wreck, was still residing at Port Oneida, the wife of Jack Barratt, great grandson of Port Oneida settler Carsten Burfiend.)

The Coast Guard beach rescue rig arrived from Glen Haven, pulled by two teams of horses borrowed from D. H. Day. A man who was asleep when the others abandoned ship was rescued by the guardsmen.

In 1988, this section, later determined to be part of the port side of the McBride, was found a mile south of Sleeping Bear Point.

By the summer of 1989, the restless bones of the McBride had worked their way to within a half mile of Sleeping Bear Point. The sandy bluff behind the point is shown in this picture. Pyramid Point is the dark land in the background. Months after this picture was taken, the section had moved to within 400 yards of the former site of the Sleeping Bear Life-Saving/Coast Guard Station.

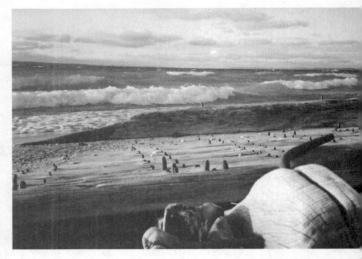

(George W

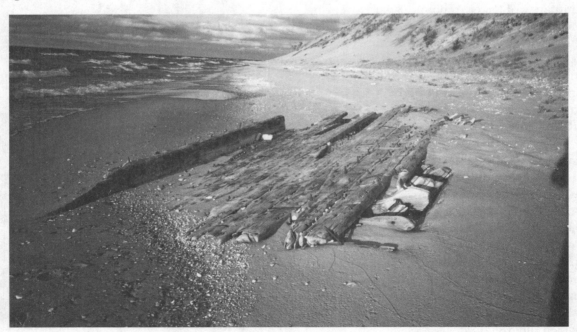

(Cottage Book Shop of Glen Arbor)

Remains of the *Rising Sun* are visible from the shore on a clear day, and are popular for recreational divers. As with other wrecks, the remains are protected objects within the Manitou Passage Bottomland Preserve.

W. B. Phelps—If there is any Great Lakes wreck deserving of mention for the role shoreline residents played in rescue, it is the schooner *Phelps*, which broke apart in a raging surf on the shore of Sleeping Bear Bay near the Glen Arbor dock in a northwest gale and fierce snow storm.

On 19 November 1879, the *Phelps* and its crew of seven arrived at the Manitou Passage with a load of wheat and beer from Milwaukee. It was hit by a sudden storm, and the sails froze in place. Unable to reach the Manitou Islands for protection, the ship was driven into Sleeping Bear Bay. As she approached the shore, the anchors failed to hold in deep water, but one caught at a place where it caused the ship to hit bottom with each wave. The captain and four crewmen were swept away.

The ship came ashore at about 7 P.M. but was not discovered until dawn, when Charles Rosman, son of a Great Lakes skipper, was walking the beach and saw the wreck. He organized a rescue effort that earned a Congressional Life Saving Medal for Rosman, W. C. Ray, W. A. Clark, John Tobin, W. W. Tucker, Howard Daniels and John Blanchfield, all of Glen Arbor.

As described by U.S. Treasury Secretary John Sherman, in the citation for the medals, this is what the men saw:

> The schooner was then lying covered with ice, and her decks completely broken up; and the two survivors of her crew of seven, were standing shouting for help on the extreme forward part of the vessel.[16]

Rosman called for volunteers, but, according to author Harold, "few responded due to the size of the waves and to the fact that everyone was collecting beer as rapidly as possible.[17] The first rescue attempt included a leaky, flat bottom fishing boat hauled to the scene by horse-drawn sleigh. Halfway to the wreck, it filled with water, and drenched rescuers returned to shore.

On the second attempt, the boat reached the stern of the *Phelps* and made fast by a line cast to the ship. The scene is described by the citation:

> Here it was seen that a mass of timbers, spars, deck planking, sails, rigging, and deck debris of all sorts hanging over the sides of the vessel and tossed about by the heavy sea, would prevent the boat from getting near the two men on the bow of the schooner, and as the fish boat was now filling with water and it was necessary to return to shore, which her company reached, wet through, chilled and covered with ice.

The citation described the third and successful attempt:

> . . . with great exertion and daring, (rescuers) forced the boat into an opening in the mass of floating debris, along side of a piece of the deck still fast to the vessel, and about 60 feet from the two seamen. In this position, constant effort was necessary to prevent the boat from being crushed to pieces by the debris tossing on each side of her. It was impossible for the two seamen to reach the boat except by crawling the distance, above named, across the mass of the stuff, constantly in motion, and over which the sea was rushing. Sustained by a line thrown from the boat, one of them succeeded in accomplishing about 40 feet of the distance when his progress was arrested, and (rescuers) then worked the boat over a piece of the broken deck along side of the fragment, upon which the sailor clung, and hauled him in.
>
> Two of your company then sprang from the boat, and leaped from piece to piece of the debris to the spot where the other sailor, weaker and more helpless than his fellow, and caught by the feet between the timbers, was vainly struggling to extricate himself. In a moment he was freed, and one of the men, seizing him by the collar, dragged him along a spar to the fragment upon which the other sailor had been where he was taken into the boat. The boat was then shoved off the piece of deck on which it partly lay, and the return to land was effected with the two men saved.

The rescued sailors, Edward Igoe and John Hourigan, continued to sail the Great Lakes, and later became Great Lakes captains.[18]

J. H. Hartzell—This 1880 wreck occurred off the Elberta Bluff, well south of the Manitou Passage and beyond the limits of wrecks listed in this book's chart. But it is worthy of mention at this point because it, too, involved dramatic shoreline work from rescuers associated with the heritage of the Sleeping Bear area. The rescue also offers a vivid example of the work of the Point Betsie Life-Saving Station.

The *Hartzel* arrived off Frankfort at 3 A.M. on 16 October 1880 with 495 tons of iron ore for the Frankfort Furnace Company. While waiting for daylight, it was hit by a sudden wind shift and storm. The ship was driven aground about 300 yards from shore.

When spotted, word was sent via horseback rider ten miles to the Point Betsie station. Townspeople built a fire on the beach, waiting to assist in the rescue. It took enormous effort of men and horse to get the rescue cart to the scene over swamps and hills. Waiting rescue, the crew clung to rigging that was whipped about by raging wind and sea. Using the Lyle gun, life car and breeches buoy apparatus (see Chapter Nine), the lifesavers rescued all but one.

The lone victim was cook Lydia Dale. Some members of the crew claimed she died of exposure before the rescuers arrived, but when her body later washed up on shore 17 days later, the coroner's report indicated she drowned. The failure to save her is examined in the 58-minute documentary "The Wreck and Rescue of the Schooner J. H. Hartzell" produced by Rich Brauer of Traverse City in cooperation with the Northwest Michigan Maritime Museum and the National Park Service.

Westmoreland—This steamer, lost 8 December 1858 was among the more notable Lake Michigan wrecks and mysteries. As with so many nineteenth century wrecks, there was no verified report on the exact location of its grave. Nor was there confirmation of the rumor that it was carrying $100,000 in gold coins.

"The *Westmoreland* could easily be the biggest practical joke ever perpetrated on the Great Lakes," said author Steve Harold. "On the other hand, it just might contain one of the largest fortunes awaiting Great Lakes adventurers."[19]

The *Westmoreland* left Chicago on 2 December with 28,000 bushels of oats, 322 barrels of flour, and 28 bags of grass seed. In Milwaukee, she took on a mixed cargo destined for Mackinac Island. Heading for the Manitou Passage, she became heavy with accumulated ice and settled so low she began taking on water and had to be abandoned. Contemporary accounts indicated that seventeen people drowned; that one life-boat capsized in heavy seas; and that survivors in another lifeboat landed on the beach of Platte Bay, said also to be eventual site of the wreck.

Despite various reports that the ship was found and her cargo salvaged, Harold said "no one has made a verified report of finding the vessel."[20] In a 1989 guidebook on the area, author/diver Steve Harrington said "the rumor persists that the ship was carrying a gold payroll worth about $4 million today. Treasure hunters from across the country have searched in vain for the Westmoreland.[21]

A detailed account on the Westmoreland, as well as thirty-three other wrecks, can be found in Harold's *Shipwrecks of the Sleeping Bear*.

Maritime Archaeology: New Discoveries of Old Wrecks

The Manitou Passage, long the site of some of the most intriguing maritime tales of Great Lakes, entered the final decade of the twentieth century with some of the most significant modern day discoveries of early Lake Michigan shipwrecks. This primarily resulted from the efforts to document wrecks and develop management techniques in the Manitou Passage Bottomland Preserve, created by the Legislature in 1988.

James McBride—One of the most interesting of the Sleeping Bear wrecks, its story contrasts with the wreck of the *Free Trader*, about which there is no documentation and no visual evidence, and the well-reported and highly-visible

Morazan. The *McBride* took underwater detective work.

This accident-plagued brigantine, launched on April Fool's Day in 1848, was believed eight months later to have carried the first cargo directly from the Atlantic to a Lake Michigan port. After the *McBride delivered* salt and codfish to Chicago, the *Chicago Journal* proclaimed on 4 December 1848: "This is the first foreign shipment ever made from the Atlantic seaboard direct to any port on our inland seas."

The *McBride* later had a number of mishaps. In 1849, she was forced to run back to Chicago in a Lake Michigan gale with two feet of water in her hold. She sank in 1855 after being hit by the schooner *C. B. Williams* near Milwaukee but was raised and returned to service. She also was re, ported to have run ashore once near South Haven and once near the mouth of the Saginaw River.

In 1857, the *McBride was* wrecked in an October gale at Sleeping Bear Point after getting a load of wood from the Manitou Islands and trying to head for Chicago. It took on water and was driven to the shore.

In 1988, NWMMM divers located, charted and identified remains of the *McBride* 200 yards offshore in 15 feet of water. A large portion of its port side broke away and became partially buried by sand on the shore a mile south of the point. Little by little, the section worked its way northward. By 1990, it had moved to within about 400 yards from a crumbled stone foundation in the vicinity of the abandoned site of the U.S. Life-Saving Service/Coast Guard Station at Sleeping Bear Point.

William T. Graves—The first bulk freighter built on the Great Lakes, it stranded at North Manitou 3 November 1885. In the fall of 1988, its remains were discovered by NWMMM staff and volunteers off North Manitou Shoal. This included a 158-foot section of the ship's star, board side, as well as a rudder that can be seen from the surface.

Alva Bradley—This 192-foot schooner, built in Cleveland in 1870 and the first with steel rigging, sank 13 October 1894. It was dis-

covered and documented in 1990 in 26 feet of water on the North Manitou Shoal, with 160 feet of its port side and much of its cabin work intact.

The year of the *Bradley* sinking, 1894, saw the total loss of forty-four vessels and sixty-eight lives in the Great Lakes and underscored a nineteenth century hazard to shipping not often heard of in the twentieth century—dense smoke from forest fires. On 6 August the schooner *A. P. Grover* stranded and was damaged in thick, smokey weather off South Manitou Island but was later freed. Dense smoke in August and September resulted in damaging and temporary stranding of these ships: 27 August at Pyramid Point, the steamer *Florida*; 1 September at Sleeping Bear Point, steamer *Robert Holland*, schooner *Fannie Neil* and schooner *S. M. Stephenson.*[22]

Supply—This brig sank in 1862 enroute to Leland with a load of bricks. It was located off Vessel Point at North Manitou Island in about 12 feet of water. Rangers of the National Park Service found additional associated wreckage. Amazingly, the bricks were still stacked in the ship's damaged hold.

Montauk—This schooner was wrecked at North Manitou on 24 November 1882 during a blinding snowstorm while carrying 22,000 bushels of grain from Chicago to Buffalo. At 3 A.M., it stranded off the north end of the island and was not discovered until seen at daylight by a fisherman who notified the island's U.S. Life-Saving Service station. The keeper dispatched a crew by large sail boat to the site, where all eight men on the *Montauk* were saved. The station's report said: "They were all very grateful to the station crew, and felt, as they expressed it, that 'they had been lifted from the grave.' The vessel and cargo were a total loss." A copy of the report is at the NWMMM. Discovery of a large section of a wooden hull that may be remains of the *Montauk was* reported in 1989. It is in about 30 feet of water on the east side of the island.

W.H. Gilcher—One of Lake Michigan's most controversial maritime mysteries involves this 300-foot, steel-hulled freighter that "went missing" with all twenty-one hands in 1892. The *Gilcher* was built in 1890 by the Cleveland Ship Building Company, which four months earlier had launched a ship of similar dimensions and construction—the *Western Reserve*. Both had steel hulls, and, while they had different owners, they were considered sister ships. The *Gilcher* quickly captured the grain-carrying record by taking 113,885 bushels of wheat from Chicago to Buffalo.

In August 1892, the *Western Reserve* sank in a summer gale on Lake Superior. It had been running light and without ballast. Lifeboats were launched after a sudden jolt, and a break appeared in the deck.

On 28 October 1892, while there was still public debate about the *Western Reserve's* sinking, the *Gilcher* cleared the Straits of Mackinac and entered gale-swept Lake Michigan carrying 3,200 tons of coal from Buffalo to Milwaukee. As described by the Northwest Michigan Maritime Museum:

> Fully laden with coal and making headway for Milwaukee, Capt. Lloyd H. Weeks, veteran master of the *Gilcher*, had no doubts as to the integrity of his vessel. The *Gilcher* was the finest vessel lakes technology could produce, and she was loaded ideally for heavy weather, unlike her lost sister which had been devoid of cargo and water ballast. Other ships were seeking shelter as the intensity of the storm increased. South Manitou Harbor was crowded with storm-beaten vessels whether at anchor or aground. Somewhere in the ragged, black expanse of northern Lake Michigan the *W. H. Gilcher* plowed on."[23]

And somewhere in Lake Michigan the *Gilcher* went under. She was never found. There were no survivors, and no bodies discovered. Some drifting wreckage was seen by other ships, and much of it was assumed to be from the *Gilcher*.

Several supports for the canvas covers of the *Gilcher's* lifeboats were found at High Island, about 40 miles north of North Manitou. The NWMMM account said "They apparently had been struck with an axe, as the crew in desperation slashed through the canvas boat cover to

gain entry. This would indicate that the *Gilcher* may have foundered very suddenly, as the crew did not have time to release the cover in the usual fashion."

Other *Gilcher* wreckage was found on North Manitou. Based on all sightings, the general location of sinking was placed somewhere northwest of the Manitous in the shipping lane.

One theory is that the *Gilcher* sank as a result of collision with the aged *Ostrich*, a 139-foot schooner found bottom up on the south shore of South Manitou Island, her seven man crew lost. Frederick Stonehouse's *Went Missing,* II calls this unlikely since the steel freighter would have sliced the schooner in two and should not have suffered major damage herself.[24] Likewise, the theory that the *Gilcher* broke up on a shoal was discounted since there was comparatively little wreckage. In either of these cases, a crew should have had a chance to launch lifeboats.

The *Gilcher* insurance loss of $180,000 was the heaviest single loss incurred by underwriters on the lakes up to that time. The future of building of steel hulls was in doubt. The "brittle steel" theory that both ships plunged to frigid graves because of faulty steel gained acceptance when lab tests indicated that the specific process used for the steel in both the *Western Reserve* and *Gilcher* left the plates brittle and was not desirable for marine use.

Although the particular process was abandoned for ship construction, the fate of some twentieth century Great Lakes freighters provided further evidence for those convinced that the nineteenth century *Gilcher* snapped apart suddenly. This is what happened to the *Carl D. Bradley* in 1958 in Lake Michigan, with loss of thirty-two crewmen, and the *Daniel J. Morrell* in Lake Huron in 1966, with loss of twenty-eight.

And then there is the 729-foot *Edmund Fitzgerald*, more than twice the length of the *Gilcher*. This most famous of modern Great Lakes wrecks disappeared with its twenty-nine crew members in 1975 in Lake Superior northwest of Whitefish Point.

Despite the Coast Guard's conclusion that the *Fitzgerald* sank by taking on water through its

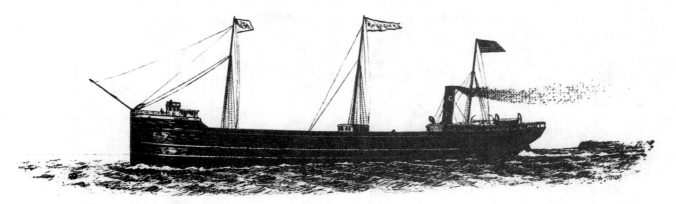

Great Lakes Steamship W.H. Gilcher, *1892.* (Dossin Great Lakes Museum)

hatches as it plowed through waves of up to 30 feet, there are those who still argue "metal fatigue" caused it to crack between the giant waves.

A $100,000 expedition was mounted in 1989 with robot camera vehicles to seek more clues about the *Fitzgerald*. The pursuit for solution to the mystery of the *Gilcher*, a nineteenth century Lake Michigan version of the *Fitzgerald* puzzle, is not as elaborate. By the mid-twentieth century, the *Gilcher* had become a relatively obscure wreck among those who wrote tales of the Great Lakes. But Manitou Passage maritime experts made pursuit of the *Gilcher* one of the priorities of their bottomland survey, and they entered the 1990s with belief that they were closing in on a solution to a century-old mystery.

"They are very similar tales," NWMMM Director Jaworski said of *Fitzgerald* and *Gilcher.* "Both were the biggest ships of their day and both met sudden, unexplained disaster with no survivors."[25]

Although it was not publicly disclosed at the time, a late 1989 sonar sounding of an apparent immense wreck, rising about 50 feet off the lake bottom, was obtained in more than 150 feet of water northwest of the Manitous in an area where bottomland specialists believed the *Gilcher* to be. Further scanning with more sophisticated equipment was inconclusive in 1990.

Few Great Lakes tales have stirred imaginations like the *Fitzgerald*, which prompted the Gordon Lightfoot hit song "The Wreck of the

Edmund Fitzgerald." But the *Gilcher*, obscure as it is today, was cited by shipwreck author William Ratigan as the inspiration for this 1892 sea-chanty:

> Of death these jolly lads
> Never once did dream;
> Brave hearts sailed under canvas
> And brave hearts sailed in steam.

> *Lost in Lake Michigan*
> *They failed to reach the shore;*
> *The gallant ships and crews*
> *Will sail the Lakes no more*[26]

Endnotes—Shipwrecks

1. Herman Melville, *Moby Dick,* (New York: Dodd, Mead and Co., 1942), 223–4.
2. Count Francis de Castlenau, as recounted in Myron H. Vent's *South Manitou Island: From Pioneer Community to National Park,* (Nassau, Del.: Manitou Publications, 1973), 16.
3. William Ratigan, *Great Lakes Shipwrecks & Survival,* (Grand Rapids, MI: Wm. B. Eerdmans Publishing Co., 1960).
4. Ratigan, 15.
5. Dana Thomas Bowen, *Shipwrecks of the Lakes,* (Cleveland: Freshwater Press, Inc., 1952), 9.
6. Dana Thomas Bowen, *Memories of the Lakes,* (Daytona Beach, Fla.: Dana Thomas Bowen, 1946), 274–75.
7. Milo M. Quaife, *Lake Michigan,* (New York: The Bobbs-Merrill Co., 1944), 254. (The sudden fury of Lake Michigan in maritime history is well documented. Not so with the oft-told tales of Indian battles. Quaife's source for the canoe disaster was a narrative of Bacqueville de la Pothrie, originally published *Great Lakes*

Steamship W.H. Gilcher, 1892. in Paris in 1722 and translated in the *Wisconsin Historical Collections*, XVI, 3–5. It said that the Winnebago's enemies "were moved by this disaster, and said that the gods ought to be satisfied with so many punishments; so they ceased making war on those who remained. ")

8. Dwight Boyer, *Ghost Ships of the Great Lakes*, (New York: Dodd, Mead & Co., 1968), 116–117, 268.

9. Steve Harold, *Shipwrecks of the Sleeping Bear*, (Traverse City, MI: Pioneer Study Center, 1984), 1.

10. Ibid.

11. A. C & L. F. Frederickson, "Frederickson's Treasure Chart," (Frankfort, MI, 1957).

12. Myron H. Vent, *South Manitou Island: From Pioneer Community to National Park*, (Nassau, Del.: Myron H. Vent, 1973), 13.

13. Harold, 9.

14. *Leelanau Enterprise*, (Leland, MI), 24 September 1885.

15. This account was provided by the Northwestern Michigan Maritime Museum, based largely on John H. Howard's 1930 *The Story of Frankfort*. The museum maintains a Ship Information and Data Record on all known wrecks of Sleeping Bear.

16. The full text of the citation was published in the *Leelanau Enteprise* 28 October 1880. A copy of that edition was obtained in 1989 from by Fred and Julia Dickinson, former publishers of the *Enterprise*.

17. Harold, 22.

18. Harold, 23.

19. Harold, 2.

20. Harold, 4.

21. Steve Harrington, *Visitors' Guide to South Manitou Island*, (Mason, MI: Beagle Publishing, Inc., 1989), 19. Harrington also is author of *Divers Guide to Michigan*, published in 1990 by Beagle Publishing. At the time, he was chairman of the Manitou Bottomland Preserve Committee. In an article for the November/December 1989 issue of *Michigan Natural Resources* magazine published by the Department of Natural Resources in Lansing, MI, he said the Manitou Bottomland is popular among divers "because more than 75 wrecks are known to have occurred in the area and only about one third of them have been discovered. "

22. U. S. Department of Agriculture, Weather Bureau, Wreck and Casualty Chart of the Great Lakes, 1895, Washington, D.C., 12 January 1894. This chart was reprinted in 1989 by the Historical Society of Michigan, Ann Arbor, MI.

23. "The Mystery of the W. H. Gilcher," *Lake Lore Newsletter* (January/February 1988) of the Northwest Michigan Maritime Museum, Frankfort, MI.

24. Frederick Stonehouse, *Went Missing*, II, (Au Train, MI: Avery Color Studiors, 1984), 152–153.

25. Jed Jaworski, director of the Northwest Michigan Maritime Museum, interview with the author, 1990.

26. Ratigan, 13.

NAME	TYPE	YEAR	CARGO	LOCATION	COMMENTS
Alice M. Beers	Sch	1902	lumber	SBB	stranded; all saved; sank four times previously in its forty-year service
Alva Bradley	Sch	1894	steel	NM	sank 13 October; first Great Lakes ship with steel rigging. Found in 1990.
Annie Vought	Sch	1892	coal	SM	stranded 12 November; total loss; all eight saved
B.A. Stannard	Bark	1864	grain	PB	stranded, probably south of PB.
Badger State	Bark	1870	corn	SBP	ran ashore 15 November; total loss
Bethlehem	Str	1888	mixed	SM	undocumented
B. H. Steel	Sch	1870	lumber	PtB	undocumented
Brig Supply	Brig	1862	bricks	NM	wreck charted in 1989 off Vessel Point at northeast end of island
Black Hawk	Sch	1847	mixed	LM	disappeared in November with all hands; undocumented
Brunswick	Str	1856		LM	foundered 9 August gale; one death; lifeboat landed Sleeping Bear
C. E. Redfern	Str	1937	lumber	LM	possibly wrecked northwest of Pt. Betsie
C. H. Hurd	Sch	1871	posts	MP	capsized in gale, all but one lost; believed southwest of SM
Caledonia	Sch	1862	mixed	SBP	undocumented
Comet	Sch	1870	wines	PB	undocumented
Congress	Str	1904	lumber	SM	burned off dock 4 October; sank in 160 feet
Diamond	Str	1871		NM	burned and sank, between NM and S. Fox
Driver	Sch	1901	wood	PB	lost 3 August somewhere between SM and Pt. Betsie; all saved
E. Kanter	Barg	1872	iron	Leland	stranded; all saved
Emily and Eliza	Sch	1910	wood	PB	stranded 9 September mouth of Otter Creek; had thirty-six years of service
Flying Cloud	Sch	1892	mixed	SBB	aground off Glen Arbor; previously capsized 1853
Francisco Morazan	Str	1960	mixed	SM	stranded 29 November; all fourteen saved; much of it remains above water
Free Trader	Sch	1835		SB	likely first wreck of Sleeping Bear; undocumented
General Taylor	Str	1862	mixed	SBP	stranded in October; all saved; total loss
Gertrude	Sch	1880	wood	PB	grounded off Platte River; one lost
Gilbert Knapp	Sch	1896	mixed	GHB	stranded off Shalda's Creek; all saved
Gilbert Mollison	Sch	1873	corn	NW	foundered 27 October; all hands lost; lifeboat found at Good Harbor
Grand Turk	Sch	1869	wood	Leland	stranded 17 November; seven saved; one lost
H. D. Moore	Sch	1907	corn	SM	Stranded 10 September; crew of four saved; 45,000 feet of lumber salvaged
H. G. Stamback	Str	1857		NW	accounts vary
Hornet	Sch	1870	grain	GHB	stranded in November; little known
James McBride	Brig	1857	wood	SB	carried first Atlantic cargo to LM; stranded 29 October; wreck charted 1988 *(continued)*

NAME	TYPE	YEAR	CARGO	LOCATION	COMMENTS
Jarvis Lord	Str	1885	ore	MP	sank in 250 feet 17 August; all 14 saved
Jennie and Annie	Sch	1872	corn	SB	wrecked north of Empire; six-seven lost
John P. Marsh	Sch	1878	coal	GHB	wrecked off Good Harbor; four of eight lost
Josephine Dresden	Sch	1907	wood	NM	first LM vessel with gas engine; stranded in November storm; all four saved; total loss
J. S. Crouse	Str	1919	lumber	SBB	burned off Glen Haven dock 15 November; all saved
J. Young Scammon	Brig	1854	mixed	SM	stranded in June gale; all saved
Kate Bully	Sch	1869	mixed	SBP	stranded in October; had earlier capsized in mid-LM
Ketchum	Sch	1883	lumber	GP	blown ashore in November storm; had capsized in LM in 1867
Lark	Sch	1857	coal	Leland	stranded 10 November; total loss
L. M. Hubby	Bark	1855	mixed	LM	capsized; ten lost; undocumented
Lomie Burton	Sch	1911	lumber	SM	stranded 17 November
Mailboat		1900s	mail	SBB	sank between Glen Arbor and Glen Haven
Margaret Dall	Sch	1906	lumber	SM	stranded 16 November; all saved
Massilon	Sch	1858	hides	SB	undocumented
Mendota	Str	1875	coal	LM	undocumented
Montauk	Sch	1882	coal	NM	wrecked 24 November at northeast end of island; all saved; total loss
M. L. Collins	Sch	1893		SM	wrecked in April; total loss
Onward	Sch	1885	wood	GP	blown ashore 21 September; total loss; all saved
Ostrich	Sch	1892		SM	found bottom up off island after 28 October storm; all seven lost
P. J. Ralph	Str	1924	lumber	SM	foundered; all fourteen saved
Pulaski	Sch	1887	coal	GHB	driven by 3 October storm from SM to GHB; total loss; all saved
R. J. Skidmore	Sch	1885		GP	blown ashore 21 September; total loss; all saved
Rising Sun	Str	1917	mixed	PPt	stranded; all thirty-two saved
St. Mary	Tug	1885		SBB	burned near Glen Haven I December; all saved; total loss
St. Nicholas	Str	1857	wheat	SBB	ran aground after springing leak 23 November; all saved; total loss
Samuel L. Mather	Str	1887		MP	accounts vary
Sardina	Sch	1874	salt	CPt	ran aground in November; total loss
Selt	Sch	1888	mixed	Leland	beached 19 October; total loss
Temperance	Sch	1857		SM	undocumented
Three Bells	Sch	1884	wood	GHB	beached at Good Harbor in November snow storm; total loss
Three Brothers	Str	1913	lumber	SM	stranded
Tribune	Sch	1848	wheat	CPt	disappeared LM; believed found offshore in 1949; all ten lost

NAME	TYPE	YEAR	CARGO	LOCATION	COMMENTS
Troy	Sch	1843	glassware	NM	believed lost near Manitous in storm
Walter L. Frost	Str	1903	grain	SM	stranded 4 November; all twenty-one saved; total loss
W. B. Phelps	Sch	1879	mixed	SBB	stranded 19 November near Glen Arbor; five of seven lost; total loss
Westmoreland	Str	1852	mixed	MP	lost 8 December with seventeen reported lost; rumored gold cargo unconfirmed
W. H. Gilcher	Str	1892	coal	NM	"ghosted" 28 October with all hands, probably northwest of island
White Pigeon	Sch	1859	bark	PB	lost in LM; undocumented
William Sanderson	Sch	1874	wheat	Empire	unsolved mystery: found on beach 26 November with crew missing
William T. Graves	Str	1885		NM	first bulk freighter built on Great Lakes; stranded 31 October; remains found 1988 off North Manitou Shoat; documented in 1990.

SOURCE: Compiled from records of Northwest Michigan Maritime Museum (NWMMM), National Park Service, and Michigan Department of Natural Resources; Steve Harold's Shipwrecks of the Sleeping Bear; Dana Thomas Bowen's *Shipwrecks of the Lakes*; Bruce D. Berman's *Encyclopedia of American Shipwrecks*; Karl E. Haden's *Directory of Shipwrecks of the Great Lakes*.

Many ships listed as wrecks in other publications have not been included because research, primarily by Harold, established they were refloated and returned to service. Those cited as "undocumented" have been mentioned in some accounts but probability of being in the Sleeping Bear area has not been authoritatively determined.

TYPE CODE: Barge—pulled by another vessel; Brig—brigantine, two-masted, square-rigged; Bark (or barque)—having 3 or more masts, square-rigged on all but aftermost; Sch—Schooner, sailing vessel having a foremast and mainmast with or without other masts; Str—Steamer, propelled by steam.

LOCATION CODE: CPt—Cathead Point north of Leland; GHB—Good Harbor Bay; GP—Gill's Pier north of Leland; LM—Lake Michigan (usually meaning suspected to be in Manitou area but unconfirmed); NM—North Manitou Island; PB—Platte Bay; PtB—Point Betsie; SB—Sleeping Bear, the shoreline south of the point; SBB—Sleeping Bear Bay; SBP—Sleeping Bear Point.

DEFINITIONS (Supplied by Northwest Michigan Maritime Museum):

Total Loss—No part of the vessel, rigging, or equipment was salvaged by the owners (or through contractual arrangement by the owners) prior to its being officially abandoned.

Loss Documented—There is evidence of later salvage.

Wreck (or site) charted—There is evidence in the historical record of the approximate location of the vessel's loss. Potential Wreck (or site) located—Physical remains have been located. This may, or may not be, in the location of the charted loss.

Wreck (or site) documented—Archaeological methodology has been used to investigate both in historical record and on site to determine conclusively the identity.

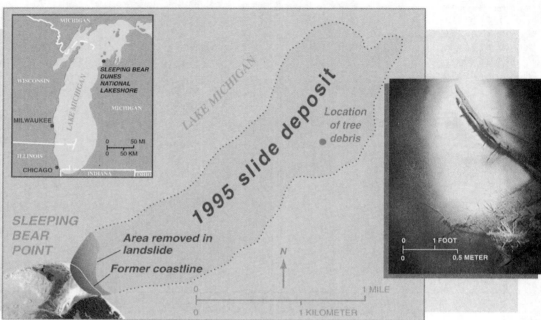

More than 35 million cubic feet of sand disappeared beneath the waters of Lake Michigan in a huge coastal landslide at Sleeping Bear Point in 1995. This composite image shows both the onshore and offshore areas removed from the point in that slide. In 1997, U.S. Geological Survey scientists found a thick blanket of debris from the slide extending more than 2 miles offshore, much farther than expected. Underwater video of the deeper part of the slide showed trees protruding from the sand (inset photo). These trees had been growing on the bluff at Sleeping Bear Point and were swept into deep water with the slide.

Sleeping Bear Point is one of Michigan's most unstable landscapes. It has had three recorded landslides in the 20th century: 1914, 1971 and 1995—all in unseasonably warm weather during the winter months.

After the 1995 slide of millions of cubic feet of sand, on a 1,600 foot stretch of the popular beach, into Lake Michigan, the U.S. Geological Survey conducted an investigation that concluded the slide was "related to increases in fluid pressure in the spaces between the grains of sand." This might have been caused by water from the snowmelt.

(U.S. Geological Survey)

CHAPTER 11

The Geology, Vistas and Trails of Sleeping Bear Dunes National Lakeshore

Sleeping Bear looks eternal, although it is not; this lake took its present shape no more than two or three thousand years ago and Sleeping Bear is slowly drifting off to the east as the wind shifts its grains of sand, swirling them up one side and dropping them on the other; in a few centuries it will be very different, if indeed it is there at all.
    —Benzie County's Bruce Catton, Waiting for the Morning Train[1]

Sleeping Bear Country remains today what it was in prehistoric yesterdays—a geologically dynamic, visually dramatic land of vistas that is a mecca for visitors and widely varied seasonal activities. It was, and is, an area of migrating people and migrating landscape.

Its migrating dunes, forming Lake Michigan's most striking scenic shoreline expanse, were sculpted upon remains of glaciers "two miles high, hundreds of miles wide and many centuries deep."[2] Remodeling by ice, wind and water is continual, especially at Sleeping Bear Point, one of Michigan's least stable pieces of real estate. As the point's dune migrates eastward, the shoreline is remodeled, sometimes overnight, by passing storms; slowly transformed by the fluctuating levels of Lake Michigan; and drastically altered by multi-acre landslides that three times in the twentieth century slumped off a massive but precarious underwater shelf into lake depths of more than 100 feet.

Great Lakes and the Great Ice Age

The relative geological youth of Sleeping Bear, and the process by which it was and is being shaped, are described in the National Park Service's proposal for creation of the Sleeping Bear Dunes National Seashore:

> The Sleeping Bear region is an extremely young landscape. Essentially it is a product of the period 20,000 to 11,000 years ago during the late stages of the Wisconsin glaciation and of events in postglacial times that have shaped and are shaping the landscape of the region.[3]

Extremely young indeed. On an earth that is three to four billion years old, Sleeping Bear was formed as recently as yesterday.

About 2 million years ago, the climate of the northern part of North America changed. As snowfall increased and did not entirely melt in the cool summers, great masses of ice accumulated in the Hudson Bay region, forming a continental glacier similar to the two-mile thick ice caps on Greenland and Antarctica.[4]

Thus began a period now known as the Pleistocene Epoch, or "most recent. (From Greek pleistos, or "most" and ceno, a combining form variation of kainos, or "recent.")

Because it is thought to coincide with a period when glacial and interglacial conditions alternated over a large part of the earth's surface, it is also called the Glacial Epoch or the Great Ice Age.[5] This geologic epoch ended about 10,000 years ago and was characterized not only by widespread glacial ice but also advent of early man. It was not a single continuous period, but rather a series of stages and substages, interspersed with cycles of melting ice.

There were four Pleistocene stages in the Great Lakes region—Nebraskan, Kansan, Illinoian and Wisconsin. The important one for Michigan was the most recent, the Wisconsin, since this stage obliterated or altered the visible evidence of previous glaciations. Of particular importance to the Sleeping Bear region is the late period of the Wisconsin Glaciation, known as the Port Huron Substage because its ice was still actively shaping the region even though most of the Lower Peninsula of Michigan was free of ice.

The Port Huron was the last major re-advance and long halt of the ice front. It built the most prominent morainic system of all and can be traced, with few breaks, from Minnesota to New York.[6]

Along borders of the ice, high ridges of glacial debris called end moraines were created. One such ridge, the Manistee Moraine, forms the high ground along much of what is now Sleeping Bear Dunes National Lakeshore. Formation of the Manistee Moraine was the climatic event of the glacial processes that shaped the Sleeping Bear area.

A moraine is a ridge, mound or other irregular mass of unstratified debris left by a glacier—chiefly boulders, gravel, sand, and clay. A glacier

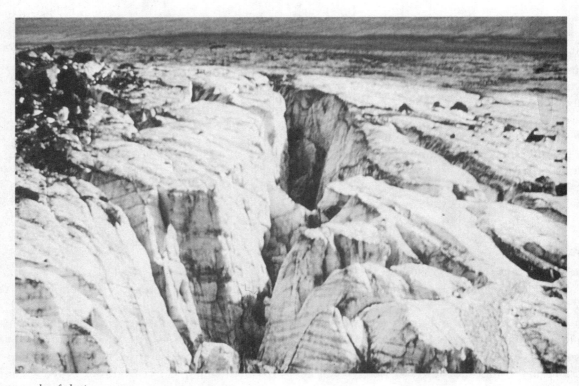

An example of glaciers. (National Park Service)

acts as a conveyor belt, carrying debris to new locations. When the rate of forward motion of the glacier is about equal to the rate of meltback at the ice front, a ridge of glacial debris known as end moraine forms around the ice margin.[7]

While the basic formation of Sleeping Bear was carved by glaciers, there also was sculpt 9 in the postglacial period 6,000 to 4,000 years ago. With the ice burden gone, the earth's crust in northern Michigan began to rise, creating what became known as the Nipissing Great Lakes.

The importance of the postglacial period to Sleeping Bear was described in 1988 by W. R. Farrand of the University of Michigan:

> The extensive belt of sand dunes along the east shore of Lake Michigan was formed mostly during the interval of lowering levels following the Nipissing stage, although some of these dunes certainly originated during the Chippewa low stage. Sands that had accumulated along the shores were exposed on now dry beaches. The prevailing westerly winds, fetching across Lake Michigan, then winnowed, lifted, bounced, and heaped the quartz grains onto the adjacent upland.[8]

(see Appendix for further geological survey material)

The Sand Dunes

The sand dunes of Sleeping Bear Dunes National Lakeshore are the product of a long and complex geological and botanical history. Visitors to the lakeshore are given this explanation of the process by the National Park Service:

> A sand dune is a wind-deposited pile of sand (mineral or rock grains ranging in diameter from 1/16 to 2 millimeters). In order for sand dunes to develop, certain conditions are necessary: and abundant supply of sand, wind of sufficient strength to move the sand, and a place for the sand to be deposited. Dunes are often associated with deserts, where lack of plant cover exposes sand to wind. Here in the humid, temperate climate of Michigan, conditions in coastal areas also favor the development of

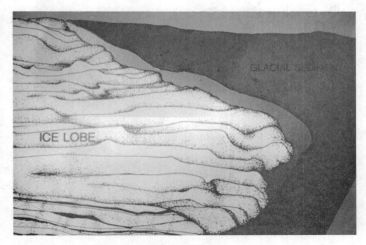

Ice lob forming bay. (National Park Service)

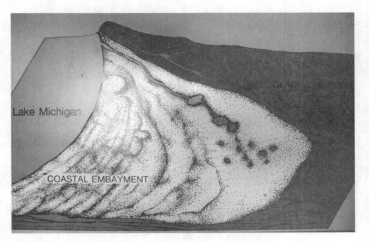

Filling in of bay. (National Park Service)

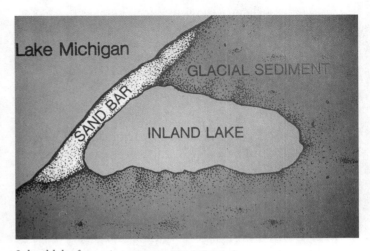

Inland lake formation. (National Park Service)

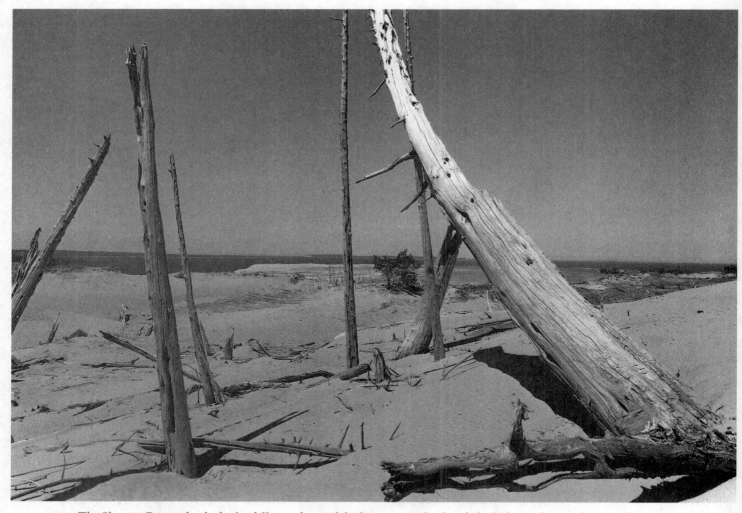

The Sleeping Bear today looks far different than it did when it was a landmark for Lake Michigan's first travelers. In this 1989 picture, looking northwest, skeletons of dead trees can be seen within the eroded bowl of the dune.

dunes. Glacial deposits provide abundant sand, Lake Michigan provides an open expanse where prevailing southwesterly winds pick up sand, and the leeward landmass provides places where sand can be deposited. Often an obstacle such as a clump of grass or a rock initiates the deposition of sand into dunes. Then the dune itself becomes an obstacle and causes more sand to be deposited. In this way a dune grows.[9]

Dune Classification

In Sleeping Bear Dunes National Lakeshore, dunes can be divided into four categories, based on their location and mode of origin: beach dunes, perched dunes, falling dunes and "deperched" dunes.

Beach dunes: They are common along Michigan's western coast, forming near lake level as onshore winds carry beach sand inland. They occasionally grow to considerable height. The Aral Dunes along Platte Bay, for example, rise more than 100 feet above Lake Michigan.

Perched dunes: They rest on a highland, often several hundred feet above lake level. They occur on the Sleeping Bear Plateau, Empire Bluffs, Pyramid Point and the west coast of South Manitou Island. The Sleeping Bear Dunes of Indian legend is a perched dune.

"Sometimes, the height of a perched dune is overestimated because confusion over where the underlying glacial sediments end and the dune begins, the National Park Service said. "The perched dunes of Sleeping Bear Plateau are actually a relatively thin blanket of windblown sand resting on a thick deposit of sandy glacial debris. When the wind reworks the upper layers of glacial sediment, sand is deposited into dunes while the coarser material remains behind as a lag gravel. Silt and clay-sized particles are so light that they remain in suspension and travel a long distance before settling. The wind is an effective sorting agent and dune sand shows little variation in size."[10]

Falling dunes: They evolve from perched dunes where sand migrates off the plateau and onto adjacent lowland, as is happening at the Dune Climb.

De-perched dunes: When dunes move beyond a plateau and rest solely on a lowland area, they may be considered "de-perched." This describes the situation over part of the Sleeping Bear Point lowlands. In the western portion of the lowland, beach dunes also develop.

"How fast are the dunes moving?"

Active dunes generally advance over time, sometimes burying trees and telephone poles. In answering oft-asked questions about the rate and direction of movement, the National park Services responded:

Rates of sand movement vary from one place to another and from one year to the next. At

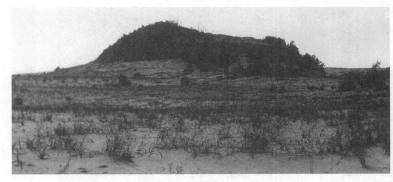

Erosion of the Sleeping Bear Dune began taking its toll in the 20th century, as indicated in this 1928 picture, taken from the east, and showing a balding crest and some dead trees.

(Photo by Frank C. Gates, Courtesy of David Gates/National Park Service)

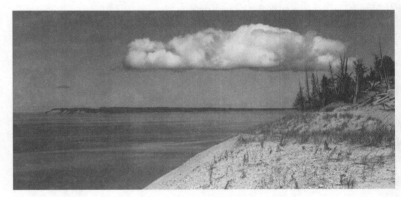

This close-up of The Bear in 1938 shows further erosion.

(Fred Dickinson)

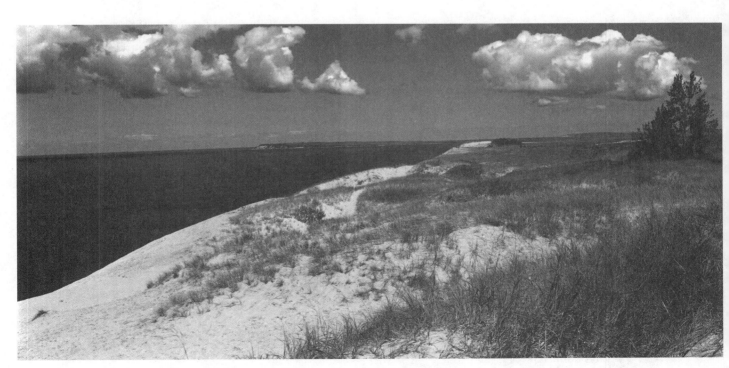

Despite the erosion, the storied dune was still discernible in this 1976 picture taken from the Sleeping Bear Dune Overlook in the Pierce Stocking Scenic Drive. Although it hardly looks like a bear in the 21st century, visitors can still see some of the thick vegetation that creates a dark shaggy look. South Manitou Island is to the left.

(Michigan Travel Bureau)

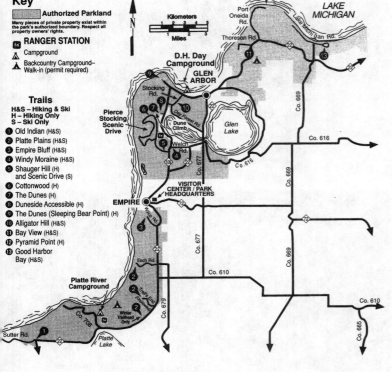

General Trail Information (National Park Service)

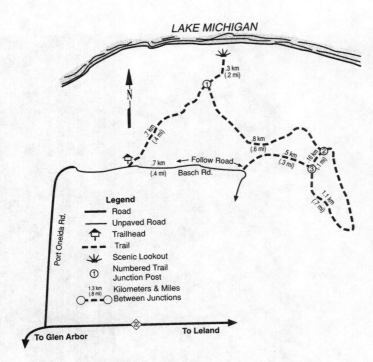

Pyramid Point Hiking Trail (National Park Service)

the Dune Climb the average rate of advance has been about four feet per year over the past few years.

Direction of sand movement also varies from one place to the next, but over the Sleeping Bear Dunes Complex the general direction of dune migration is northeasterly in response to the prevailing southwesterly dune-forming winds. The shapes of dunes reveal the direction of the formative winds. Dry, loose sand can take on a maximum slope of 34 degrees, known as the angle of repose. As sand piles up on an unvegetated dune, the leeward (downwind) slope approximates the angle of repose, while the windward slope is more gradual. Ripples in the sand show a similar asymmetrical shape.

Dune sand moves primarily by a process called "saltation," literally "jumping." Wind sets grains of sand rolling and in subsequent collisions some grains bounce into the air, are driven downwind as they fall, and upon landing strike other grains to produce a chain reaction. On a windy day you can see a hazy zone of sand moving just a foot or two above the ground.[11]

Sands that have buried trees, and then moved on, have created exposed "ghost forests" of stark, bleached trunks. Telephone poles that once carried lines to the Sleeping Bear Point Coast Guard Station are also buried. The station's buildings themselves had to be moved from the point to Glen Haven because migrating dunes were beginning to cover them.

Dune Ecology: The Cutting Edge and a Stabilizing Factor

Quartz, notable for its resistance to physical and chemical breakdown, is the most abundant mineral in the sand of Sleeping Bear. Because of its hardness, it is an effective agent of erosion. On the Sleeping Bear Plateau, windblown sand has produced ventifacts, rocks with one or more smooth flat surfaces like the facets of a gem.

One of the major limiting facts in dune movement is plant cover. It is hard to imagine a more hostile environment for plants: strong sunlight; low soil fertility; drying and eroding winds; limited soil moisture; and build-ups of sand that can bury plants.

Among the first plants to appear on dunes are beachgrass, sand cherry and cottonwood. Beachgrass is the most abundant plant on the dunes. But the most conspicuous is the eastern cottonwood, whose seeds are transported by the wind and sprout in the damp basins in the dunes. Other plants get started in the basins, but often dies out. The cottonwood, the only common tree of the dunes, grows rapidly enough to stay above the sand and create a barrier that accumulates sand and forms a dune. The cottonwood can reproduce by cloning, sprouting new trunks from roots. The role of the cottonwood in stabilizing the dunes is an example of the many things that can be observed on the trails of Sleeping Bear.

TRAILS OF SLEEPING BEAR:
Past is Prologue

The newest trails in the Sleeping Bear area are also the oldest. Adapting old railroad beds and Indian and logging trails, the National Park Service (NPS) has provided 90 miles of varied trekking terrain, including 27 miles on the Manitou Islands.

Nationally, the number of miles of hiking trails declined during the last half of the twentieth century. But thanks to preservation and sensitive development, hiking, skiing and snowshoeing opportunities are abundant in Sleeping Bear Country. Maps are available at trailheads and at the NPS headquarters in Empire. Motorized vehicles and bicycles are prohibited on the trails.

PIERCE STOCKING SCENIC DRIVE

From spring to fall, the Pierce Stocking Scenic Drive provides a way to experience the Sleeping Bear Dunes from the comfort and convenience of a car. Hiking is permitted but not encouraged because of heavy automobile traffic. The extreme right portion of the paved roadway is reserved for bicyclists, joggers and hikers.

During the snow season, though, the road links up with the Shauger Hill trail and becomes a 7.6-mile cross-country ski trail system offering long downhill runs and scenic overlooks of the dunes, Lake Michigan, North Bar Lake and Glen

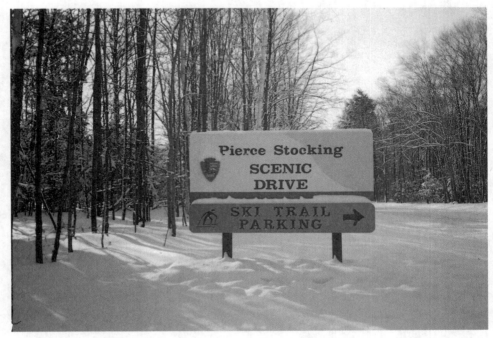

In the winter, the Pierce Stocking Scenic Drive links with the Shauger Hill Trail and becomes a 7.6 mile cross country ski trail system offering long downhill runs and scenic over looks.

(The Cottage Book Shop of Glen Arbor)

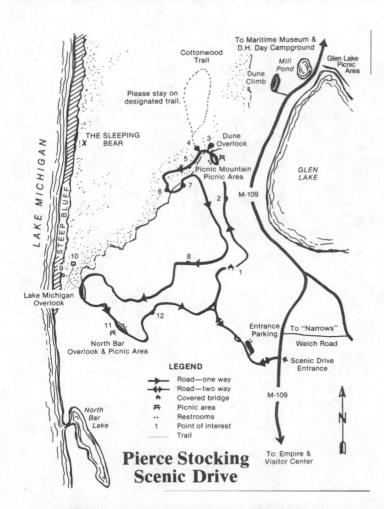

Pierce Stocking Scenic Drive

To Maritime Museum & D.H. Day Campground

Mill Pond

Glen Lake Picnic Area

Cottonwood Trail

Dune Climb

Please stay on designated trail.

THE SLEEPING BEAR

GLEN LAKE

LAKE MICHIGAN

STEEP BLUFF

Dune Overlook

4 3

5

Picnic Mountain Picnic Area

6 7

2 M-109

8

1

Lake Michigan Overlook

10

9

12

North Bar Overlook & Picnic Area

11

Entrance Parking

To "Narrows"

Welch Road

Scenic Drive Entrance

M-109

North Bar Lake

To: Empire & Visitor Center

LEGEND

Road—one way
Road—two way
Covered bridge
Picnic area
Restrooms
1 Point of interest
Trail

N

The location and attractions of the 7.4 mile Pierce Stocking Scenic Drive, between Lake Michigan and Glen Lake, are shown on this map. Named after a lumberman who developed the drive's first road and operated the scenic drive from 1967 until his death in 1976, it provides spectacular overlooks of Lake Michigan and the Sleeping Bear Dunes. In 1977, the road became part of Sleeping Bear Dunes National Lakeshore, which completed extensive road rehabilitation in 1986.

The numbered "Point of interest" designations, which will help in orienting some of the pictures in this chapter, are: 1—Covered Bridge, 2—Glen Lake, 3—Dune Overlook, 4—Cottonwood Trail, 5—Dune Ecology, 6—Leaving the Sand Dunes, 7—Beech-maple forest, 8—Changes over time, 9—Lake Michigan Overlook, 10—Sleeping Bear Dune overlook, 11—North Bar Lake, 12—Pine plantation. (National Park Service)

Facing east from the Dunes Overlook, Little Glen Lake, the Narrows, and Big Glen Lake. Alligator Hill is to the left. (Michigan Travel Bureau)

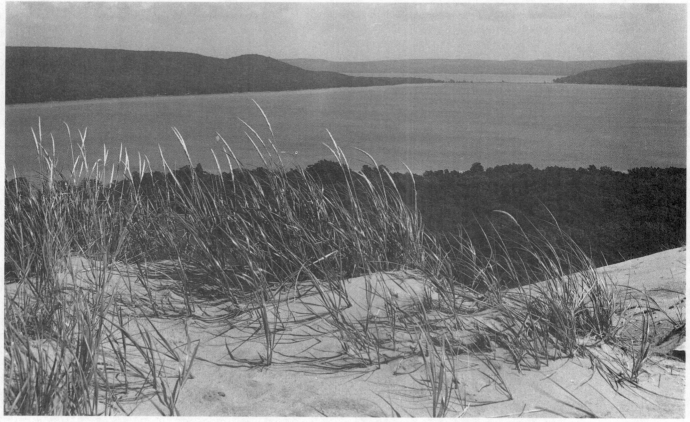

Facing east from the Dunes Overlook, Little Glen Lake, the Narrows, and Big Glen Lake. Alligator Hill is to the left.

(Michigan Travel Bureau)

Lake. Steep dunes are not part of the ski trail system due the danger of avalanches.

The roads of the scenic drive were built in the 1960s by Pierce Stocking, a lumberman with large holdings of land in the Sleeping Bear Dunes area. Stocking offered vistas of the dunes to automobile drivers from 1967 until his death in 1976.

The National Park Service purchased the drive in 1977, closed a portion of the road that was especially susceptible to drifting sand, widened and paved other portions, and moved the entrance to the drive two miles south to provide safer and less steep access to the dunes.

In addition to views of the lakes and dunes,

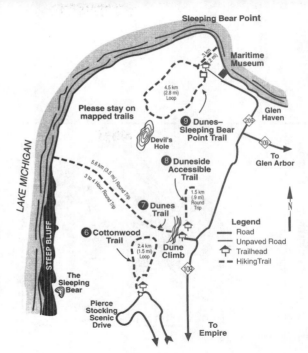

DUNES CLIMB & TRAILS: This map of the Dunes Trail System shows the entrances to the Dune Climb and the Sleeping Bear Point Trail.

(National Park Service)

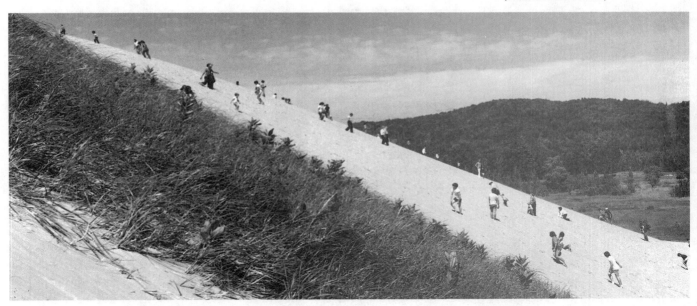

For generations, one of the most popular attractions of the Sleeping Bear Dunes has been the Dune Climb, a 130 foot high sand hill shown here in 1974. Some visitors climb the hill and continue along a strenuous 1.5-mile trail to Lake Michigan. (Michigan Travel Bureau)

Entrance to Dune Climb on M-109, which in 2001 was designated by the State of Michigan as D. H. Day Highway.

(George Weeks)

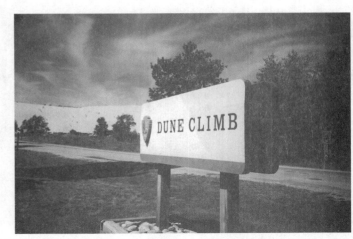

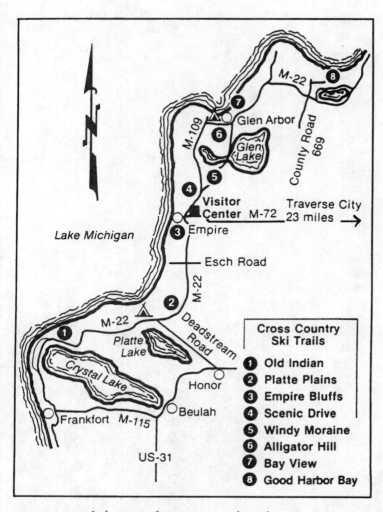

Index map of cross-country ski trails.

(National Park Service)

**Cross Country
Ski Trails**

1 **Old Indian**
2 **Platte Plains**
3 **Empire Bluffs**
4 **Scenic Drive**
5 **Windy Moraine**
6 **Alligator Hill**
7 **Bay View**
8 **Good Harbor Bay**

the Pierce Stocking Scenic Drive provides another interesting sight: a covered bridge. Stocking included this New England-style bridge as a special touch; the NPS has maintained it and increased its vertical clearance to 13'6".

SHAUGER HILL

The Shauger Hill trail is a 2.4-mile loop which passes through hardwood forests, pine plantations and small fields. Going south from the trailhead, the first half of the trail has some moderate uphill slopes; the second half has a few steep downhill sections. It twice crosses Dune Valley

Road. Motorized vehicles and bicycles are prohibited on the trails.

In the winter, Shauger Hill becomes part of the Pierce Stocking Scenic Drive ski trail.

COTTONWOOD

This 1.5-mile loop showcases the variety of vegetation native and alien to the dunes. Hikers on this trail will see some of the grasses and flowers that grow on a sand dune, such as beach grass, sandreed and little bluestem. Shrubs on the more stable part of the trail include the common juniper, bearberry and buffaloberry. This is also one of the few places on the dunes where paper birch trees grow.

White sweet clover, spotted knapweed and Queen Anne's lace are among the foreign wildflowers that grow here along an abandoned road which is gradually being buried by sand. The road was part of the Pierce Stocking Scenic Drive. A cherry orchard once grew here, too.

On its way to the overlook of Glen Lake and the surrounding countryside, the Cottonwood trail passes a dune restoration study area. It was set up in 1984 to study methods of restoring native plants to damaged dunes.

GOOD HARBOR BAY

The Good Harbor Bay trail is a 2.8-mile loop between Little Traverse Lake and Lake Michigan's Good Harbor Bay. For a short distance east of the trailhead, it goes across a foredune on the shoreline. Turning south, it crosses a creek and passes through a wetland area.

In the winter, the Good Harbor Bay trail is a beginner cross-country ski loop, with grades not exceeding ten percent.

PYRAMID POINT

The Pyramid Point trail is a 2.7-mile loop through wetlands, meadows and beech-maple forests. A .2-mile spur leads to a steep bluff over-

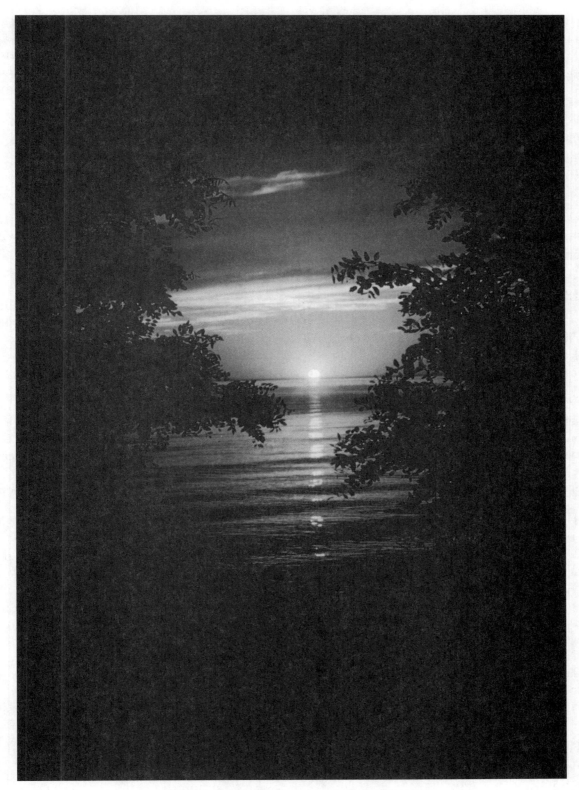

Sunset on Lake Michigan (National Park Service)

looking Lake Michigan used as a launching site for hang gliders.

BAY VIEW

This eight-mile system of loops passes through hardwood forests and open farm country. One loop leads to Lookout Point, with a fine view of Lake Michigan. In the winter, it is the only park trail for which there is a charge. Under a concession agreement with the NPS, the Home, stead Resort grooms the trails and is allowed to charge a fee on weekends and holidays. The trail system offers easy, intermediate and advanced skiing segments.

ALLIGATOR HILL

This hill between Little Glen Lake and Lake Michigan is so-named because the southeast corner resembles the snout of an alligator resting its chin on the shore of Glen Lake at the Narrows.

Alligator Hill was intended to be the site of a resort complex. Evidence of the fairways of a planned 18-hole golf course can still be seen. Prominent lumberman David Henry Day began the venture in the 1920s, but it failed during the Depression. (see Chapter six)

The 7.7 miles of trails of Alligator Hill follow old roads, some of which were built for the intended resort. There are several sawmill sites on the hill, and some of the trails follow old logging roads.

A short spur leading to an overlook begins near the site of a water tower built to water the fairways of the golf course. The remnants of the tower were removed by the park service around 1977.

At one point, the trail following the north ridge of the hill provides a view of Sleeping Bear Bay and the Manitou Islands.

THE DUNES

Walking across the dunes, either on the 2.8-mile loop or the 1.5-mile trail from The Climb to Lake Michigan (and 1.5 miles back), is like a stroll in a different world. The vegetation alone creates a unique setting, from the endangered Pitcher's Thistle to the ghost forests of bleached cedar trunks. Looking like planted driftwood, they are what's left of a forest that was buried by the moving sand. Subsequent winds have uncovered some of the trees, showing how well wood can be preserved when entombed in sand.

The terrain of the dunes can be a strange sight, too, with its drifts of sand, gulley-like blow-outs and deep depressions.

The loop follows portions of the route across the dunes taken by cars and trucks which for 43 years beginning in 1935 offered dune rides (see Chapter six). The trail from The Climb to the lake, though only 1.5 miles, can take as long as four hours round trip because of the many hills and valleys it traverses.

WINDY MORAINE

The 1.5 miles of the Windy Moraine trail reflect the developmental history and biological diversity of the Sleeping Bear area. Near the beginning of the trail, a few apple trees and remnants of an old sawmill can be seen. A pine plantation, likely planted after the forest was cleared by loggers, borders the field near the trailhead. The trail also passes a giant sugar maple tree nearly two hundred years old.

The variety of habitats contained within the trail area—fields, old orchards, pine plantations and hardwood forest—support a rich diversity of plants and wildlife.

About half way through the trail, an overlook provides a view of much of the Sleeping Bear Dunes National Lakeshore.

EMPIRE BLUFF

This is a relatively straight 3/4-mile trail from Wilco Road to the bluff just south of Empire. Near the trailhead is the site of an old farm which probably grew hay, one of the few crops supported by the sandy soil here.

On the other side of a beech-maple forest is the site of an old cherry orchard which once extended all the way to the village. Around 1910, the Empire Lumber Company planted fruit trees on much of its logged-over land.

At the end of the trail is the Empire Bluff overlook, 400 feet above Lake Michigan. This is a popular launching site for hang gliders. To the north, you can see the beach at Empire, South Bar Lake, the Sleeping Bear Dunes and South Manitou Island. To the south is Platte Bay.

PLATTE PLAINS

The extensive trail system of 14.7 miles within the Platte Plains area follows roads once used in the harvest and transportation of wood. One of the trails is an old railroad bed used to haul lumber from a sawmill on Platte Lake to a dock on Lake Michigan.

Several small lakes are within this system; one loop circles Otter Lake and its outlet into Lake Michigan, Otter Creek. Another trail goes to the White Pine (walk-in) Campground.

Many of the east-west portions of the system follow the crests of dunes which mark former positions of the Lake Michigan shoreline.

Trailheads are at the Platte River Campground, Esch Road near the mouth of Otter Creek and Trail's End Road near Otter Lake.

OLD INDIAN

The two short loops covering 5 miles pass through hardwood- and pine-covered ridges. These ridges are the crests of beach dunes which were at the various receding shoreline positions of Lake Michigan in early post-glacial times.

The trails are generally flat, but cross-country skiers should note that the northeast corner has a steep hill containing a sharp turn.

These trails were established by early Indians for travel up and down the shoreline to fishing camps.

In addition to these maintained trails on the mainland, there are the 1.5-mile Valley View Trail to camping sites north of Glen Arbor and the 1-mile Old Grade Trail between Little Glen Lake and the Dunes. There are 27 miles of trails on North Manitou Island and 3 miles of trails on South Manitou Island.—Don Weeks

CONCLUSION

A took at the trails of Sleeping Bear Dunes National Lakeshore is an appropriate way to conclude *Sleeping Bear: Yesterday and Today*. They reflect both the splendor and heritage of the Lakeshore. Some trails were used by the first people of Sleeping Bear; some by loggers and settlers. All are available for enjoyment by today's residents and visitors.

More than 100 years ago, a geological report called the dunes of Sleeping Bear far and away the grandest along Lake Michigan, and described their soft flowing contours a "restless maze." For those interested in a closer look at the geological formation of the dunes, scientific information is offered in the Appendix. In a more spiritual vein, the Appendix also offers an anthology of Sleeping Bear in verse and prose.

Endnotes—Geology, Vistas and Trails

1. Bruce Catton, *Waiting for the Morning Train*, (Garden City, NY: Doubleday & Co., 1972), 15. (Geologists indicate that glacial depth of the Sleeping Bear area was less than the two miles that it was elsewhere.)
2. Catton, 15.
3. United States Department of Interior, National Park Service, *Sleeping Bear National Seashore: A Proposal*, Washington, 1961.
4. W. R. Farrand, "The Glacial Lakes Around Michigan," Geological Survey Division, Michigan Department of Natural Resources, *Bulletin 4*, Lansing, MI, revised 1988, 4.
5. *Encyclopedia Britannica*, Vol. 18 (Chicago, 1964), 73.
6. Farrand, 8.
7. "The Story of the Sand Dunes," a 1988 brochure of the Sleeping Bear Dunes National Lakeshore.
8. Farrand, 13.
9. "The Story of the Sand Dunes," (Empire, MI: Sleeping Bear Dunes National Lakeshore, 1989). This brochure is the basis for most of the dunes classification material in Chapter eleven.
10. Ibid.
11. Ibid.

Geologic Map

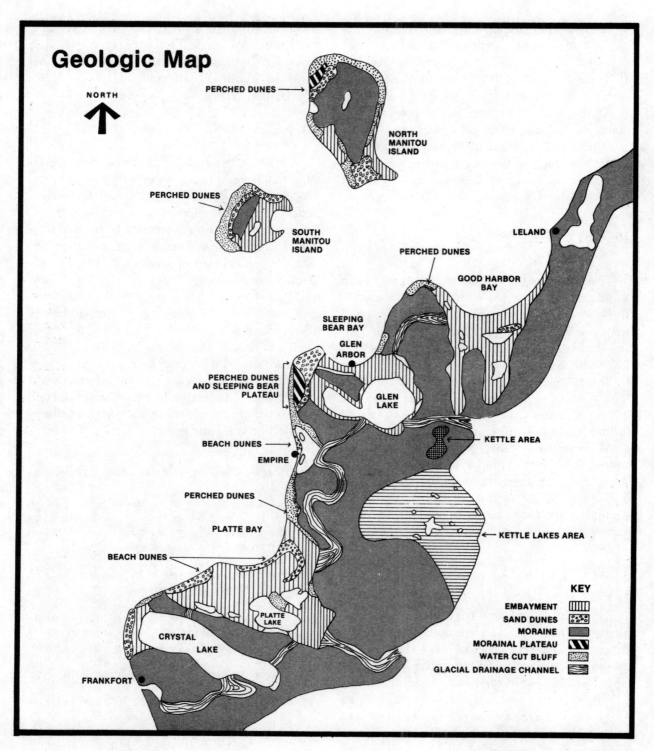

NORTH

PERCHED DUNES →

NORTH MANITOU ISLAND

PERCHED DUNES →

SOUTH MANITOU ISLAND

LELAND

PERCHED DUNES

GOOD HARBOR BAY

SLEEPING BEAR BAY

GLEN ARBOR

PERCHED DUNES AND SLEEPING BEAR PLATEAU

GLEN LAKE

KETTLE AREA

BEACH DUNES →

EMPIRE

PERCHED DUNES

KETTLE LAKES AREA →

PLATTE BAY

BEACH DUNES →

PLATTE LAKE

CRYSTAL LAKE

FRANKFORT

KEY

EMBAYMENT

SAND DUNES

MORAINE

MORAINAL PLATEAU

WATER CUT BLUFF

GLACIAL DRAINAGE CHANNEL

(National Park Service)

APPENDIX I—Geology

In 1961, as part of its investigation of the feasibility of including Sleeping Bear in the National Park System, the National Park Service (NPS) of the U. S. Department of Interior published A *Proposed Sleeping Bear National Seashore: Natural History Report*. It drew extensively on previous geological surveys, going back to an 1889 study by H. C. Cowles, who called the dunes of Sleeping Bear "far and away the grandest along Lake Michigan," and described their soft flowing contours a "restless maze."[1] The NPS report also includes the work of James L. Calver[2] in 1946, Helen M. Martin[3] and Richard Foster Flint[4] in 1957, and Jack L. Hough in 1958.[5]

Following, presented in cooperation with Superintendent Richard Peterson of the Sleeping Bear Dunes National Lakeshore, are excerpts and illustrations from the geology section of the 1961 NPS report, with particular emphasis on the Wisconsin Glaciation, the Port Huron Substage, and the Manistee Moraine:

Wisconsin Glaciation

The evidence indicates that ice of the Wisconsin stage lasted approximately 50,000 to 10,000 years, with the ice having disappeared from the Sleeping Bear region about 11,000 years ago. During and following the recession of the ice, the waters of the Great Lakes fluctuated as they sought the lowest outlets, with the final adjustment as we know them today taking place about 2,000 years ago.

During its maximum extent, Wisconsin ice completely blanketed the state of Michigan, extending far south into Illinois, Indiana, and Ohio. Though all stages of glaciation wrought changes in the landscape of any given point affected by them, it is with the later substages of Wisconsin glaciation that we are concerned, for these are the ones which have left their indelible marks on the landscape of the study area.

Hough (1958) lists seven substages of the Wisconsin stage, each characterized by the occurrence of some distinctive evidence. These substages occurred generally successively further north, the last being north of the Great Lakes. The fifth, the Port Huron or Mankato substage, is the most

important in the study area though the sixth or Valders phase touched upon it.

Port Huron Substage

The Port Huron substage is marked by a highly developed morainic system from south of Manistee on Lake Michigan northward around the tip of the lower peninsula and then southerly around the Saginaw Bay lobe to the vicinity of Port Huron. Within this system is a well-defined series of end moraines, ground moraines, outwash areas, glacial channels, deltas, and glacial lake beds. During the early part of the Port Huron substage much of the lower peninsula was free of ice and by the close of the substage the ice had melted back from the lower peninsula completely. Thus it was during this time that the characteristic topography of the study area was fashioned.

From Portage Lake in Manistee County to Little Traverse Bay in Emmet County, the northwestern corner of the lower peninsula is indented by a series of lakes, lowlands and bays. So prominent are these features that they immediately set this region apart from the area to the south. The reasons for the prominence of this "interlobate" area, as it is called, stems most probably from two causes: pre-glacial topography and the lobate nature of the ice of the Port Huron substage.

During successive advances of glacial ice a tremendous amount of inorganic rubble known as till was transported by ice movements from within the zone of glaciation to the periphery of the glaciated region. As the ice melted back, the till was deposited in a variety of ways. If the rate of wasting of the margin of glacial ice approximately equalled the cumulative advance of the glacier, till deposited along its margin would form a high ridge known as and end moraine. If wasting away of the ice exceeded its advance and a general continuous retreat of ice ensued, till would be deposited unevenly over the resurrected landscape as a ground moraine. Between two adjacent lobes of a glacier, an interlobate moraine would be created. Other glacial features such as kettle holes, ice block lakes, outwash Plains, glacial drainage channels, eskers, kames, kame terraces and drumlins are part of the landscape of the area of continental glaciation. Through glacial transport a tremendous amount of glacial debris covered the bedrock of the study area to depths exceeding 500 feet, while the amount of drift that covers the Great Lakes region as a whole has been estimated to average forty feet in depth (Flint, 1957).

The Effect of Pre-Glacial Topography

Though our knowledge of the pre-glacial landscape is obscure, it is generally accepted that the direction of ice movement was largely predicated by existing topography (Flint, 1957). Whatever the exact nature of the pre-glacial Great Lakes basins, it is almost certain that erosional processes and not diastrophic action or crustal warping were primarily responsible for their being (Hough, 1958). It is, of course, obvious that structure affects erosional processes.

The immediate region of the study area and northern Lake Michigan in general " . . . may appropriately be called a ridge and valley province."

This area contains a number of islands and its bottom topography is characterized by a number of deep troughs, 250 to 500 feet deep, separated by ridges with 25 to 50 feet of water over them. The valleys are connected in what appears to be a drowned drainage system: the master valley, or deepest trough, extends along the south shore from a point west of Petoskey, Michigan, west-southwestward along the northern face of Grand Traverse Bay, and thence westward to the deep northern basin. (Hough, 1958).

So we believe a number of streams in the area in what are now Little Traverse Bay and the deep gorges now filled with Walloon, Charlevoix, Torch, Elk, and Intermediate lakes were tributary to the main river in the Lake Michigan Valley. The little evidence we now have from drilling through the drift shows their gorges extend for several miles southeastward. (Martin, 1957)

In view of the foregoing, the deeply indented shoreline takes on new significance. Glacial ice advancing south along the larger topographic features of the Great Lakes, by following the lines of least resistance, should be expected to show a highly lobate nature. And, indeed, lobation is a well-marked characteristic of Wisconsin ice.

As the main lobe of the Port Huron substage pressed southward in the Lake Michigan basin, lateral lobes entered these tributary lowland valleys, pushing their accumulated load of glacial debris upstream. Between the lobes a well-defined series of interlobate moraines was formed. Eventually the ice lobes merged and pushed south along a united, if still lobate, front to the Port Huron maximum. In these valleys the ice was thicker and consequently had more power to shape the landscape. After the thinner upland ice melted, the valley lobes remained and this had an important bearing on the glacial topography of the study area.

Ice Border Lakes and Glacial Drainage

At the Port Huron maximum the ice had advanced far to the south in the Lake Michigan basin, but only lapped upon the margin of the northern highlands of the Lower Peninsula, leaving the formerly glaciated region free of ice. Melting of the retreating ice forms lakes between the ice margin and the end moraines. Waters of these lakes, in turn, rose until they cut outlets through the moraines, forming outwash plains and glacial channels along the morainal front. Thus new drainage systems, independent of the pre-glacial system, came into being. The duration of active flow in these channels was controlled by the volume, the continued supply, and the extent of melting of the glacier. The direction of flow was controlled largely by glacial topography, moraines being cut through when water dammed sufficiently deep behind them. Channels flowed between moraines formed by the immediate stage or substage and those of previous substages. That many of these channels were excavated so deeply that they still carry important rivers is dramatic proof of the tremendous volume of water held captive in the glacial ice. As the ice melted back, however, lower elevations were exposed and many streams abandoned the old glacial channels for lower levels, leaving them high and dry. Others ceased to flow actively once their source of supply, namely the glacial ice, disappeared.

The Port Huron ice did not retreat evenly and continuously. There were retreats, halts, and advances all along the line; however, three principal halts are recognized in the general region (Martin, 1957). The first two were south of the study area. The third and its consequent retreat occurred on, and was tremendously important in shaping, the landscape of the Sleeping Bear region.

The Manistee Moraine

The final halt of the Port Huron substage formed the Manistee Moraine and must be considered the climactic event of the glacial history of the Sleeping Bear region. At that time the southern end of the Lake Michigan basin was free of ice and was occupied by Lake Chicago at an elevation of about 640 feet. The glacial ice entered the Lake Michigan basin somewhere in the vicinity of Manistee.

In the formation of the well-defined Manistee Moraine, the edge of the ice had attained a nearly static position where melting equalled advance. This implies a tremendous amount of run-off which through seeking the lowest possible outlets would finally find its way southwesterly to glacial Lake Chicago.

Meltwater Drainage

The original drainage pattern had been obliterated by previous glaciation, though outwash channels were beginning to form a new drainage system, much of which is still active today. Along the ice margin a vast river of meltwater was flowing south between Port Huron and Manistee moraines.

As this water reached the south end of Grand Traverse Bay it became constricted between the Port Huron Moraine at 1, 100 feet elevation and the massive lobe of ice at the south end of the East and West arms of Grand Traverse Bay. To the west of this point lay a plateau-like area between 900 and 1,200 feet in elevation along the northern morainal border and dropping in elevation southerly to about 750 feet above sea level in northern Manistee County. As the ice retreated from the area south of the moraine, large blocks of stagnant ice were left behind. These were buried, in the outwash plain and upon their eventual melting formed the series of lakes now found in western Grand Traverse, northern Benzie, and southern Leelanau Counties.

During the formation of the Manistee Moraine and the early stages of retreat of Manistee ice, drainage was southwesterly down the ancestral channel of the Boardman River, thence westerly along the front of the Port Huron Moraine at an elevation of about 870 feet to the vicinity of Duck and Green Lakes where it probably entered a large ice border lake at an elevation of about 840 feet above sea level.

In the Lake Michigan basin there was a tremendous mass of ice with a total depth at its deepest point of well over 900 feet (the deepest point in the lake) and probably well over 1,200 feet. Lobes of this vast reservoir of ice fingered into Grand Traverse Bay, covered the Leelanau Peninsula, and filled Glen Lake, Platte Lake, Crystal Lake and the other shoreline depressions (Fig. 3).

The deeper the ice the more resistant it was to melting, and the greater was its ability to alter the landscape. It must be remembered that even as vast volumes of ice melted along the morainal margin, the main mass of ice was still advancing sufficiently to maintain the glacier's position along the morainal border.

Drumlin Fields

From Petoskey southwesterly to Good Harbor Bay on the Leelanau Peninsula, the base of the glacial ice had ridden out of the depths of Lake Michigan to an elevation of from 600 to 900 feet above sea level. The ice in this area was thus the thinnest of any in the area behind the Manistee Moraine other than the interlobate moraines, being perhaps less than 100 feet deep in places. It was beneath this near stagnant ice preceding the final retreat of the glacier into Lake Michigan that the curious drumlin fields, the largest in the lower peninsula of Michigan, were formed. These drumlins were built atop ground moraine, indicative of a rather rapid advance of the ice. The forward movement of the original covering of shallow ice, of insufficient mass to continuously grade the surface of the glacial till, may have met locally with minor barriers in the form of accumulated drift, or may have scooped up sufficient till in minor depressions to form barriers to the flow of the ice. By flowing faster around the margins of the barriers than over them, it created alternating streamlined hills aligned with the direction of ice flow. These drumlins were highly compacted by the ice and thus are extremely durable, perhaps to the extent

that ice might advance over them more than once, giving them a stratified or laminated appearance in cross section.

Ice Border Lakes

At a given time in the process of retreat of the Manistee ice, its level fell below that of the terminal Manistee Moraine. At that stage, about 900 feet above sea level in the study area, the high ridge of the moraine would form an effective dam, and the meltwater from the glacier would be trapped between the moraine and the glacier forming ice border lakes. The meltwater would consequently rise higher until it found the lowest possible outlet to the outwash plains. Originally this was probably at the southern tip of the Grand Traverse lobe where the meltwater cut through the moraine and flowed southwesterly at about 870 feet above sea level in the old intermorainal drainage. Eventually the ice melted back sufficiently far to connect the dammed-up meltwater of the Leelanau and Grand Traverse lobes, and a drainage was established from the end of the Leelanau lobe at 840 feet southwesterly to Lake Ann, thence down the Platte River to a point about 2 1/2 miles southeast of Honor beyond which it entered the Manistee ice border lake which may have been somewhat lowered from its previous level.

As the Manistee ice dropped below the level of its moraine, the era of the constantly fluctuating ice border lakes came into being. These lakes must be considered as varying in level, of fusing when two or more adjacent bodies of water rose high enough to top off an ice lobe or interlobate moraine, or for a single body of water to be fragmented by lowering the water level. Originally most of the meltwater would have derived from the edge of the ice and from its surface. However, as melting continued, the tops of the interlobate moraines south of Pyramid Point and the low spine of the Leelanau Peninsula must certainly have been exposed. This undoubtedly hastened melting by providing additional surfaces for the warming air to attack. As this ice melted, it would have been blocked both east and west by the deep ice lobes in Grand Traverse Bay and Lake Michigan.

Glen Lake Channel

Originally the top of the Manistee Moraine was probably everywhere at about 900 feet minimum elevation above sea level, but meltwater eventually cut through the morainal dam via the two channels already mentioned, and, most importantly, through the Glen Lake Channel south of Glen Lake. This channel undoubtedly maintained a level of about 860 feet during the early stages of its existence; but for some reason, probably through receiving the greatest proportion of the Leelanau Peninsula meltwater, it undercut the other ice border drainages and became the outlet for the area west of the Grand Traverse Bay for a long while. While the Glen Lake Channel was cutting down to its base elevation of 770 feet (70 feet below any other outlet at that time), the Manistee ice border lake was also dropping to an elevation of somewhere around 760 feet above sea level.

Thus a slow river of meltwater—if the hypothetical reconstruction is accurate—meandered southward from Glen Lake, through the Sleeping Bear Moraine, skirted the ice filled Empire Embayment, cut behind the Empire Moraine, flowed over the outwash plain east of Otter Lake and around the inner margin of the ice of the Platte lobe, found its way into the ice filled Crystal Lake depression, flowed west of Benzonia and south along what is now the northward flowing Betsie River and joined the shallow upper end of the Manistee ice border lake.

From how large an area the Glen Lake channel gathered its water is debatable. Certainly most of the Leelanau Peninsula meltwater flowed through this channel. The Grand Traverse Bay ice lobes may have proved sufficient to have kept waters from the northward as far as Charlevoix from flowing in this direction or more probably kept the Leelanau Peninsula waters from flowing northeasterly via Burt and Mullet Lakes into Lake Huron or into a Lake Huron ice border lake. How long the Glen Lake Channel was operative in not known. The outside edge of the large meander at Empire is bordered by a sheer cut back, 100 feet high. It seems possible that eventually the ice in the Bar Lake Embayment might have receded far enough lakeward to permit the waters to flow around the lakeward side of the Empire Moraine and thence into the Platte Embayment bypassing the Empire meander and that portion of the channel south to the Platte depression. This would ultimately bring the channel bottom down to the 720 feet level through the Sleeping Bear Moraine and to 700 plus feet through the Crystal Lake Moraine. It would then be impossible for the water to flow over the 770 foot divide between the Betsie River and Bear Creek, indicating drainage to the mouth of the Betsie River and thence south along the ice in the Lake Michigan basin to the 640 foot level of Lake Chicago. There seems to be some evidence of this at the east end of Crystal Lake, the circular basin along the Betsie River south of Benzonia and remnants of a lake plain along the Manistee River at 680 feet above sea level. All the foregoing is extremely logical but needs substantiation by further study.

The Valders Substage

Eventually the ice in Lake Michigan melted back sufficiently to vacate even these ice border channels and the Port Huron substage came to an end. Later, Valders ice flowed far to the south in the Michigan basin but neither built conspicuous moraines nor altered the landscape of the study area in any important fashion. It did, however, leave evidence of its passing in the form of red, slightly pebbly clay deposits in ice margin lakes of the area. Such evidence may be found at Betsie Point, the Empire Bluffs and between Glen Arbor and Port Oneida.

It is thought that during the retreat of Valders ice, Lake Huron may have drained into Lake Michigan through Mullet and Burt Lakes and the northern interlobate lakes by a system of connecting channels to Grand Traverse Bay, thence from south to north through Lake Leelanau and along the front of the ice at an elevation of about 620 feet (Hough, 1955). This interesting possibility would have the combined waters of takes Erie and Huron (Lake Lundy) passing into the Calumet stage of Lake Chicago along the lakeward margins of the study area.

Post-Glacial Lake Stages

Following the retreat of Valders ice, the Grand Traverse region was never again to be glaciated. Though the continental glacier continued to diminish to the northward, its net effect on the study area was not entirely lost, for, though the inland topography had been ordained by Port Huron ice, the shoreline was to undergo tremendous changes in the maturation of the glacial and post-glacial Great Lakes.

Four Important Lake Stages

Lake Chicago existed south of the study area during the Port Huron and Valders substage but had no effect on it other than that the drainage from the study area flowed southwesterly toward it. It is with the beginning of early Lake Algonquin that the post-glacial shore features began to be developed. Those changes were continuous but are left in visible evidence by four lake stages: the Algonquin, the Nipissing, the Algoma and the present Lake Michigan. The changes are connected with the static levels of the lake of sufficient duration to create prominent shore features in the form of wave-cut terraces and beaches. Such evidence is found everywhere on the Great Lakes in one form or another, but is probably nowhere any better developed than in the Platte Embayment, Glen Lake, Good Harbor Bay and the bordering moraines of the Sleeping Bear, the Empire Bluffs, Pyramid Point and on South Manitou Island. The maturation of the shoreline is still continuing and its influences have had a marked effect on the botanical history of the area.

Endnotes—Appendix I, Geology

1. H.C. Cowles, from a 1989 paper on ecological relations of the vegetation on the sand dunes of Lake Michigan.
2. James L. Calvet, from a 1946 paper on the glacial and post-glacial geology of the Platte and Crystal Lake depressions, Benzie County, MI. Publication 48, Geological Series 38, Geological Survey Division, Michigan Department of Conservation.
3. Helen M. Martin, "Outline of the Geologic History of the Grand Traverse Region", Geological Survey Division, Michigan Department of Conservation, 1957.
4. Richard Foster Flint, *Glacial and Pleistocene Geology*, (New York: John Wiley and Sons, Inc., 1957).
5. Jack L. Hough, *Geology of the Great Lakes*, (Urbana: University of Illinois Press, 1958).

APPENDIX II—Anthology

ANTHOLOGY: Sleeping Bear in Verse and Prose

Oh, Sleeping Bear, what dreams must come to you!
—Harry R. Dumbrille, The Poet of Leelanau

The richness of the lore of Sleeping Bear has been passed through the centuries by oral repetition, and preserved in diverse publications—many of them not readily available. For those who inhabit and visit Sleeping Bear Country today, here are some recollections from yesterday.

The Sleeping Bear

Oh, Sleeping Bear, what dreams must come to you,
Whose sleep has been so many ages through!
Forgotten is the vigil you should keep;
The place unguarded where your children sleep!

The seasons pass, the plant life turns to green,
The strong winds blow, the great waves roll between;
And yet, you lie unmindful of it all,
The spirits of your babes invainly call.

Perchance you dream of that far distant time
When, with your cubs, you left Wisconsin's clime
To swim to Leelanau's inviting shore,
To see your native dwelling place no more.

Are not your slumbers broken with the fear
Of the flaming forests, charred and sear,
That drove you, halting, to the seething foam,
In distant lands to seek another home?

The Manitous, out yonder 'gainst the sky,
Now mark the places where your off-spring lie,
Two monuments, up-standing in the haze!
Oh, cast the shroud of centuries from your gaze!
—Harry R. Dumbrille[1]

Sleeping Bear Pinnacle

There on your pinnacle, towering high,
Above the great sand dune, in slumber, you lie,
Asleep, undisturbed, by the world's din and blare,
High on your pinnacle, oh, Sleeping Bear.

Above you, the skies do not seem far away,
Below, the blue waters of Sleeping Bear Bay,
Around you are billowy oceans of sand,
Drifting unceasingly over the land.

The sound of the surf on the beach down below,
The sough of the winds, overhead, as they blow,
Have lulled you to sleep through the long passing years,
Like soft soothing music have come to your ears.

Will not the great storms as they beat round your lair,
The lightning's forked flash, as it goes through the air.
The shock of the thunder, arouse you from sleep?
The call of your loved ones out there in the deep?
—Harry R. Dumbrille[2]

Bearwalk

Bearwalkers, known as "me-coub-moose" to the Ottawa and Chippewa and as "man-doz-it" to the Potawatomi, can with herbs and special words which only they know, instantly transform themselves into balls of fire or assume animal forms. Once transformed, they are able to travel great distances quickly and go unrecognized to inflict bad luck, disgrace, poverty, sickness and even death on their enemies or on people who they believe have wronged them. In either their human forms or one of their assumed forms,

161

they can inflict their "bad medicine" by personal contact with their victims, or they can simply spread their bad medicine in places where they know their victims will pass.
—From *The Tree That Never Dies*[3]

LEELINAU, OR THE LOST DAUGHTER
An Odjibwa Tale

(*Author's note:* Much of the beauty of this legend has been lost in more than a century of re-telling and re-publishing. In subsequent writings, Henry Rowe Schoolcraft himself changed what he published in 1839 in the classic *Algic Researches*. Following is the full text of the original version of the legend, with spellings and punctuation unchanged.)

LEELINAU was the favourite daughter of an able hunter who lived near the base of the lofty highlands called Kaug Wudjoo, on the shore of Lake Superior. From her earliest youth she was observed to be pensive and timid, and to spend much of her time in solitude and fasting. Whenever she could leave her father's lodge she would fly to remote haunts and recesses in the woods, or sit upon some high promontory of rock overlooking the lake. In such places she was supposed to invoke her guardian spirit. But amid all the sylvan haunts, so numerous in a highly picturesque section of the country, none had so great attractions for her mind as a forest of pines, on the open shore, called Manitowak, or the Sacred Grove. It was one of those consecrated places which are supposed to be the residence of the PUK WUDJ ININEE, or little wild men of the woods, and MISHEN IMOKINAKOG, or turtle-spirits, two classes of minor spirits or fairies who love romantic scenes. Owing to this notion, it was seldom visited by Indians, who attribute to these imaginary beings a mischievous agency. And whenever they were compelled by stress of weather to make a landing on this part of the coast, they never failed to leave an offering of tobacco, or some other article.

To this fearful spot Leelinau had made her way at an early age, gathering strange flowers or plants, which she would bring home to her parents, and relate to them all the little incidents that had occurred in her rambles. Although they discountenanced her visits to the place, they were unable to restrain them, for they did not wish to lay any violent commands upon her. Her attachment to the spot, therefore, increased with her age. If she wished to propitiate her spirits to procure pleasant dreams, or any other favour, she repaired to the Manitowok. If her father remained out later than usual, and it was feared he had been overwhelmed by the tempest, or met with some other accident, she offered up her prayers at the Manitowok. It was there that she fasted, supplicated, and strolled. And she spent so much of her time there, that her parents began to suspect some bad spirit had enticed her to its haunts, and thrown a charm around her which she was unable to resist.

This conjecture was confirmed by her mother (who had secretly followed her) overhearing her repeat sentiments like these.

> Spirit of the dancing leaves
> Hear a throbbing heart that grieves,
> Not for joys this world can give,
> But the life that spirits live:
> Spirit of the foaming billow,
> Visit thou my nightly pillow,
> Shedding o'er it silver dreams,
> Of the mountain brooks and streams,
> Sunny glades, and golden hours,
> Such as suit thy buoyant powers:
> Spirit of the starry night,
> Pencil out thy fleecy light,
> That my footprints still may lead
> To the blush-let Miscodeed,
> Or the flower to passion true
> Yielding free its carmine hue:
> Spirit of the morning dawn,
> Waft thy fleecy columns on,
> Snowy white, or tender blue
> Such as brave men love to view.
> Spirit of the green wood plume
> Shed around thy leaf perfume
> Such as spring from buds of gold
> Which thy tiny hands unfold.
> Spirits hither quick repair,
> Hear a maiden's evening prayer.
>
> * (Claytonia Virginica)

The effect of these visits was to render the daughter dissatisfied with the realities of life, and to disqualify her for an active and useful participation in its duties. She became melancholy and taciturn. She had permitted her mind to dwell so much on imaginary scenes, that she at last mistook them for realities, and sighed for an existence inconsistent with the accidents of mortality. The consequence was, a disrelish for all the ordinary sources of amusement and employment, which engaged her equals in years. When the girls of the neighbouring lodges assembled to play at their favourite game of pappus-e-kowaun, (a game played with sticks and two small blocks on a string by females) before the lodge door, Leelinau. would sit vacantly by, or enter so feebly into the spirit of play, as to show plainly that it was irksome to her. Again, in the evening, when the youths and girls formed a social ring around the lodge, and the piepeendji-gun (a game played with a piece of perforated leather and a bone) passed rapidly from hand to hand, she either handed it along without attempting to play, or if she played, it was with no effort to swell her count. Her parents saw that she was prey to some secret power, and attempted to divert her in every way they could. They favoured the attentions paid to her by a man much her senior in years, but who had the reputation of great activity, and was the eldest son of a neighbouring chief. But she could not be persuaded to listen to the proposal. Supposing her aversion merely the result of natural timidity, her objections were not deemed of serious character; and in a state of society where matches are left very much in the hands of the parents, they proceeded to make the customary arrangements for the union. The young man was informed, through his parents, that his offer had been favourably received. The day was fixed for the marriage visit to the lodge, and the persons who were to be present were invited. As the favourable expression of the will of the parents had been explicitly given, and compliance was certainly expected, she saw no means of frustrating the object, but by a firm declaration of her sentiments. She told her parents that she could never consent to the match, and that her mind was unalterably made up.

It had been her custom to pass many of her hours in her favourite place of retirement, under a low, broad-topped young pine, whose leaves whispered in the wind. Thither she now went, and while leaning pensively against its trunk, she fancied she heard articulate sounds. Very soon they became more distinct, and appeared to address her.

> Maiden, think me not a tree
> But thine own dear lover free,
> Tall and youthful in my bloom
> With the bright green nodding plume.
> Thou art leaning on my breast,
> Lean for ever there, and rest!
> Fly from man, that bloody race,
> Pards, assassins, bold and base;
> Quit their din, and false parade
> For the quiet lonely shade.
> Leave the windy birchen cot
> For my own, light happy lot,
> O'er thee I my veil will fling,
> Light as beetle's silken wing;
> I will breathe perfume of flowers,
> O'er the happy evening hours;
> I will in my shell canoe
> Waft thee o'er the waters blue;
> I will deck thy mantle fold,
> With the sun's last rays of gold.
> Come, and on the mountain free
> Rove a fairy bright with me.

Her fancy confirmed all she heard as the words of sober truth. She needed nothing more to settle her purpose.

On the evening preceding the day fixed for her marriage, she dressed herself in her best garments. She arranged her hair according to the fashion of her tribe, and put on the ornaments she possessed. Thus robed, she assumed an air of unwonted gayety, as she presented herself before her parents. I am going, said she, to meet my little lover, the chieftain of the green plume, who is waiting for me at the Spirit Grove; and her countenance expressed a buoyant delight, which she had seldom evinced. They were quite pleased with these evidences of restored cheerfulness, supposing she was going to act some harmless freak. "I am going," said she, to her mother, as she left the lodge, "from one who has watched my infancy, and guarded my youth. Who has given me medicine when I was sick, and prepared me food when I was well. I am going from a father who has ranged the forest to procure the choicest skins for my dress, and kept his lodge supplied with the best food of the chase. I am going from a lodge which has been my shelter form the storms of winter, and my shield from the heats of summer. Adieu! adieu!" she cried as she skipped lightly over the plain.

So saying she hastened to the confines of the fairy haunted grove. As it was her common resort, no alarm was entertained, and the parents confidently waited her return with the sunset hour. But as she did not arrive, they began to feel uneasy. Darkness approached, and no daughter returned. They now lighted torches of pine wood, and proceeded to the, gloomy forest of pines, but were wholly unsuccessful in the search. They called aloud upon her name, but the echo was their only reply. Next day the search was renewed, but with no better success. Suns rose and set, but they rose and set upon a bereaved father and mother, who were never afterward permitted to behold a daughter whose manners and habits they had not sufficiently guarded, and whose inclinations they had, in the end, too violently thwarted.

One night a party of fishermen, who were spearing fish near the Spirit Grove, descried something resembling a female figure standing on the shore. As the evening was mild, and the waters calm, they cautiously paddled their canoe ashore, but the slight ripple of the water excited alarm. The figure fled, but they recognised, in the shape and dress, as she ascended the bank, the lost daughter, and they saw the green plumes of her lover waving over his forehead, as he glided lightly through the forest of young pines.

—Henry Rowe Schoolcraft[4]

Legend of the Great Lakes

As this demi-god was walking along the shores of Lake Michigan one day in search of food, he came to a patch of a certain kind of sea weed that he greatly relished. He gorged himself on his favorite dish and lay down to rest. He slept for a long time, until the water, by its gradual movement, nearly submerged him, and awoke just in time to save himself from a watery grave. He was highly incensed at this action of the water, and, rising to his full height, extended his hands over the lake and said:

"Hereafter, that you may fool no one else in this manner, you will become smaller and smaller until you are as a draught of water in the palm of my hand."

Since that time the water in the Great Lakes has receded, and it is believed that the day will come when nothing but the great sea basins will remain to show where the lakes existed.

—From *The Crooked Tree*[5]

How the Moon and Stars Came

Formerly the rabbit was a beautiful and graceful animal, having no superior in personal comliness in the forest. But one bright day it came out into the open to lie down and sleep in the warm sunshine.

At that time the sun was larger and brighter than it is today and it beat down upon the poor rabbit so fiercely that it burnt off his tail and bent his legs out of shape.

The little animal was awakened by the scorching sensation and jumped up and hopped around in great anger.

At that time the rabbit carried little magic pellets which it threw at its enemies to destroy them.

Resolving to avenge itself upon the sun, the rabbit traveled to the end of the earth and when it got as near as it could it threw one of its magic pellets at the great orb and struck it full in the face. This caused a great combustion and broke off a large piece which lodged in another part of the sky and became the moon, and the sparks flying in every direction from the explosion filled the firmament with stars.

Since that time the rabbit never comes out of its hiding place in the day time, but at night it sallies forth to play and gambol, because it is not afraid of its friends—the moon and stars—which it created.

—From The *Crooked Tree*[6]

The Legend of the Indian Summer

High up in the heavens the Sun-god, he whose symbol is the white bird Wakehon, looked down upon the earth one day, smiling to see how well he had finished his labors of the year. Now, the Sun-god is not the *One*—Ta-ren-ya-wa-go, Holder of the Heavens; no, he is only the Manito of the sun which, as we know, is the heart of the sky. He is fat and fair and lazy; then also he sometimes is very cross and out of temper, and at such times, sky, air, and water all feel his frowns. Often, however, he is good humored; and then it is that all things rejoice in his smiles. But looking down this day and seeing all so well done—all the grain ripened and gathered, all the fruit perfected and stored, the meadows lying tranquil, the forests still and peaceful, the game abundant, then it was that the Manito grew restive and bethought himself that he was much in need of a respite from such exceedingly good behavior—of which he sometimes grew very tired.

He was not much given to thinking, because he was fat and lazy, but now he set himself to it to find some speedy way of indulging such mischievous pranks as he felt disposed. The better to help his meditations he filled and lighted his great calumet, his mighty peace-pipe, that should not have been smoked except in the council lodge, and so sat down to his musings. After a long time he hit upon a plan that filled him with glee.

"Aha!" he cried, "I will get me up and away into the far, frozen Northland where my brother Peboan (the winter) reigns, and I will help him strip these forests, still these

rivers, and send the icy blasts sweeping over the great lakes and waters, drifting the powdery snow through the villages and piling it high about the wigwams. I'll nip the hunter's fingers and make the old men cower over the coals and the women and children wail in the storm. It will be rare sport to see my brother Seegwan (the spring) work till he sweats to repair my mischief—the lazy fellow!"

After this, overcome by the labor of thinking out things for himself to which he was not accustomed, and besides being still surfeited with the great feast of the Medway that was held but lately in the month of the Sturgeon when all the fruits and grains, the game and fish are most abundant and delicious, the lazy Sun-god failed to note the sly approach of Weeng, the Spirit of Sleep, who with his many hued pinions came fluttering softly in the air with a gentle, murmuring noise that in time stole away the senses of the Manito, and while not at all meaning to linger he yet drifted away into peaceful slumber.

Then, as he thus slept, summer gaily tarried, flaunting her most vivid colors in the very face of the stupid Sun-god; the waters laughed softly, the winds murmured in gentle undertone, all things in nature conspiring together to laugh at and mock him, yet always so quietly as not to disturb his slumbers.

While he dreams the smoke from his great peace-pipe fills the air—you see it resting on the far hills and craggy uplands in a purple haze, there in the still valleys, there in the quiet waters over all the landscape like a shimmering veil. And not till his mighty calumet is smoked out to its very last spark will the fat and lazy Manito awake.

This then is the Indian summer.

—From *Historic Michigan*[7]

Indian Prayer

O GREAT SPIRIT,
Whose voice I hear in the winds,
And whose breath gives life to all the world,
hear me! I am small and weak, I need your
strength and wisdom.
LET ME WALK IN BEAUTY, and make my eyes
ever behold the red and purple sunset.
MAKE MY HANDS respect the things you have
made and my ears sharp to hear your voice.
MAKE ME WISE so that I may understand the things
you have taught my people.
LET ME LEARN the lessons you have hidden in every
leaf and rock.
I SEEK STRENGTH, not to be greater than my
brother, but to fight my greatest
enemy—myself
MAKE ME ALWAYS READY, to come to you with
clean hands and straight eyes.
SO WHEN LIFE FADES, as the fading sunset,
my spirit may come to you without shame.[8]

Endnotes—Appendix II, Anthology

1. Harry R. Dumbrille, ("The Poet of Leelanau"), *The Sleeping Bear and other Poems*, (Beulah, MI: Record Publishing Co., 1927), 7.
2. Dumbrille, 52.
3. The *Tree That Never Dies: Oral History of the Michigan Indians*, (Grand Rapids Public Library, 1978), 82.
4. Henry Rowe Schoolcraft, *Algic Researches, Comprising Inquiries Respecting the Mental Characteristics of the North American Indians*, Vol. II, (New York: Harper & Brothers, 1839), 76–84.
5. John C. Wright, *The Crooked Tree: Indian Legends and a Short History of the Little Traverse Bay Region*, (Harbor Springs, MI: Matthew A. Erwin, 1917), 35.
6. Wright, 153.
7. George N. Fuller, ed. *Historic Michigan*, Vol. I, (Lansing, MI: National Historical Association, Inc., 1924), 67–68, a legend originally recounted by Mary E. Chamberlain in *Michigan Pioneer and Historical Collections*, XXXII, 392.
8. Indian Prayer, Immaculate Conception Church, Peshawbestown, MI.

INDEX

ABOUT THE AUTHOR

Author George Weeks, columnist for The Detroit News and a member of the Michigan Journalism Hall of Fame, has long chronicled the state's contemporary events and history, including that of Sleeping Bear. A Traverse City native and longtime resident of Glen Arbor, he is a former member of the Sleeping Bear Dunes National Lakeshore Advisory Commission.

During 14 years with United Press International, he was Lansing bureau chief and then foreign editor in Washington. He has a journalism degree from Michigan State University and was a Kennedy Fellow at Harvard University's Institute of Politics. He also was press secretary and then chief-of-staff to Gov. William G. Milliken.

Weeks also is author of *Sleeping Bear: Its Lore, Legends and First People*; *Stewards of the State: The Governors of Michigan*; and *Mem-ka-weh: Dawning of the Grand Traverse Band of Ottawa and Chippewa Indians*.

He is co-author of *The Milliken Years: A Pictorial Reflection*, and contributing author of *Michigan: Visions of Our Past*, and *A Handbook of African Affairs*.

He also was a member of the Board of Governors of the Clarke Historical Library at Central Michigan University.